ALEXAND

ALEXANDER CARTWRIGHT

THE LIFE BEHIND THE BASEBALL LEGEND

MONICA NUCCIARONE Foreword by **JOHN THORN**

UNIVERSITY OF NEBRASKA PRESS | LINCOLN AND LONDON

Library of Congress Cataloging-
in-Publication Data
Nucciarone, Monica.
Alexander Cartwright : the life behind
the baseball legend / Monica Nucciarone ;
foreword by John Thorn.
p. cm.
Includes bibliographical references and index.
ISBN 978-0-8032-3353-9 (cloth : alk. paper)
1. Cartwright, Alexander Joy, 1820–1892.
2. Baseball—United States—Biography.
3. Baseball—United States—History.
I. Title.
GV865.C32N83 2009
796.357092—dc22
[B]
2008050109

Set in Scala.

For
my parents
Tullio and Theresa
and
my friends
Susan and Mary

For we are here but a short time on this earth

CONTENTS

Part 2. The Mythography of a Man

FOREWORD

Abner Cartwright, Alexander Doubleday . . . these composite
names stand for an exceedingly odd couple whose identities
have been stolen, accomplishments merged, and stories inter-
twined for more than a century now. In truth, Abner Doubleday and Alexander Cartwright were entirely separate, histori-
cally significant individuals who were born and died one year
apart but never met each other in life. What both men share is
that their hard-won fame was hijacked after their deaths by un-
principled advocates with ulterior motives, and as a result each
was credited with something he did not do: invent baseball.

There is no need to recite here the full story, amply reported
elsewhere, of how Abner Doubleday was anointed the Father
of Baseball by the Mills Commission at the end of 1907, fourteen years after he left this life having had little to say about the
game to anyone, not even his old friend Mills. What left Abraham G. Mills holding his nose while affirming Doubleday's

paternity was the lately produced recollection of Abner Graves, offered into evidence by Albert Goodwill Spalding, that in 1839 (when Graves was five years old), he had witnessed Doubleday sketch out a new game that he called baseball.

"Until my perusal of this testimony," Mills wrote in the December 30, 1907, report of his commission, whose mandate was set to run out at year's end, "my own belief had been that our 'National Game of Base Ball' originated with the Knickerbocker club, organized in New York in 1845, and which club published certain elementary rules in that year; but, in the interesting and pertinent testimony for which we are indebted to Mr. A. G. Spalding, appears a circumstantial statement by a reputable gentleman, according to which the first known diagram of the diamond, indicating positions for the players, was drawn by Abner Doubleday in Cooperstown, N.Y., in 1839."[1]

Mills's personal knowledge that the Knickerbocker club had been an innovative force in baseball made him wary of the Spalding/Graves claim. Toward the end of his report he wrote:

> I am also much interested in the statement made by Mr. Curry, [first president] of the pioneer Knickerbocker club, and confirmed by Mr. Tassie, of the famous old Atlantic club of Brooklyn, that a diagram, showing the ball field laid out substantially as it is to-day, was brought to the field one afternoon by a Mr. Wadsworth. Mr. Curry says "the plan caused a great deal of talk, but, finally, we agreed to try it."

1. Abraham Mills, "Final Decision of the Special Baseball Commission," December 30, 1907, in *Spalding Official Base Ball Guide*, ed. Henry Chadwick (New York: American Sports Publishing, 1908), 47.

It is possible that a connection more or less direct
can be traced between the diagram drawn by Doubleday in 1839 and that presented to the Knickerbocker
club by Wadsworth in 1845, or thereabouts, and I wrote
several days ago for certain data bearing on this point,
but as it has not yet come to hand I have decided to delay no longer sending in the kind of paper your letter
calls for, promising to furnish you the indicated data
when I obtain it, whatever it may be.

The requested data about the mysterious Mr. Wadsworth never
emerged. As the author of this book details, a baseball writer
whose 1877 interview with Curry had been the source of Mills's
mention of Wadsworth reversed course in 1905 and said that
Curry had meant to credit Cartwright rather than Wadsworth.
A weary Mills ruled on baseball's paternity suit in a somewhat
contingent fashion by stating that "the first scheme for playing
it, according to the best evidence obtainable *to date*, was devised by Abner Doubleday at Cooperstown, N.Y., in 1839" (em-
phasis added).

One week after issuing the report, Mills wrote to the baseball writer whose memory had improved twenty-eight years after the fact (Will Rankin):

You quote Mr. Curry as stating that "some one had presented a plan showing a ball field," etc., and, in the second letter, Mr. Tassie told you that he remembered the
incident, and that he "thought it was a Mr. Wadsworth
who held an important position in the Custom House,"
etc. Taking this as a clue I wrote sometime ago to the

Collector of Customs, asking him to have the records searched for the years '40 to '45, for the purpose of ascertaining from what part of the State the Mr. Wadsworth, in question, came.[2]

Mills was wondering whether an upstate Wadsworth, perhaps one of the Geneseo clan, might somehow have brought the Doubleday diagram to New York.

Not even ten years later, on February 2, 1916, an unnamed writer in the *New York Times* hilariously mashed up Mills's equivocal support for Doubleday with his suspicions about baseball's creation myth:

> Baseball before the days of the National League dates seventy-seven years back to 1839, when Abner Doubleday, at an academy at Cooperstown, N.Y., invented a game of ball on which the present game is based. Doubleday afterwards went to West Point and later became a Major General in the United States Army.
>
> The game as played at the school in Cooperstown consisted of hitting the ball and running to one base. First it was called "One Old Cat," then with two bases "Two Old Cat," and finally with three bases "Three Old Cat."
>
> Another boy at the Cooperstown school, Alexander J. Cartwright, one day evolved a rough sketch of a diamond and the boys tried it with great success. From

2. Letter from Abraham Mills to Will Rankin, January 6, 1908, in Mills Correspondence, Giamatti Research Center, National Baseball Hall of Fame, Cooperstown NY.

that day to this the general plan of the diamond has changed only in a few details.

It was at Mr. Cartwright's suggestion in 1845 that the first baseball club was formed.

Is it any wonder that delegates for Doubleday and Cartwright went on to contend so fiercely for primacy? In the present work, Monica Nucciarone provides a strong account of the bickering and machinations that led, on the strength of the claim for Doubleday, to the founding of the Baseball Hall of Fame in Cooperstown, while the Cartwright faction, led by his indefatigable grandson Bruce, as formidable a propagandist as Spalding had been, won for their champion a plaque in the Hall that was denied to Doubleday.

General Doubleday went to his grave with an undeniable record of military accomplishment, especially in the Civil War; he was also known for his belief in spiritualism. His only documented intersection with baseball came in 1871. While in command of the 24th U.S. Infantry's "Colored Regiment" at Fort McKavett, Texas, he addressed a request on June 17 to General E. D. Townsend, Adjutant General, U.S. Army, Washington DC:

> I have the honor to apply for permission to purchase for the Regimental Library a few portraits of distinguished generals, Battle pictures, and some of Rogers groups of Statuary particularly those relative to the actions of the Colored population of the south. This being a colored regiment ornaments of this kind seem very appropriate. I would also like to purchase baseball implements for the amusement of the men and a

Magic Lantern for the same purpose. The fund is ample and I think these expenditures would add to the
happiness of the men.[3]

Cartwright, on the other hand, was a real baseball person-
age. He was present at the creation of the Knickerbocker club
and possesses genuine claims to organizational and playing
prowess, though the lengths to which his supporters have gone
to make him the Isaac Newton of baseball have rendered his
myth more difficult to deconstruct than Doubleday's. We may
look to the mid-nineteenth century's obsession with science,
system, business, and organization to answer the question of
who was thought, back then, to have created the game, and why.
The Knickerbockers' claim to being the "pioneer organization"
was not asserted because they were the first to play the game
of baseball (children had been doing that for a century), or because they were the first club organized to encourage men to
play what had been a boys' game.

Today we know that baseball was invented by no one man in
a feat of spontaneous inspiration. We know that the New York,
Gotham, Washington, Eagle, Magnolia, and Olympic clubs all
preceded the Knickerbocker club. We know that baseball was
played under that name by two teams of grown men in New
York City in 1823 and that the game had become so pervasive
that playing it within eighty yards of the town meeting house
of Pittsfield, Massachusetts, was banned in 1791. We know that
baseball was the name for the game as it was played in England
before anyone had heard of rounders.

3. Regimental Book of Letters Sent, addressed to Brigadier General E. D. Townsend,
Adjutant General, U.S. Army, Washington DC, National Archives.

In short, recent scholarship has revealed the prior history of early baseball to be a lie agreed upon, with first Doubleday and then Cartwright and his playmates as a contrived starting point. The Knickerbockers were proclaimed first because they had a formal set of rules, regular days of play, a firm roster of members, and sundry other bourgeois, upstanding values. And Alex Cartwright—rather than Duncan Curry, or Louis F. Wadsworth, or D. L. Adams, or William R. Wheaton—became the standard bearer for the Knickerbocker club because he had a more dedicated press corps in the person of his grandson.

To separate the man from the myth, Nucciarone has accepted at face value none of the claims made for him by those scholars who, in debunking Doubleday, have elevated Cartwright beyond the demonstrable record of his accomplishment. For example, Cartwright assuredly did not do any of the three central things credited to him on his plaque in the Baseball Hall of Fame: "Set bases 90 feet apart. Established 9 innings as a game and 9 players as a team." The plaque goes on to add: "Carried baseball to Pacific Coast and Hawaii in pioneer days." I will not spoil a special pleasure of this book by commenting on that, but you may sense a raised eyebrow.

Alexander Joy Cartwright was twenty-nine when he left New York for the Gold Rush and his eventual home in Hawaii, where he lived for his remaining forty-three years. His mercantile, cultural, and political involvements are on display here, and the magnitude of the man cannot be understood if one looks only to his baseball years (the same may be said for Doubleday). It is a signal accomplishment of the author that while diminishing the legend, she has enlarged the man.

John Thorn

ACKNOWLEDGMENTS

My gratitude extends to a great many people for help in researching and writing this book. From those who provided small pieces of the puzzle to those who added the many larger pieces, this book would not be what it is without the help of so many.

At the beginning, when I did not know where my research would lead me, two members of the Bruce Cartwright family line (Alexander IV and his mother Anne) loaned me photographs, letters, and tattered papers upon which the gold rush journal was transcribed via typewriter. I thank them very much.

A few individuals rise to the top of my gratitude list for their countless hours and efforts to help uncover information. To these individuals, I give enormous thanks. Nanette Napoleon and Joyce Salmon have done research for me over and over again in various locations in Honolulu. To me, they are treasures themselves. *Mahalo* to them. Other than these contacts in Hawaii, those who provided the most information and help,

often going out of their way through the years, are my fellow
SABR members Angus Macfarlane, Fred Ivor-Campbell, David
Block, and most aptly, John Thorn, who gave me numerous
newspaper reference referrals and was a fountainhead of answers to my many questions.

Two individuals from the National Baseball Hall of Fame who
repeatedly provided me with help during my research were Tom
Sheiber and Jim Gates. Many thanks to them.

I am indebted to the individuals who work at the Hawaii
State Archives, Hawaiian Historical Society, Mission Houses
Museum, Punahou Archives, Masonic Public Library, and the
Bishop Museum. The individuals whom I ran ragged are: Lu-
ella H. Kurkjian, Gina S. Vergara, Barbara Dunn, Carol White,
Kylee Omo, Rudy McIntyre, and the keeper of the Cartwright
diary at the Bishop Museum, DeSoto Brown.

I am extremely grateful for the cooperation of those individuals who are members of the Oregon-California Trails Association, and those who assist at historical sites in Independence,
Missouri: David W. Jackson, John Mark Lambertson, Kathleen
Tuohey, Travis Boley, Kathy Conway, Jim and Sallie Riehl, and
Dr. Dan Purdom, whose remarkable timing motivated me to
research in Independence in the first place.

Some very special people along the way were supportive as
well as helpful. Dorothy Seymour Mills, a woman who researched
and wrote baseball history long before there was a Society for
American Baseball Research, provided not only information
but inspiration as well. Kathy Keller was a great help early on
as an instructor within a writers' critique group; she was a great
support of my writing and its morphing into what it's become.

Barbara Perkins, whose library research talents soared above my expectations, was always ready to help. Phil Hatori, a great grandson of Robert Wilcox and Princess Theresa, provided me with significant and intriguing facts with encouragement and support in the spirit of Aloha. Matt Mattice, a descendent of Alexander III, was a helpful and pleasant surprise to meet in Honolulu. Tom Coffman's excellent research about the annexation movement proved invaluable, as did his supportive attitude when we met. Reed Hayes and his professional approach to analyzing the Cartwright diary were awe-inspiring. Donald and Samantha Metcalf were of great help in sharing and copying many artifacts in their possession.

Many thanks go to my developmental editor, Jeff Campbell, who provided a great working relationship upon which to build the manuscript far beyond my expectations. Sabrina Stellrecht, my project editor at the University of Nebraska Press, was terrific. The talents and personality of my copyeditor, Beth Ina, made me feel assured through the tedious process of editing. My acquisitions editor, Rob Taylor, believed in this project from the start and was patient for me to deliver, and his editorial assistant, Katie Neubauer, was a great help, too.

Many people provided or assisted me with small yet key pieces of information; although these details were sometimes germane only to a small portion of the larger text, they were critical nonetheless. To the people who provided me with them, I am very grateful: Frank Ardolino, Maritza Baida, Tokiko Y. Bazzell, Richard Bordner, Peggy Bowen, Nan Card, Stuart Ching, Paul Conley, Kathy Daniel, John Freyer, Laura Gerwitz, Dan Gilbert, Yaeko Habein, Carl Hallberg, Dennis Ing, Steven

Johnson, James Lewis, Robert Lifson, Joan Manke, Rochelle Monsarrat, Christopher Moore, Brian Niiya, Richard K. Paglinawan, Barry Pavelec, Debra Peterson, Anne Pulfrey, Cynara Robinson, Rosa Say, Corey Shanus, Michelle Skrovan, Edward Steele, Daigo Takagi, James Tootle, April West-Baker, and Shannon Wilson.

Last, but not least, a special thanks to my daughter Rhonda, my sister Sabrina, my brother Joe, and my friends Barbara, Tanya, Cynthia, Mary G-B, Maritza, and Mary G. Their help and support throughout this long journey helped make this book a reality.

INTRODUCTION

A Baseball Diamond at Madison Square

Staring into the intersection of Twenty-seventh Street and Park Avenue in New York City, I hope to see an ethereal image of men in their early twenties sporting muttonchop whiskers and wearing long-sleeved white bib shirts tucked into pin-striped pants with suspenders to hold them up. I watch and concentrate. At least in my mind's eye I can see the men gather about the dirt, while one steps off the parameters of their playing field. Madison Square Park once extended to this corner and beyond between 1814 and 1845.[1] Park Avenue, in its previous incarnation, was Fourth Avenue. I imagine one lanky gentlemen square up to pitch while his fellow fielders shuffle in anticipation and the batter waves a wooden stick, eager for the ball.

In reality, yellow taxi cabs zoom through the streets around me, and people, some still wearing winter coats against the cool morning of early spring, walk in every direction. No one is playing games. The New York Life Building, with its pointed golden

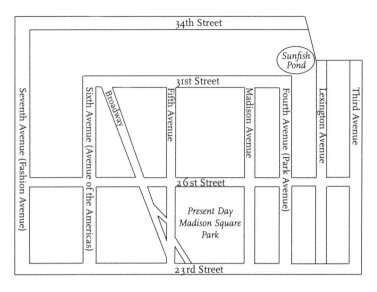

Madison Square Park, adapted from Berman, *Madison Square.* This diagram shows Madison Square Park in three phases: 1) In 1807 its boundaries stretched from Twenty-third to Thirty-fourth streets and from Seventh to Third avenues. 2) In 1814 its boundaries fell between Twenty-third and Thirty-first streets and between Sixth and Park avenues. 3) In 1845 and up to the present day, the park extends from Twenty-third to Twenty-sixth streets and from Fifth Avenue to Madison Avenue. Murray Hill (since leveled) was located at what is today Park Avenue and Thirty-sixth Street, though the district encompasses a much broader area that includes Lexington Avenue to somewhere between Madison and Fifth avenues (approximately). Sunfish Pond no longer exists.

dome and neogothic architecture, occupies an entire city block, with Park Avenue on one side and Madison Avenue on the other. Twenty-sixth and Twenty-seventh streets encase it on the other sides. The imposing building has stood on this site since it was completed in 1928. In 1837, the site was occupied by the Union Depot of the New York and Harlem Railroad Company.

The harsh shrill of a police siren echoes between the high-rise buildings as the car speeds down Park Avenue. The sight and sound prompt me to turn in its direction. I walk down Park

Avenue, but by the time I reach Twenty-sixth Street, the sound of the emergency is long gone. Walking west on Twenty-sixth brings me to the corner of the current Madison Square Park. Just beyond the park I can see the famed Flatiron Building, completed in 1902, with its narrow end pointing in my direction.

In the northeast corner of the park is a colorful playground where the laughter and shouts of children mingle with the traffic noise around me. A park bench seems to be waiting, so I stop and rest. From this vantage, I look up between the still winter-bare tree branches at the tall buildings. It may be early spring, but a small bite of leftover crisp winter cold pierces through the morning sun, which casts fresh rays across the massive buildings that envelop the park.

Madison Square Park is surrounded by historical structures. From early childhood, I have been fascinated by historical landmarks and the stories behind them. Not to be confused with present-day Madison Square Garden, this six-acre public park in lower Manhattan was named after James Madison, fourth president of the United States. During the 1830s and 1840s, it was here, and in green spaces like it in other East Coast cities, that the game of baseball developed into the form we know today.

A child's scream interrupts my thoughts. I look to the playground with concern, but giggles replace the frantic shriek, and I shake my head with relief that no one was hurt. It was just play.

My father, a first-generation Italian American, instilled in me an interest in the past. My Italian grandparents came to America via Ellis Island in New York in the early 1900s, and my second-generation German American mother's roots were in rural

Wisconsin. My parents met and married in Southern California where they raised their family of three children—I was the eldest, followed by a brother and sister.

When I was ten years old, our family took a two-month cross-country trip from the West Coast to the East Coast, visiting nearly every major historical site along the way—most of them made famous during the nineteenth century. What could have been the most boring trip imaginable became, through my father's influence, a key childhood experience that led to my fascination with American history. For example, after learning about the California Gold Rush in school, history came alive for me when we visited Sutter's Mill, where gold was first discovered in 1848. A few years later, I saw the original gold rush diary of Charles Glass Gray when our family visited the Huntington Library in San Marino, California, where it was on display.

Not all our family trips were devoted to history. Each summer we went to Disneyland, and another destination was Anaheim Stadium, home of the new Angels baseball team (new to Anaheim, anyway). However, what stayed with me, and still fills my senses with awe, is imagining the history of a place arising out of a modern scene before me, just as right now, I am imagining the nineteenth-century birth of baseball occurring in a New York City park where children play on slides and swings, making up their own games and their own rules.

Just beyond the northwest tip of the park is the location where Delmonico's Restaurant once stood in the 1800s. Mark Twain often dined there. All the corner contains now is another tall building reaching for the clouds, yet in my mind I see Delmonico's as it might have been in 1889, during a banquet held to honor the return of Albert Spalding's Chicago White Stockings baseball team from their world tour, which included a stop in Honolulu. A crowd of three hundred joined the occasion, including Mark Twain, who at one point rose to address the group and reminisced of his own Hawaii visit years earlier:

> I have been in the Sandwich Islands—twenty-three years ago—that peaceful land, that beautiful land, that far-off home of solitude, and soft idleness, and repose, and dreams, where life is one long slumberous Sabbath, the climate one long summer day, and the good that die experience no change, for they but fall asleep in one heaven and wake up in another. And these boys have played baseball there!—Baseball, which is the very symbol, the outward and visible expression, of the drive and push and rush and struggle of the living, tearing, booming nineteenth, the mightiest of all the centuries!

Twain obviously did not realize at this point that the young men did not have the opportunity to actually play baseball in Hawaii. He went on to remark about the islanders and their ways, and ended his speech trying to capture the strong memories that permanently inhabited his soul:

> No alien land in all the earth has any deep, strong charm for me but that one; no other land could so longingly and so beseechingly haunt me, sleeping and waking, through half a lifetime, as that one has done. Other things leave me, but it abides; other things change, but it remains the same. For me its balmy airs are always blowing, its

summer seas flashing in the sun; the pulsing of its surf
is in my ear; I can see its garlanded crags, its leaping
cascades, its plumy palms drowsing by the shore, its
remote summits floating like islands above the cloud-
rack; I can feel the spirit of its woody solitudes, I hear
the splashing of the brooks; in my nostrils still lives the
breath of flowers that perished twenty years ago.[2]

Twain spoke to this crowd in New York as passionately about the
Sandwich Islands (Hawaii) as he did about the game of baseball.
New York, Hawaii, and baseball? Do they belong together? One
man embodies this seemingly strange combination: Alexander
Cartwright. Long considered the founder of modern baseball,
Cartwright has deep connections with all three, and any story
of his life needs to travel to these places, bringing them to life
as they were in the best way we can today.

Alexander Joy Cartwright Jr. was inducted into the National
Baseball Hall of Fame in 1938 in Cooperstown, New York. In
Honolulu, Hawaii, a street as well as a park are named for him,
and each year his gravesite is visited by hundreds of baseball
fans, both locals and tourists. They leave baseball mementos
and notes thanking him for the sport. Since at least the 1930s,
his reputation as the primary founder of modern baseball has
seemed solid and accepted, and his accomplishments are of
mythic proportions.

As the Hall of Fame and history books tell it, the legend goes
like this: Cartwright drafted modern baseball's first rules in 1845;
he designed the baseball diamond, set the distance between

the bases, and established the nine-inning, nine-player game,
among other things. Also in 1845, he organized the first baseball club, the Knickerbocker Base Ball Club of New York, who
played the first match game. When Cartwright joined the California Gold Rush in 1849, he became the "Johnny Appleseed"
of baseball, teaching and playing the game at every stop along
the way, thus spreading it across the continent and creating a
truly national sport. Lastly, after Cartwright settled in Hawaii,
he introduced and instituted baseball throughout the Hawaiian Islands.

That's what we have been told. As for Alexander Cartwright's
later life in Hawaii, not much has been revealed. Baseball, clearly,
was the main focus of his life, and his baseball accomplishments
alone are enough legacy for any person. The one published book-
length biography of Cartwright—*The Man Who Invented Baseball*, by Harold Peterson (1973)—provided a broad description
of early baseball and an overview of Cartwright's life from New
York to Hawaii, but Peterson did not elaborate on Cartwright's
life *in* Hawaii. Still, Peterson's work immediately became the
primary reference about Cartwright for most baseball historians, researchers, presenters, and writers.

Initially, my goal was simply to write the first full biography
of Alexander Cartwright, which had never been done before. It
would include both his early baseball accomplishments and his
later time in Hawaii, which in fact constituted the bulk of his
life. I felt that a fuller account of Cartwright and of the times
in which he lived, especially in Hawaii, would provide a better
understanding of the man, of baseball, and of America during
the nineteenth century.

My nearly eight years of researching Cartwright led me to places such as New York, Hawaii, Washington DC, and Independence, Missouri. I also made numerous connections with archivists, writers, collectors, and researchers all over the world via the Internet. I have experienced the fervor of many individuals, both male and female, whose interest in Cartwright and curiosity about his life equaled mine. Yet the more I researched, the more I came to realize that many aspects of baseball's history typically attributed to Cartwright are *not* verifiable. In case after case, direct evidence and primary sources are lacking. How could this be?

In fact, Harold Peterson did not provide citations for his research, and he died an untimely death shortly after publication of *The Man Who Invented Baseball*. Since then, verifying Peterson's research has been difficult at best. Similarly, I found that most historical and other accounts of Cartwright and baseball's creation are nearly impossible to confirm. And the more research I did, the more I found conflicting or competing versions of events. Eventually, I couldn't help but ask: Could it be that the most basic tenets of baseball history regarding Alexander Cartwright are not based on actual evidence but instead have become more of a legendary story that was created after the fact? Are Cartwright's baseball accomplishments actually more myth than reality?

As this was happening, I was also finding that Cartwright's life in Hawaii was far more compelling and interesting, and even quite important, than most people realized. Cartwright arrived in Hawaii in 1849, as the nation was just opening its society to foreigners, and he became a highly respected, successful businessman in Honolulu. He enjoyed close, at times intimate, relations with the Hawaiian monarchy while also becoming a member of the annexation movement that would overthrow the monarchy and bring Hawaii into the fold of the United States. While there are still significant gaps in the record of his later life, Cartwright's legacy in Hawaii is by comparison richly documented, certainly more so than his early life in New York.

To do justice to the complexity of Alexander Cartwright's life and legacy, and to tell his story in the fullest possible way, I have divided this book into two parts, each with a different focus.

Part 1 tells the whole story of Cartwright's amazing life, from his birth in Manhattan to his death in Honolulu, creating as full a biographical portrait as is possible to date. This includes what will be, for some, familiar territory: Cartwright's years in New York as a volunteer fireman, bank clerk, and bookseller, and of course his time with the Knickerbocker Base Ball Club of New York. We will then follow Cartwright across the country during the 1849 Gold Rush and on to Hawaii, where we will get to know the Alexander Cartwright very few have met: the one who became a financial advisor to a queen, a leader of Honolulu society, and a colleague of Lorrin Thurston, Sanford Dole, and other members of Hawaii's annexation movement.

Throughout part 1, Cartwright's involvement with baseball is described, but the evidence, or lack thereof, shows that it played a much smaller role throughout his life than most realize, and many times, there is controversy over the exact nature of what he did or did not do. So as not to interrupt the narrative flow of Cartwright's full biography in part 1, when it comes to baseball,

I describe only what the existing documents and research I have been able to uncover reveal as verifiably true.

The chapter titles for part 2 come from Cartwright's 1865 letter to Charles DeBost, which is the only existing document we have thus far in Cartwright's own hand that references baseball. Each title pertains to segments from that letter that represent Cartwright's involvement with baseball and from the time periods of his life in which they correspond.

In part 2, I focus specifically on Cartwright and baseball's founding: I dissect each significant aspect of Cartwright's legacy—examining the documentation that exists, how reliable the evidence is, and what it reveals, as well as bringing up any competing claims. At times, the lack of documentation is itself significant, both because it calls into question particular claims made for Cartwright and also because it has provided an open space for speculation and mythmaking.

In part 2, I also examine what has been written by previous baseball historians—such as Charles Peverelly, Alfred Spink, Harold Peterson, and others—and I provide new information and research that in some cases may not have been seen before by those reading this work. Sometimes, the state of the evidence is completely contrary to the commonly held beliefs about Cartwright's baseball accomplishments.

For example, in *The Man Who Invented Baseball*, Peterson mentions in passing that there are a few transcriptions of Alexander Cartwright's gold rush diary, which he said characterizes Cartwright as the "Johnny Appleseed of baseball." What he does not emphasize or make clear is that the earliest and *perhaps* most authentic transcription doesn't mention baseball at all,

and that the other transcriptions (those that *do* mention baseball) were typed by a family member who included his own remembrances of the stories his grandfather had told woven into
the text. This family member was also at the time advocating
for his ancestor in hopes of gaining recognition during the development of the National Baseball Hall of Fame.

As the title of part 2 indicates, I believe that in significant ways,
Cartwright's fame as the "founder" of modern baseball is based
on *some* elements of myth *as well as* reality. At times, baseball
fans and historians have taken a kernel of truth about Cartwright and sown a field of dreams. I think that the reasons any
mythic portions developed are quite complex—Cartwright's story
evolved over time, in different contexts and involving many people with sometimes unrelated agendas.

One reason this happened may be much like the game of
"telephone." One person begins by whispering a phrase to the
next person in a circle, and each person passes it along in secret until it reaches the last person, who announces to the group
what he or she has heard. More often than not, the final phrase
is quite different from the original one, which is what makes
the game amusing.

Over and over, in the several books I've collected and reviewed
for conducting my research, I found that some writers and historians published what they believed to be true based on another
writer's public declaration. What is disturbing is that because
of this, certain stories have come to be treated as established
"facts" without citation of primary sources. But what about the
first source in the chain? Is that story based on an eyewitness

account or can the research be corroborated with documentation? Or, are such accounts believed regardless, possibly based on their authors' stature as historians or journalists? When it comes to baseball's founding, the early historians rarely named their sources, making it almost impossible to know who they talked to and why they made the claims they did—and also, most important, making it extremely difficult to verify the information today. Despite this, later historians often repeated the accepted version of baseball's founding as if it were true, without, seemingly, verifying it for themselves.

When Hawaiians sit down to chat with one another, they call it "talking story." To "talk story" isn't merely to describe the events of your day to your friends, it is to make a story out of them, one that captivates the imagination and evokes the truth of the teller's emotional experiences. In the process, some of the actual facts or events might become exaggerated, but as in the game of telephone, this is part of the fun. It's not done intentionally to mislead but to entertain and provide a more satisfying "true" story. This, I think, is part of how the Cartwright story or any elements of myth develop: over time, the story of Cartwright founding baseball was gradually elaborated into a satisfying, entertaining tale that had the ring of truth.

In addition, some in this particular game of telephone seem to have their own reasons for telling the story the way they did. As the "national pastime," baseball is tied to America's national identity, and at one time it served the purpose of baseball's promoters to create a history of the sport that was fully American and clearly linked to a particular individual and a moment in time.

On a more exclusive level, some descendents of Alexander Cartwright have conveyed their ancestor's baseball legacy through the years based mainly on oral history and family stories that were passed down through the generations. And this, of course, leads us back to Alexander Cartwright himself. What did he say when he "talked story" about baseball, and how much mythmaking was involved when he described his role to his friends, his children, and his grandchildren? Mythmaking is something we *all* do, of course, and not necessarily in a deliberate manner to omit any truth. With Alexander Cartwright, there are some things we may never know, because as yet, no written documentation has been found in which Cartwright tells his version of baseball's founding in his own words.

Separating and distinguishing personal and cultural myths from actual fact is one of the purposes, and joys, of biography. As the historian and biographer Shirley A. Leckie writes, "For without historians' insights, the public will formulate its views on the basis of myth." She states as well: "We also value biography as a way of encountering the personal myths of others, so that we might reflect on our own personal mythmaking and perhaps achieve a deeper understanding of ourselves through others."[3]

Yet the quote of Leckie's I like best, and the one that seems particularly important for this examination of Cartwright's legacy, is the following: "Many have little understanding that both history and biography are the result of constant interpretation and reinterpretations based on new questions and concerns that arise in every decade and generation."[4]

Many, many popular "myths" that circulate through American

culture continue to be accepted as truth despite the sometimes heated debates of historians. Was Paul Revere the *only* "midnight rider" who warned townsfolk about the British coming, or were there others who joined in the effort? Was John Wilkes Booth solely responsible for Lincoln's assassination, or was it a conspiracy? Is Henry Chadwick's claim true that baseball was derived from the British game of rounders—or did baseball spring fully formed from the mind of Alexander Cartwright? In time, we may discover sufficient documentation to decide on all these issues, while others may never be resolved. However, when we lack documentation, the interpretation of history is open to anyone, and mythmaking can run rampant. Yet, as Leckie says, it behooves all of us to recognize when we are mythmaking and when we are not, so that we don't come to mistake our myths for reality.

ALEXANDER CARTWRIGHT

PART 1

A LEGENDARY LIFE

ONE

Alexander Joy Cartwright Jr. and Nineteenth-Century New York

Originally named "New Amsterdam" by the Dutch colonists who settled in North America in the seventeenth century, New York only gradually developed into one of America's, and then the world's, largest and most important cities. In the early nineteenth century, the only means of mass communication was through newspapers and books; Samuel Morse wouldn't demonstrate the telegraph to the public until 1844, and Alexander Graham Bell wouldn't invent the telephone until 1876. New York was home to a host of newspapers, and two of the most prominent were the *New York Evening Post* and the *New York Times*. It was in the *Post* in October 1809 that what eventually became a well-known nineteenth-century term was apparently first introduced.

An elderly gentleman named Diedrich Knickerbocker was missing. Seth Handaside, landlord of the Independent Columbian Hotel, placed a notice in the newspaper regarding his tenant's disappearance. Two weeks later, Mr. Handaside placed a second notice declaring he would publish the contents of a "very curious kind of written book" found in Mr. Knickerbocker's room to pay off his bill for boarding and lodging if his tenant did not return. Another posting was published shortly thereafter in the *New York Evening Post* to declare the soon-to-be-published book, entitled *A History of New York* by Diedrich Knickerbocker.

In reality, Washington Irving, who is best known as the author of *The Legend of Sleepy Hollow* and *Rip Van Winkle*, created the fictional Diedrich Knickerbocker to narrate his satirical *A History of New York*. It is quite likely that this book was the source of the term *Knickerbocker*, which soon became synonymous with the city and the people in it. In the following decades, Knickerbocker became a common title for everything from magazines and newspapers to steamboat companies, schools, and volunteer fire departments. Eventually, the term came to define the era, providing the title for Abram Dayton's posthumously published book *Last Days of Knickerbocker Life in New York* (1880). In it, Dayton reminisced of life in New York "forty years earlier," before the city's expansive growth changed it forever from a cozy village to a bustling financial and industrial center.

New York was in a constant state of expansion during the first four decades of the nineteenth century. The continuous sounds of hammering and construction could be heard in every corner of the city, which served to punctuate the laments of New Yorkers for "the good old days." But New York's rapid commercial growth frequently hit barriers to progress in the form of the city's antiquated infrastructure, necessitating major changes to its water sanitation, refuse disposal, and travel routes.

Important milestones in the city's development were the construction of the Erie Canal, which began in 1810, and of the New York Central Railroad in 1828. In 1825 gas pipes were buried underground to feed the streetlamps, which illuminated sidewalks and building fronts. Beginning in 1837, the Croton River was dammed near its mouth and diverted through 150 miles of pipe to provide fresh water throughout the city. The construction of sewers, aqueducts, and reservoirs—among many other things—made New York's urbanization possible.

Communication broadened as well. In 1837 New Yorkers could choose to read any of seventeen daily newspapers. In 1844 one of these papers, the *Evening Mirror*, could boast Edgar Allen Poe on its staff and published Poe's poem "The Raven" in January 1845. Poe later became the editor of the *Broadway Journal*, which failed in 1846.

As the city grew, so did its social life and entertainments. From the early 1800s onward, Broadway developed into the entertainment center of New York, producing plays and musicals as well as hosting a wide variety of amusements. In 1841 P. T. Barnum purchased Scudder's American Museum on Broadway and installed extremely popular exhibits highlighting natural and artificial curiosities from around the world. It was not until years later that he took the "Greatest Show on Earth" on the road as a traveling circus, by which time P. T. Barnum had himself become a quite famous and wealthy celebrity.

Since as early as the eighteenth century, New York City's financial hub was located on Wall Street. The street was named for the wall that the Dutch built in 1653 as protection from unfriendly Indians. Eventually, the street became home to banks, stock exchange brokerages, and insurance offices. By the 1830s, despite the city's galloping expansion, Wall Street and the surrounding area still contained numerous vacant lots and open spaces, where it was common to see men gathering for a game of ball after their workday. One of these young men was Alexander Cartwright.

Alexander Joy Cartwright Jr. was born in New York City on April 17, 1820, to Captain Alexander Joy Cartwright and Esther Burlock Cartwright. Captain Cartwright was from the island of Nantucket, and before his marriage to Esther, he had been involved in the War of 1812. In fact, he had been captured by the British Navy. This war disrupted Nantucket's primary industry, whaling, and the local economy had a hard time recovering even after peace was restored.

This prompted Alexander Sr. to venture to the city of New York to earn a living in the shipping business.[1] There, he married Esther, and their family grew by seven children. Alexander Joy Cartwright Jr. was the eldest. His siblings were Alfred, Benjamin, Katherine, Esther, Mary, and Ann. At the time of Alexander Jr.'s birth the family lived on Lombardy Street, which later became Monroe Street.[2] But they would move within the city several times over the years. They later moved to Rivington Street, and then later settled on Cherry Street, on Manhattan's southeast corner.

In 1832 the Cartwright family again moved, this time to Mott Street, near Bleecker Street and Washington Square. Now part of New York's Chinatown, this area was then a place where one could spot cows roaming freely. In 1837 an economic downturn caused Captain Cartwright to lose most of his business investments, and the Cartwrights moved back to more modest quarters on Rivington Street. Captain Cartwright took a job as an inspector for the Marine Insurance Company in 1838, and years later for Hone's American Mutual Insurance Company.[3]

In 1836, at the age of sixteen, Alexander Cartwright Jr. went to work to help his family, becoming a clerk in the stockbroker's office of Coit and Cochrane on Wall Street. Over the next few years, the younger Alexander moved up the career ladder from a lowly clerk to a bank teller at Union Bank of New York with Daniel Ebbets, who was a cashier (and second only to the president).[4] Banker's hours afforded bank employees, more than other workers and manual laborers, abundant free time to spend outdoors before heading home by nightfall. One area popular for playing ball was a vacant lot at Twenty-seventh Street and Fourth Avenue (Madison Square), and later at Thirty-fourth Street and Lexington Avenue (Murray Hill).

Once Alexander had established himself at the bank and felt financially comfortable, he proposed marriage to his sweetheart, Eliza Ann Gerrits Van Wie. Eliza was the daughter of a prominent family in Albany, New York, yet as a young child, she was taken to New York City to live with her Uncle Robinson. On June 2, 1842, twenty-two-year-old Alexander Cartwright married Eliza Van Wie at the Third Free Presbyterian Church.[5] Less than a year later, on May 3, 1843, they gave birth to their first child, a son, DeWitt Robinson Cartwright. They would have two more children born in New York: Mary Groesbeck Cartwright (born June 1, 1845), and Kathleen Lee or "Kate Lee" (born October 5, 1849).[6]

In addition to his work as a bank clerk, Alexander Cartwright was a volunteer fireman. And indeed, many of the young men who gathered to play ball in the late afternoons in New York City were amateur fire fighters who knew each other from the same firehouse. The first firehouse that Cartwright was associated with was Oceana Hose Company No. 36. Later, he joined Knickerbocker Engine Company No. 12, located at Pearl and Cherry Streets.[7]

Fighting fires in New York during the early 1800s was a difficult challenge, but competition between companies to arrive first on the scene became almost a sport. From the moment the fire bell rang in the cupola of city hall, citizens would line up on either side of the street to cheer for their favorite company to take the lead. Though camaraderie developed between fire companies, fights often broke out as well because of the fierce competition, since they were paid for their services by the insurance companies or the property owners.

In July 1845 a huge fire destroyed the Union Bank where Cartwright was employed. Consequently, Alex went into the bookselling business with his brother Alfred on Wall Street.[8] Their business was across the street from the office Poe worked in for the *Evening Mirror*. Earlier that year, Alfred married Rebecca Layton; the two of them later had a daughter together named Mary.

Another source of camaraderie or "brotherhood" in New York at this time was the Masons. Though often thought of today as a religious or "secret" society, Masonry is more of a fraternity. Men became members based on their good reputation in the community, and at the invitation of someone who was already a Mason. Freemasonry's basic philosophy consists of brotherly love, caring for the community through philanthropy, and truth.

The Masons trace their origins to medieval times, when stonemasons traveled around Europe to build cathedrals. They were known as "freemasons" because they traveled from place to place as they were hired for specific jobs, not unlike the way "free agents" switch teams in modern-day baseball. Freemasons used secret passwords and handshakes to identify themselves; these signs indicated their level of skill and experience, which ranged from Entered Apprentice, to Fellowcraft (Fellow of the Craft, known today as "Journeyman"), to Master Mason (Master of the Craft).[9] The secrets of each level were closely guarded because higher levels earned higher wages, and that secrecy carried over to the fraternal Freemasons order. The difference between the terms "Free" and "Accepted" masons distinguished those who were actually "stonemasons" from those who were not.

In nineteenth-century New York, Masonry's popularity grew rapidly, so that by 1827 there were forty-five Masonic lodges, and many more were established by midcentury.[10] Cartwright was likely a member of one of these, particularly considering his deep involvement with the Masons later in his life, although this can't be confirmed. For instance, today's Livingston Masonic Library in New York City organizes their archives by lodge name and number, but over time, many lodges merged and formed new lodges with new names, and this can sometimes make it almost impossible to trace members to their original lodge associations.

This is true for Cartwright, whose later lodge memberships in Hawaii have not revealed what his prior memberships in New York might have been.

Ultimately, all these types of organizations provided a sense of community. They were sources of camaraderie and even of entertainment in the age before television and the Internet made these available in the home. However, if at first volunteer fire companies and Masonic lodges provided their members with friends and opportunities to gather casually for the sake of community, recreation, and playing ball, ball games themselves eventually grew to be their own organizing force.

At the time of this writing, the earliest known indigenous use of the term *base ball* in America was a reference within a 1791 law passed in Pittsfield, Massachusetts, adjacent to upstate New York. The ordinance stated that "base ball" was not permitted within eighty yards of the city's new meetinghouse (for fear that the windows would be broken).[11]

It's possible that any of these versions of bat and ball might have emerged to become modern-day baseball. For instance, Massachusetts had its own ball game with a different set of playing rules than the New York game (as played by the Knickerbocker club). In the Massachusetts game, the playing field was rectangular-shaped with bases sixty feet apart; a mere thirty feet separated the thrower's stand from the striker's (or batter's) stand.[12] However, the New York game eventually replaced all other forms of base ball played in North America, including the Massachusetts game.

Why? Speculation flourishes among historians. Some think that the New York game contained a few rules that just made more sense, such as making an out by tagging a runner instead of throwing the ball at him. However, whether owing to common sense or not, the New York game's rules were first standardized at the 1857 convention that also established the National Association of Base Ball Players, and from then, it was only a matter of time before all baseball games looked like the one in New York.

The New York game's rules are often called the "Knickerbocker Rules" because they reflected the way the Knickerbocker Base Ball Club played the game. The Knickerbockers organized as an official club and codified their rules in 1845. Since it has long been presumed that Alexander Cartwright was responsible for many, if not all, of the baseball rules that the Knickerbockers developed, they are also sometimes called the "Cartwright Rules." We will take a closer look at these rules, and how they might have developed, in chapter 12.

But we have gotten ahead of our story. In the mid-1840s, at the same time that the informal ball playing of the city's young men was growing to the point where it inspired the formation of independent clubs of its own, the city was getting too crowded for the game. Manhattan was steadily expanding and eating up all the vacant lots where ball clubs liked to gather. In name, the Knickerbockers might embody an entire era of New York, but Manhattan itself didn't have room for them any longer. So even as they were forming, the Knickerbockers looked across the Hudson River, to Hoboken, New Jersey, where there was a popular and roomy spot that would fit their needs perfectly: Elysian Fields.

TWO

The Knickerbocker Base Ball Club
of New York

In 1866 Charles Peverelly published *American Pastimes*, which
covered the history of baseball, cricket, rowing, and yachting
clubs in the United States. Peverelly's description of Alexander Cartwright's involvement with the Knickerbocker Base Ball
Club is the earliest known, though the source for his account
hasn't been verified.[1] He begins by mentioning Alexander Cartwright very prominently as the person who suggested organizing the club they would name the Knickerbockers, and yet Peverelly's list of the club's first officers does not name Cartwright
among them.

I will look at what specific role Cartwright might have played
in the formation of the Knickerbockers and of baseball's rules
in chapters 11 and 12. At a minimum we know that Cartwright
was there, and using Peverelly's description (reprinted in full
in chapter 11) and other accounts and reminiscences by players, we can speculate *one possible scenario* for what might have

occurred on Murray Hill, under a still-bright sun, at perhaps two or three o'clock on a late summer's afternoon:

As usual, the men gathered casually, one at a time, as they wrapped up their work, changed their clothes, and headed for Murray Hill. They were for the most part doctors and lawyers, bank clerks and booksellers; they were middle-class professional men who spent most of their days at a desk or in a chair. Many knew each other from other social clubs—from Masonic lodges or as volunteer fire fighters—which was how most had come to be invited to the Murray Hill ball games.

As three, four, and five men gathered, they began to toss a ball around, and played around with different rules, taking games they knew from childhood and updating them (particularly "three-cornered cat" or "three old cat"). Their bases were whatever rocks, tree stumps, and parts of the landscape presented themselves. It didn't much matter, though games rarely started without some discussion, a few times lengthy, about how the field should be arranged and what rules they should play by.

No one knew exactly who would turn up, or how many. In the early days, it had been a dozen or so, but eventually the numbers grew to well over thirty men. Some were known for always being late and so had to be accommodated after serious play had begun. These men were sometimes forced to wait until a second man arrived, so that the sides would remain equal. This, too, led to pauses in play and debate about how to arrange the players, particularly when the late arrivals were unhappy about having to stand and watch.

Some had taken to calling their group the Gotham Club (or sometimes the New York Club or the New York Nine), but the "club" was very informal. There were no officers, and no one was in charge; it was more of a team name to use when they played competitive "stump matches" with other clubs, such as with the team from Brooklyn. It gave the New Yorkers an identity and a sense of belonging, but otherwise they were just a loose group of coworkers, acquaintances, and friends in want of exercise. Each time they got together, they'd choose captains (leading to some arguments), and the captains would pick their players (leading to more arguments), and when they played another group, they had the most arguments of all over who would compose the Gotham "team." Players and sides changed nearly every game.

Most of them didn't mind, and even liked it this way; it kept things relaxed and fun. But the assembly on Murray Hill had grown; word had spread, and sometimes so many more men than necessary showed up vying to play that they wasted half their time getting organized enough to start. Some grumbled that there were too many men now, and too many opinions on the best way to play, and that they were having too many discussions they'd already had many times before.

So, on this afternoon, with the sun still firm in the sky and the air still hot, one of the regulars showed up—on time, like he always did—with a piece of paper in his hand. On the paper was a crude diagram, a rough diamond shape similar to the one shown in *Boys Book of Sports* from 1835. The gentleman explained his idea: he wanted to use sandbags for bases and keep the distances between them the same every time. This way, they wouldn't have to play around rocks and trees, and they wouldn't have to argue whether balls were fair or foul—the invisible

lines from the home plate to the first and third bases would always mark this.

Further, the man wanted to establish fixed positions; he was
tired of arguments over who would play where and how many
could take the field. Now, there would be a fixed number of men
on the field, a fixed number of outs per side, and a fixed number of outs per game—which would regularize the whole thing
and put an end to the arguments. This way, they could get to
playing and exercising instead of milling around and debating
each time—and in particular, having play come to a standstill
whenever someone disagreed with where a ball landed and all
the players gathered in a group, pointing at the grass and at the
landmarks, arguing over what was in play and what was not.

A few players agreed with the man and nodded, jumping in
with comments of their own; they'd discussed some of these
ideas together before. But others laughed. Why did they have to
play in a regular way? They enjoyed their games as they were.
They were only having some outdoor fun and exercise. Why be
so highfalutin?

The man persisted, however. His earnestness was such that
even his friends laughed a bit. Overnight, he seemed to have
become quite attached to his scheme, more so than his friends
were. He had brought bags, and he began filling them, and despite the ribbing he was receiving, he walked off the paces, drop-
ping the bags at each corner.

Then he began to tell the men where to stand. They all were
laughing now, even the man. But the players humored him
and took their spots. The man pointed out how the tosser's position would always be the same, and that this would improve

the toss. More men had shown up as the demonstration progressed, and they were now watching this strange sight—an organized field.

Then, they played. And while the game wasn't so much different than usual, it unfolded smoothly, with fewer debates, and by the end, most agreed that the field was an improvement. A few days or weeks later and away from the field, the same man suggested to a few others that they should organize the club better as well. Wouldn't everything be improved if they could limit play only to members, who would be the most dependable and dedicated players anyway, so they didn't have to deal with all the latecomers, no-accounts, and rambunctious loons? If they had a president and rules to abide by, then they'd be a real club, just like the Masons or any respectable organization. Above all, their raucous gatherings had ceased to feel like they quite reflected the standing of their class. If they conducted themselves like an actual club, one founded to promote healthy exercise rather than competition, then their games could become fit social occasions for their families.

A handful of men agreed, and in the ensuing weeks, they recruited only those members whom they thought fit for the new club. As they held their first meetings, they elected officers, formed a rules committee, decided on a new name (the Knickerbocker Base Ball Club), and came to the conclusion that, ideally, they needed a new place to play. It would be best to make a break from the Gotham Club and Murray Hill, because the city had not only grown to surround the park but also reduced it in size. A few members did scouting runs, and in the end, it was felt that the most promising site was across the river in New Jersey.

This scene, as imagined here, is a combination of known facts and conjecture based on those facts. It is meant as an evocative imagining of what *may* have happened, not necessarily what did happen. The idea of one person arriving with modern baseball diagrammed on a single sheaf of paper one glowing afternoon may contain less truth than fanciful legend concocted decades after the fact. As we will see in chapters 11 and 12, it is very difficult today to confirm exactly what did happen on Murray Hill, which forms the center of Cartwright's legacy.

What we do know, and with much more verifiable detail, is that when the Knickerbockers formed, they immediately shifted the site of play to Hoboken, New Jersey, to the well-kept and spacious playground known as Elysian Fields.

In New Jersey, Elysian Fields bordered the Hudson River, and in the 1820s it had been developed into a prosperous pleasure resort by its owner, Colonel John Stevens. Together, Stevens and his sons (who inherited Elysian Fields after Stevens's death in 1838) landscaped this sloped, wooded area into an attractive countryside complete with meadows, walking paths shaded with lush foliage, and an area where refreshments were served. Decades before baseball arrived and into the 1850s, Elysian Fields was a popular afternoon destination and diversion for city-weary New Yorkers.

Stevens's ferryboats landed at the foot of a small hill on which stood the '76 House. This tavern overlooked a beautiful lawn, or "The Green," as it was called, which was the home to popular amusements supplied by the Stevens family.[2] Cool breezes off the water and plenty of shaded areas made for a relaxing escape. One of the area's attractions (beginning in 1836) was Sybil's Cave at Castle Point, a spot no one would miss when visiting Hoboken. Hewn out of solid rock, the cave featured a spring of sparkling water that bubbled up, and visitors could quench their thirst daily in the summer for a penny a glass.[3]

By 1829 the town of Hoboken had one post office, four hotels, four groceries, three smithies, one wheelwright, two carpenter shops, one livery stable, one distillery, one steel factory, three schools, and between four and five hundred inhabitants.[4] How much the town swelled with visitors from New York to Elysian Fields, records do not say. In total, the town and countryside encompassed 564 acres.

In 1830 Colonel Stevens erected a pavilion called the Colonade Inn, later known as McCarty's Hotel in the 1840s and 1850s. Its Grecian architecture made a spectacular setting in which to escape from rain showers, and the hotel provided some entertainment and refreshments for visitors. The expansive open areas nearby allowed children to romp and play in unfettered glee, and these fields were what captured the attention of the newly formed Knickerbockers. All in all, considering its many amenities, Elysian Fields would make the best spot for playing ball games that they had ever enjoyed.

The Stevens family made quite a profit from their Elysian Fields—from the visitors who arrived by ferryboat at six cents a trip to glasses of spring water at a penny a glass. And after 1845, they added renting large playing fields for ball games at seventy-five dollars per year. Three or four ball grounds were laid out by the Stevens family for ball playing, and the Knickerbocker club's business meetings were held at Madame Fijux's Hotel, rented for two dollars a meeting.[5] After their games, the ball-players retreated to McCarty's Hotel to dine with one another. One receipt (currently in private collection) is signed by McCarty himself and made out to the Knickerbocker Base Ball Club for twenty dinners at $1.50 each, dated December 5, 1845.[6]

The club met monthly during their playing season, and officers were elected annually by majority vote for one-year terms. The board's responsibilities included selecting the days and hours of play, necessary equipment, style of uniform, and the arrangement of dressing-room facilities. They also determined what other ball clubs to play, chose players and team captains, and controlled member conduct. Annual dues for all members were five dollars and the initiation fee was two dollars.[7]

If proper conduct was not upheld, members could be fined, suspended, or expelled. For instance, a player could be fined fifty cents for refusing to obey his captain and twenty-five cents for disputing the decision of the umpire. The penalty for swearing was six cents, which Knickerbocker J. W. Davis paid during the team's very first outside match. However, in spite of this attention to proper conduct, it wasn't yet considered respectable for ladies to watch the game.

The president of the club had the authority to pick two captains after assembling on the field. However, if a captain neglected his duty, he was charged one dollar.[8] Those who came to watch the games were not charged until the 1870s.

As for the game itself, runs were calculated as "aces," and the first team to score twenty-one aces across home plate won the game. A batter, or "striker," was out after swinging and missing a pitched ball three times. An out was also attained if the opposing team caught a hit ball even after it bounced once on the field. If a struck ball was not caught on a fly or a first bounce, the batter made a run for first base. Originally, the fielders tried to get the runner out by hitting him with the ball before he made it to the base, but a Knickerbocker innovation was to throw the ball to the base ahead of the runner or else to touch or tag him with the ball to make an out. An inning was considered over when the third "hand," or player, was put out.[9]

One of the best depictions of early baseball and of spectators watching the game is the famous Currier and Ives lithograph "The American National Game of Baseball" from 1866. It depicts a championship game between the Brooklyn Atlantics and the New York Mutuals at Elysian Fields.[10] People who came to watch gathered along the outfield boundaries. Elite fans appeared in their Sunday best; gentlemen wore tuxedos and bowties and (later) ladies came in long gowns. Some sat in their carriages or wagons, while others stood. There were no fences to keep the spectators from mingling with the players or from interfering with the game, for that matter. As today, they were there to cheer for their preferred team as well as to be entertained for an afternoon.

It took less than a year for the Knickerbockers to engage in match play with other clubs. It's easy to imagine the appeal as the Knickerbockers grew accustomed to playing each other. Duncan Curry, the first Knickerbocker Base Ball Club president, vividly described this event:

> At a special meeting held June 5, 1846, Messrs. Curry, Adams, and Tucker were elected as a committee to

arrange for a match game, or a series of home and home games, with the New York Club. It was finally agreed to play the first game on June 19, at Elysian Fields, Hoboken, N.J.

Well do I remember that game, the first regular game of baseball ever played hereabouts, and the New Yorks won it by a score of 23 to 1.

An awful beating you would say at our own game, but, you see, the majority of the New York Club's players were cricketers, and clever ones at that game, and their opponents too cheaply and few of us had practiced any prior to the contest, thinking that we knew more about the game than they did. It was not without misgivings that some of the members looked forward to this match, but we pooh poohed at their apprehensions, and would not believe it possible that we could lose. When the day finally came, the weather was everything that could be desired, but intensely warm, yet there was quite a gathering of friends of the two clubs present to witness the match. The pitcher of the New York nine was a cricket bowler of some note, and while one could use only the straight arm delivery he could pitch an awfully speedy ball. The game was in a crude state. No balls were called on the pitcher and that was a great advantage to him, and when he did get them over the plate they came in so fast our basemen could not see them.[11]

Alexander Cartwright's time as a "hand" on the Knickerbocker Base Ball Club would be relatively short. He would play and serve as a club officer only until 1848. As was often the case, members performed the role of umpire in some games and served in the lineup in others, and the last time Cartwright is recorded umpiring a game was on September 26, 1848. He also played with the team at their "Thanksgiving Match" that year.[12] Then, before the 1849 baseball season began, an entirely different adventure lured Cartwright away, not only from Elysian Fields, but from New York, his work, and his family.

As for the Knickerbockers, they played enthusiastically for years at Elysian Fields. Yet by 1860, urban development crept up on the lovely grounds in the form of brownstones. The Knickerbockers would play their final season in 1882, and by 1890, virtually all of Elysian Fields had vanished. By the twentieth century, a triangle of trees overshadowed by a coffee factory was all that remained. In Hoboken today, Elysian Fields exists in memory only: the intersection of Eleventh and Washington streets is paved to look like a baseball diamond, and a nearby park is named Elysian Park.

THREE

The Rush for Gold

Excitement filled the banquet room at the City Hotel in Newark, New Jersey, on February 19, 1849.[1] Nearly a year before, in January 1848, gold had been discovered in California. The country—already in the throes of Manifest Destiny—now shook with excitement over this mother lode of precious ore. Almost immediately, thousands of fortune seekers began heading west, and the reports they sent back had fired the nation's imagination. The next year, Alexander Cartwright became one of the tens of thousands who decided to pack up and leave everything they knew for the prosperity and new life now promised out west.

That February night in Newark in 1849, General John Stevens Darcy toasted to the future fortunes of the Newark Overland Company, which in little more than a fortnight would be embarking west for California. Of the approximately forty-one men from New Jersey and New York who composed this gold-dust-seeking group, Cartwright was one of three New Yorkers,

along with several other men from Newark. Cartwright left behind two children and a wife who, by then, was about two months
pregnant with their third child. Meanwhile, Alexander's brother
Alfred had also decided to head west to become a forty-niner,
but he would travel by boat around the tip of South America to
reach the West Coast.

The Newark Overland Company departed New Jersey for
Philadelphia, Pennsylvania, on March 1, 1849.[2] The company
traveled by train through Baltimore, Cumberland, and Pitts-
burgh, and then by steamboat down the Ohio River and up the
Mississippi River to St. Louis, Missouri.[3] Late in the evening
on March 18, they reached St. Louis (as reported the next day
in the *St. Louis Daily Union*), and the members of the Newark
Overland Company dispersed to find lodgings. A. J. Cartwright
stayed the night at Planters' House.[4]

At the time of this writing, only four diaries have been uncovered from those who began their gold rush journey with the Newark Overland Company. Those men were Robert Bond, Cyrus
Currier, Charles Glass Gray, and Alexander Joy Cartwright. Piec-
ing together dates from their diaries and from accounts reported
in the *Newark Daily Advertiser*, a timeline of their travels can be
determined. When traveling by steamboat on the Mississippi
and Missouri rivers, the company apparently was not always
together on the same boat. Bond's diary has him landing in Independence, Missouri, on March 29, while Currier arrives on
April 4. Cartwright's and Gray's diary entries don't begin until
the actual journey west from Independence launches.

A portion of a letter printed a few weeks later in the *Newark
Daily Advertiser* describing the Darcy party's St. Louis stay gives

a sense of the eye-opening excitement the travelers must have been experiencing: "California emigrants arrive daily, and the hotels, there are only two, are crowded. We have them from all parts of the Union from Maine to Texas. Most of them are boarding at private homes, and with the farmers in the neighborhood. Six of our number board with a Kentuckian about half a mile from town. It is a very pleasant place, plenty of Negroes for waiters. We are growing fat."[5]

It is quite likely that Cartwright, and most if not all in the Darcy party, encountered slaves in everyday life for the first time in St. Louis. In 1799 New York had passed the Gradual Emancipation Act, and all northern states were of course "free" states. As a result of the Missouri Compromise, Missouri had been admitted to the Union as a slave state in 1821 (in exchange, Maine was admitted as a free state, and slavery would be excluded from most of the northern territory acquired in the 1803 Louisiana Purchase). But this hadn't resolved the national crisis over slavery, which had only grown more urgent over the next two decades and had remained focused on whether new slave states should be admitted into the Union. Indeed, in 1849 California was itself petitioning for statehood, and this set off another round of fierce national arguments over slavery's expansion (California became a state in 1850, but only after another compromise).

There is no record of what Alexander Cartwright felt when, perhaps for the first time, a black slave served his meal and then cleared his plate as he dined in St. Louis. However, though we don't know Cartwright's views on slavery, his April 1865 letter to Charles DeBost indicates that he was vehemently pro-Union during the Civil War, though also "Sound on the Goose," which was a term for slavery.

Continuing westward, the journey along the Missouri River and across the state to Independence by steamboat took approximately six days to travel the 450 river miles. Then, from Independence, all three overland gold rush trails began: the California, Oregon, and Santa Fe trails. Nicknamed the "Queen City of the Trails," Independence had a population of 1,500, and it was where emigrants outfitted for the overland journey. In his letters home, General Darcy described Independence as a pretty place built on high land three miles from the river.

However, were these East Coast businessmen prepared, mentally and physically, for the arduous wagon train journey that awaited them, so different from the train and steamboat travel they'd enjoyed till now? Poised on the edge of wilderness and the western deserts, what sort of figure did they cut? Fortunately, from the diary of another emigrant who apparently was aboard the same steamboat as some members of the Newark Overland Company party, we have at least one person's impression:

> There is a party of New Yorkers on board dressed in uniform of Blue Cassimere, armed with Government Rifles, Bowie Knives, and Colt Revolvers who are the most lackadaisical Milk and Waterish fellows I ever saw. They are in fact to use the words of M. Morrison, as green as a pumpkin vine. From their appearance one would suppose they had never seen more of the world than can be seen from behind the counter of paltry Dry Goods or Thread and Needle Store and their ridiculous

affection of Military Style and Etiquette joined to their
egregious vanity, Hoggishness of Manners and evident
high estimation of themselves of all and almost tempts
me to deny my Country. It is my private opinion that
before they arrive at their destination they will be perfectly well acquainted with the "Elephant."[6]

To say you had "seen the elephant" meant that you had experienced firsthand the hardship of the overland trails leading
west.

Arriving on April 4, Cyrus Currier wrote in his diary that after he took a stage into town, he saw Darcy's party encamped in
an old church built of logs near the town. Currier lodged that
night at a house with William Evans and party from Browns-
ville, Pennsylvania.

The following day, on April 5, Currier united with the Darcy
party again, only to witness a heated debate over whether to use
mules or oxen for the overland journey. Hearing that one group
of men decided on mules and the other group of men decided
on oxen, Currier stated, "It was no use to argue the point." Currier must have needed to take a break from listening to the arguments and went to town the following day to take a look around.
Seeing Independence, he said, "It stands on high ground and
is laid out very regular with a public square and Court House
in the centre. The inhabitants are enterprising and industous
[sic] the soil rich and fertile."[7]

The argument over mules or oxen had begun even before
the Darcy party's arrival in Independence.[8] Once in Independence, Charles Gillespie and George W. Martin made the case

for mules, and in the end, approximately thirteen men broke off from the original forty-one-member company, and they were thenceforth known as the "mule" or "jackass" party (indicating their preferred choice of pack animal). According to his diary, Cartwright joined this rebel group, which was led by Colonel Russell.[9]

As was the case with the Newark Overland Company, travelers did not always remain in their original company. Even well into their journey to California, some might become impatient and strike off by themselves or in smaller new parties. In other cases, separate parties might merge and travel or camp together after meeting up along the way. As a result, reliably verifying who was where and when is not always possible. Most of the information we have comes from diaries, which are not always themselves reliable, and sometimes diarists might begin in one party together and then split up in new combinations.

Charles Glass Gray was one of Cartwright's fellow New Yorkers, but in Independence, Gray joined the oxen party—which was led by General Darcy, who was Gray's uncle—and so Gray did not travel with Cartwright overland. Robert Bond also traveled with Darcy, but he died partway through the trip.

Cyrus Currier's and Alexander Cartwright's diaries mention similar time frames, places, people, and events on the same dates, which makes Currier's diary the only known journal in existence that coincides precisely with Cartwright's. And yet, even with two diaries to compare, we are left having to infer much about events.

For instance, Cyrus Currier admits that he refused to join Colonel Russell's rebel "mule" party in the beginning, but on

April 30, he caught up with them less than a week after starting out (Currier says he left on April 26th).[10] Still, it is unclear whether Currier left Independence with Darcy's party or a different group altogether; and then, by May 5, Currier notes in his diary that he had decided to split from the mule party again—now joining a group that included a Captain Woolsey and Mr. Emery. Did Cartwright join Currier in this new group? Most likely. Unfortunately, there are no journal entries in Cartwright's diary between April 28 and May 17 with which to compare events. However, throughout Cartwright's diary, he mentions Emery, making it reasonably safe to presume that Currier and Cartwright traveled quite awhile together with the same men, and that they also ventured away from Colonel Russell's party early on. Ultimately, Cartwright's gold rush diary ends on June 5, and Currier's journal entries end on July 24.

The Newark Overland Company party stayed in the town and surrounding areas of Independence, Missouri, for the better part of a month as they purchased supplies and got ready to continue their journey. Louis J. Rasmussen, in his Ship, Rail, and Wagon Train series, mentions that the Newark Overland Company (including Cartwright) camped outside of Independence on April 9, 1849.[11] Cyrus Currier writes that between the 4th and 24th of April, he was occupied with buying and harnessing mules, buying oats and corn as feed for the mules, going to church to hear an address delivered to Masons and Sons of Temperance, hunting and fishing, and conversing with Colonel Russell.

But more to the point, what was Alexander Cartwright doing while waiting to embark on the next leg of his gold rush adventure? According to baseball legend and Cartwright family history, he spent part of his time playing the game he had come to love—baseball. Indeed, it's easy to imagine him, twenty-nine years old, eagerly trying to gather enough players to make teams and explaining the rules to those who'd never heard of it before, all so he could enjoy a small taste of the kind of fun he was probably sorely missing. If there was any moment in the journey when the organization of a full-fledged baseball game was possible, it would have been during Cartwright's stay in Independence. But one could also imagine this occurring, to a lesser extent, during the overland journey; perhaps, once the group was settled into camp for the afternoon, Cartwright pulled out the ball he used when he played with the Knickerbocker club, found a large stick on the ground to use as a bat, then talked whomever he could into joining him for a little practice before nightfall as a deserved break from the stress and rigors of the day—unless, of course, blistered feet prevented anyone from doing so.

And yet, while it's easy to imagine Cartwright playing baseball when he could and spreading the new game across the country as he went, it's much more difficult to prove he did this. The evidence is scant and inconsistent. Examining this evidence and the truth of this claim is the focus of chapter 13. Cartwright's original diary no longer exists, but multiple transcribed versions survive: one handwritten version is in the Bishop Museum in Honolulu, and a few typed versions are in the possession of the Cartwright family, collectors, and the Baseball Hall of Fame. These diaries do not always match each other exactly, and this is the case for the following diary entry, which is from

the family's typed copy and was evidently the entry the day before Cartwright left Independence:

> **April 23, 1849** During the past week we have passed the
> time in fixing the wagon covers, stowing away property
> etc., varied by hunting, fishing, swimming and play-
> ing base-ball. I have the ball and book of Rules with
> me that we used in forming The Knickerbocker Base-
> ball Club back home. Tonight we held council and de-
> cided to strike out for California along the Santa Fe
> Trail until we reached the Oregon Trail, then follow
> that to the South Pass and then to the Sierra Nevadas
> to California.[12]

The transcription of this entry from Cartwright's handwritten diary in the Bishop Museum in Hawaii is similar, but it
varies significantly in two ways. One is that there is no date
provided for the description of Cartwright's activities in Independence. And the second is that those activities make no mention of baseball:

> Left Independence and traveled to the Boundary line,
> where we camped with Colonel Russell Co. for over a
> week, nothing of note occurring. Time passed in fix-
> ing wagon covers, stowing away property etc, varied by
> hunting, fishing, and swimming.
>
> On Tuesday the 24th of April 1849 the weather be-
> ing clear and warm and all nature smiling prosper-
> ously, at 7 O'clock a.m. we started under the guidance
> of Col Russell, the company consisting of 32 waggons

with 110 men for the "Gold Diggins" of California. Our
trail lay over a fine prairie on the "Santa Fe" route, 12
O'clock brought us to "Lone Elm" a poor solitary in a
wide expanse of Prairie.[13]

What seems beyond dispute is that on April 24, Cartwright left
Independence, Missouri, as a member of Colonel Russell's party.
Currier also notes in his diary that Colonel Russell's company
left at 8 a.m. on the 24th, though he says that they consisted of
30 teams and 120 men.[14]

Initially, all the trails destined for Oregon and California began as one route and only diverged much later in the journey.
The least treacherous route to begin the trek was via the Santa
Fe Trail, also known as Independence Road. Starting in a south-
erly direction, crossing rivers and roads, Independence Road
eventually turned north to intersect the St. Joe Road west of
present-day Marysville, Kansas. From there, emigrants began
the long journey west via the South Pass Route.

Heading west from Independence, also called the "jumping
off point," was essentially leaving civilization as they knew it.
Emigrants were moving from their homeland to settle in what
was then desolate territory. They faced typically three or four
months of difficult terrain and unpredictable weather; it was a
given that some would die along the way. When it comes to the
difficulties of the trip and the struggle with the elements, many
gold rush diaries describe common problems and themes.

Wagons typically were loaded with provisions that included
cooking equipment, weapons, and barrels of cornmeal (which
also doubled as packing material for fragile items, such as eggs
and china). Trunks full of clothing and personal treasures also

were brought along. Food was the most important item; standard provisions included 100 pounds of flour for each adult, 70 pounds of bacon, 30 pounds of "pilot bread" (unleavened bread, which lasts longer without spoiling), beans, rice, coffee, sugar, dried fruits, baking soda, and vinegar.[15]

In diaries, Indians were mentioned as interested in trading handmade items for food or other necessities. Though travelers were wary because of the stories they heard about Indians being cruel and dangerous, many diarists noted that their interactions were far from problematic.[16]

The troubles that did arise were mostly with the terrain. Crossing rivers and venturing up or down mountain slopes or hills made the trip very difficult. In addition, there were long stretches without enough water to drink between stops, especially when the weather was hot. Wagons broke down, and the animals that towed them became exhausted or died.

In both the Currier and Cartwright diaries, the beginning of the trip consisted of crossing the Kansas River, where Indians owned and managed a flat boat that would ferry the wagons over to the other side. Currier noted that the Indians were of the Pottawatomie tribe but that they had intermingled with French Canadians, and so some were nearly white.

As mentioned before, Currier wrote that he left Colonel Russell's "mule" party and joined Captain Woolsey and Mr. Emery on May 5, noting that Colonel Russell knew no more about the country than they did, and he knew less about managing a train. While Cartwright's journal entries are missing until May 17, he later mentions Mr. Emery repeatedly and likely joined Currier in switching parties at this time.

On their way to Fort Kearny (within present-day Nebraska), the overlanders followed the Little Blue, a river they camped beside along the way. This was Pawnee country. Not many days later, on May 11, the wagon train arrived in Fort Kearny, home to fifty U.S. troops and a building built of sun-dried bricks plastered over with mud. The travelers were furnished with a room, paper, pens, and ink to write letters. Not staying long, they left to make their camp beside the Platte River. They were now 330 miles from Independence.

Currier's and Cartwright's journals are in sync on May 17. Both men's entries for that day mention crossing the South Fork of the Platte in the rain. A portion of Cartwright's journal entry for that day describes their experience traveling above the junction of two roads that merged from the west and were crowded with emigrants:

> This morning we crossed the South Forks of Platte, about 20 miles above the junctions, it having rained heavily for the past three days, and still continuing. The river was quite high. We are now 5 waggons in company. We were the last to attempt the crossing, but the first to succeed. The superiority of our animals was here very apparent. After a few moments rest on the other side we returned to the middle of the stream to the assistance of those who were unable to advance further because of the weight of their waggons or the weakness of their animals. With a great deal of labor, and by doubling teams, we at last succeeded in landing all safely on the opposite shore. I am still suffering from dysentery caused by eating too freely of buffalo.[17]

On May 23, both Cartwright and Currier mention seeing Chimney Rock, as it was called by emigrants, which is located along the North Platte River in Nebraska. However, Native Americans at the time called it "Elk Penis." On May 25, both Cartwright and Currier mention encountering a trader named Mr. Rubidoux (near what is now Scottsbluff, Nebraska). Rubidoux, living in a log cabin and in possession of a few blacksmith tools, was a fixture in many emigrant diaries.

On May 26, Cartwright's party arrived at Fort Laramie, a trading post for the American Fur Company. At this point, Cartwright seemed to have seen enough of the elephant to pass some judgments of his own:

> The Fort is beautifully situated on the banks of the Laramie River, with plenty of wood in the vicinity and good pasture for stock. There is no game of any consequence within considerable distance of the Fort. Its principal trade is with the "Sioux." This is the first post for trading on the trail and I must say that I was not very favorably impressed either with the Fort itself or its occupants. A poor miserable set they appeared indeed, however these are not the real "Mountain Men." In the distance we can see the tall "Peak of Laramie," the highest point of the "Black Hills," with its top covered with snow.[18]

On June 2, the team met up with a "Crow Tribe of Indians," and Cartwright and Currier describe their encounter in a similar fashion. Currier states that they smoked a pipe of peace with signs and words after they exchanged gifts of buffalo meat and crackers. Cartwright mentioned that he found smoking the sage pipe so pleasant that he smoked the pipe out. He also exchanged a pocket handkerchief for a necklace of beads.[19]

On June 4, they passed Independence Rock and Devil's Gate. June 5 would be the last entry in the Cartwright's diary (or, at least, in the transcribed versions that remain). Cartwright mentioned that grass and water were scarce on the 5th, and that they followed Captain Paul's trail (Captain Paul was the leader of another emigrant party they met). They struggled getting through this heavy, sandy road, and once they did, they camped at noon.

After June 5, we know little of what Cartwright did or experienced until he reached San Francisco. Currier continued to Sutter's Mill, California, the site of the original gold discovery. It is not known if Cartwright stayed with Currier all the way to Sutter's Mill and then went to San Francisco, or if he broke off separately at some point. It is likely, though, that they continued together for at least the next few weeks.

Currier wrote that Captain Paul's company was from St. Louis and had started two weeks before they did, which indicates that they had picked up the pace along the way. On June 22, Currier states that his company came to Fort Hall at noon. Fort Hall was located in what was then Oregon Territory but which would later become the state of Idaho. From Fort Hall, emigrants bound for Oregon continued along the Snake River, while those bound for California turned southwest at the Raft River; this led to the Humboldt River and then to the gold diggings. Cartwright probably accompanied Currier to Fort Hall and then went southwest on the California Trail, leaving the Oregon Trail behind.

On July 1, Currier wrote that they struck the head of the Humboldt River. On July 4, Currier sounded homesick and tired; he said his thoughts were of home most of the day, at the end of which he "took a glass of Whiskey to keep the 4th and went to bed."[20]

On July 13, Currier wrote that the party arrived at Carson River, a fine clear stream. He stated, "all happily rejoicing to think we had crossed the desert so well." The team had successfully passed through the "Forty Mile Desert." But their jubilance was short-lived. Currier told a tale that caused the men to "arouse a warlike spirit":

> At midnight just as the moon was rising, the Guard that was herding the animals in a fine meadow by the banks of the River gave the alarm of Indians. We all rushed out of our tents and secured the mules to the wagons. We found one of Capt. Paul's Mules shot with 3 arrows. One of them stuck in the thigh about 6 inches. Capt. Paul had been back to our last stopping place after a mule and had just returned with an arrow pulled out of him. As this was the first aggression, it aroused our warlike spirit and some said they would shoot the first Indian they saw. We hunted the woods and bushes a part of the night and in the morning. No sign of Indians could be seen. The Indians on this river are called the Digger Tribe. They live mostly on roots, but are fond of horse and mule flesh when they can get it. We left the old mule for them to eat wishing that every mouthful of old Ned, as he was called, would choke them.[21]

Currier finally arrived at Sutter's Mill on July 24 and wrote, "here was our first sight of the gold diggings and life in California." He balked at the high prices for items such as sugar compared to prices in Newark, his hometown. The last lines in his diary that day remark, "I took a glass of Porter and sat down and read the newspaper which was a rare treat. I almost felt myself at home again."[22]

Many years later, Alexander Cartwright joined the Society of California Pioneers. On his membership certificate in his handwriting it states that he arrived in California on July 4, 1849.[23] This date nearly matches the date when Currier says he reached the Humboldt River, which was within California's boundaries at the time (though later Nevada's borders would encompass that area of the river).

The Newark Overland Company, Cartwright and Currier's original party, apparently followed the Lassen Trail through California, north of Sutter's Fort, whereas Cartwright and Currier took the Carson Route, east of the mill. The diary of Charles Glass Gray (who remained with General Darcy and the main Newark Overland Company group) reports on October 11 that his company was ready to start from San Francisco toward the "Yuba" and Sacramento City, a distance of another 125 miles. By October 21 he reports that his party had finally seen gold diggers at work on the Yuba River.[24]

A diverse multitude of men were mining side by side for gold. Gray described them as "American, French, Spaniards, and Indians," with a "vigorous and sun burnt healthy appearance." On October 25 the Newark Overland Company set up camp alongside the river. Gray declared it "our home till next spring" and christened it "Darcy." Their "home" did not last long, as they ventured to other locations, including Sacramento City. General Darcy and his nephew were almost tourists at this point, rather than gold miners.

During their travels General Darcy became ill and lost nearly seventy pounds. During November in Sacramento City, he accepted the invitation of James R. Hardenbergh to recover for the winter aboard his vessel, *Isabel*.[25] The ship was anchored in the Sacramento River opposite Sacramento City. In a letter from Darcy dated December 24 and 28, 1849 (which was published in the *Newark Daily Advertiser* on February 11, 1850), Darcy provided information on the whereabouts of some of the men from his party: "December 28th—Mr. Cartwright from our camp on the Yuba came down today. All our friends up there are well, and have got to work. The Lewis's, Fowler and Jobes make, when they work, two ounces a day, equal to eight dollars per man. They have no quicksilver, but will procure it soon; and by that means will probably treble their receipts. A few pounds of that article will run a machine for several months if carefully used and separated from the gold."[26]

It is unlikely that the "Mr. Cartwright" mentioned in Darcy's letter is Alexander Cartwright.[27] Furthermore, it is also unlikely to be Alfred Cartwright, Alexander's brother.[28] Alfred had sailed to San Francisco from New York rather than making the overland trip. By December 1849, all the evidence shows that both Alexander and Alfred had already given up on mining and were embarked on an entirely new adventure in an entirely different land: they had kept going west to Hawaii.

But again, this is getting ahead of our story. In 1892, after Cartwright's death, one of Cartwright's sons provided an account to the newspapers of Cartwright's initial gold-mining prospects and business efforts in 1849 after reaching California. According to family notations, this information was originally written by Cartwright himself:

> When we reached the "Embarcadero" the first wooden building was being erected for Barten, Lee & Co on the site of the city of Sacramento. Captain Seeley and I turned our attention to mining, but after looking over the field we wisely decided that other openings offered greater inducements to men of our class. We proceeded down the Sacramento River to San Francisco. Here I met my younger brother Alfred DeForest Cartwright who had preceded me to California by way of Cape Horn.
>
> My first business venture was the purchasing, with my brother Alfred, of the interest of J. Ross Browne in a mining enterprise which was being inaugurated by the party that came to San Francisco in the ship Pacific. This venture was soon given up.
>
> Shortly after my arrival in California I was attacked by dysentery and was advised by my friend Charles Robinson, who had previously lived in Honolulu, to go to the Hawaiian Islands of which he gave a glowing account. I decided to follow his advice intending to proceed to China as soon as I had regained my health, and from there secure a passage to New York.[29]

J. Ross Browne was a shipmate of Alfred Cartwright while the two journeyed to San Francisco via Cape Horn. Browne was a writer and was broke when they arrived in San Francisco on August 5, 1849. He soon gained employment with Colonel Allen, Special Agent of the Post Office, and he accepted a temporary commission to establish a line of post offices and post routes as far south as San Diego (at the pay rate of six dollars a day). However, he was primarily hired to go to Monterey, California, to document the state's constitutional convention. Browne began his duties on August 10.[30]

The existing documentation about Browne and his mining enterprise is not specific, but it may well be the mining enterprise that Cartwright mentioned. As the *Hawaiian Gazette* later stated it, "This venture did not result as was expected, and was soon given up."[31]

What is interesting about Cartwright's description of his initial California ventures is that he very quickly seems to have decided to leave California. Mining hadn't worked out "as was expected," he was sick, and it's hard to imagine that San Francisco itself was in the least attractive to him. Compared to the industrious bustle and commerce of New York and to the well-tended playgrounds of Elysian Fields—and even, perhaps, compared to the respectable game of baseball—San Francisco must have appeared exactly as it was: the suddenly overcrowded home of a dirty, greedy rabble for whom larceny, gambling, and prostitution were a way of life.

Many first-time visitors remarked that beautiful San Francisco Bay looked "large enough to hold all the Navies of the world," but in 1849, it was a navy of abandoned ships—once loaded with hopeful argonauts, they had now been anchored and simply left to rot by passengers and crew. The shore was also noteworthy for its neglect. It was piled high with empty boxes, old clothing and trunks, and spoiled or unwanted cargoes. All this garbage decayed in the rain and mixed with mud.

In the first half of 1849, San Francisco's population soared by an estimated 15,000, but that was nothing compared to the second half of the year, when 4,000 people arrived every month by sea alone. Altogether, nearly 40,000 people arrived in San Francisco during 1849, more than 90 percent of them men.[32] Their "homes" were mostly canvas tents strewn along the slopes and valleys of the sand dune that surrounded Yerba Buena Cove. A more practical solution to housing was solved by turning the hundreds of abandoned ships into hotels. The downside was the cost and the unreliability of getting a rowboat ride out to the ship.

San Francisco did not have paved streets, gas lighting, or enough fresh water, but it did have a grid street plan, which was laid in 1847. This helped newcomers find locations such as the post office at Portsmouth Square, more familiarly known as "The Plaza" on the corner of Pike and Clay Streets.[33] When mail arrived from the Atlantic states, which usually occurred once a month, people would wait hours for their turn to reach the delivery window. Some secured a place in line the night before, standing all night in the mud and the pouring rain.

The winter of 1849–50 was reportedly one of the wettest in San Francisco's recorded history. Approximately fifty inches of rain fell on the city. Since not a single street was paved or planked, everyone walked ankle-deep in mud. The city became so filthy that it was known for three things: rats, fleas, and empty bottles.

In 1849, there was a shortage of women in San Francisco, and most females who did arrive were saloon girls and prostitutes. Like the men, they had come to San Francisco to make money and get rich. Eventually, the cost of hiring a woman to sit with a customer at a bar or card table was $16 an evening. And for that, she needed to do nothing else. A whole night with a woman would cost a customer $200 to $400.[34] There were scores of gambling saloons in town, most of them large tents with dirt floors. By comparison, brothels were among the most comfortable and homelike structures in town.

Drawn as well by the lure of gold, Arthur M. Ebbets, the brother of Knickerbocker Edward A. Ebbets, arrived in San Francisco on the ship *Pacific* on August 5, 1849,[35] the same ship as Alfred Cartwright. Ebbets soon bought a lot on the south side of California Street, where he established a mercantile store that sold items they had brought with them from New York to gold miners. Keeping the throngs of emigrants fed and sheltered made for big business in the West, and it would eventually become an important business for the Cartwrights.

Arthur Ebbets later referred to his beginnings as his "gold rush trade built out of discarded packing cases," from which they first sold their goods. Arthur's father was Daniel Ebbets, for whom Alexander Cartwright had worked at the Union Bank in New York. And it would be Arthur's cousin's son, Charlie, who would build Ebbets Field in New York in the early twentieth century.[36]

FOUR

The Allure of Paradise

Less than two months after arriving in California, in half the time it took him to reach the West Coast, Alexander Cartwright departed. Landing by ship in Honolulu, Cartwright would have seen the tall palm trees growing closer and rising higher until they framed the bright blue sky, the lush greenery creating a backdrop for the tropical flowers spread across the foliage. As the strip of white sand hugging the island's shore drew nearer, he would have heard the rhythmic crashing of white-crested waves on the beach. Ultimately, the golden sun of Hawaii came to entice Cartwright more than any gold nuggets to be found in California.

He arrived in Honolulu from San Francisco on August 30, 1849, aboard the brig *Pacific*. His occupation was listed as merchant.[1] Cartwright initially remained in Honolulu nearly a year, and in that time he began the process of establishing himself permanently in Hawaii and, indeed, as a merchant. All thoughts of continuing to China or returning to New York seem to have faded.

Ship records in Honolulu and San Francisco do not indicate that Cartwright traveled back to San Francisco by December 1849 to engage again in mining, as General Darcy's letter suggests. Instead, in December 1849, Cartwright was in Honolulu petitioning for membership in a Masonic lodge.[2] Initially, Alexander's brother Alfred remained in California, but that same December, Alfred joined him in Honolulu.[3]

Alexander began working with a former acquaintance from New York, Aaron B. Howe, who was a commission merchant and auctioneer. Howe sailed to San Francisco, and on his return coaxed Cartwright into going to California as supercargo on the brig *Pacific* with a load of sweet potatoes.[4] Howe had learned that it was a very profitable endeavor to bring Hawaii's abundance of fruits and vegetables to the hungry miners in California.

In the back of Cartwright's gold rush journal there is a section titled "Journal of a voyage from San Francisco to Sandwich Islands." This is dated June 15, 1850.[5] Quite likely, Cartwright was accompanying sweet potatoes and perhaps other delicious cargo, but again, he was not tempted to remain on the mainland. The ship manifest lists Cartwright as landing back in Honolulu on July 2, 1850.[6]

Cartwright's life in Hawaii coincided with a very significant period in the island's history, and he would come to play a role in how that history continued to unfold. Cartwright arrived during the rule of King Kamehameha III. Until the 1790s, the islands of Hawaii were ruled separately. But then, Kamehameha I (also known as Kamehameha the Great), the ruler of the island of Hawai'i (or the "Big Island"), unified all the islands through warfare and negotiation. From then until his death in 1819, King Kamehameha established a rare period of peace and stability in Hawaii. At his death, Kamehameha the Great said, "Endless is the good I have given you to enjoy."[7]

Kamehameha's son Liholiho became King Kamehameha II at the age of twenty-two, becoming coruler of Hawaii with Queen Ka'ahumanu, who was Kamehameha the Great's wife. Influenced by the arrival of Protestant missionaries in 1820, Liholiho and Ka'ahumanu renounced Hawaii's two-thousand-year-old religious *kapu* system and ordered the destruction of the temples and religious idols. This created a period of intense upheaval in Hawaiian society during which Hawaiians increasingly embraced Western ways and education.

Liholiho died in 1824 after contracting measles. In 1825 his brother, Kauikeaouli, succeeded him to the throne as King Kamehameha III when he was only twelve years old. Missionaries had taught Kauikeaouli reading and writing, along with the Christian religion. As more missionaries arrived in the 1820s, they spread the teachings of Christianity and began imposing American ideas of proper society and civilization.

Native Hawaiian religion centered on a pantheon of nature gods, such as Pele, the goddess of fire; Lono, the god of agriculture; and Kane, the god of sunlight, fresh water, and winds. However, after the destruction of the temples and under the influence of the missionaries, the Christian religion was soon adopted by many Hawaiians.

In addition to embracing Christianity, King Kamehameha III

passed several significant government acts. In 1840 he helped create Hawaii's first constitution, which established a monarchy with limited citizen representation, a nascent form of democracy. He also enacted land reform in 1848 (called the Great Mahele) and in 1850 (with the Kuleana Act), which swept aside the old system and allowed both private citizens and foreigners to own land. Further, in 1845, the king allowed foreigners to become naturalized Hawaiian citizens.

These changes in effect abolished Hawaii's previous class system and allowed foreigners unprecedented access and influence in Hawaii. The changes were also an indication of Hawaii's growing relationship with America, which was pressuring Hawaii to open its economy and to shape itself into a Christian democracy similar to itself. Alexander Cartwright arrived at the precise moment when Hawaii was opening its doors—to foreign business, foreign land ownership, and foreign citizenship.

As mentioned, one of the first signs that Alexander Cartwright was immediately interested in staying in Hawaii, and perhaps in establishing himself there permanently, was his petition in December 1849 to join Hawaii's first—and, at the time, only—Masonic lodge, mere months after his arrival in Honolulu.

Primarily composed of Americans, the Masonic lodge was named Lodge le Progres de l'Oceanie No. 124, Ancient and Accepted Scottish Rite (AASR). It was founded April 8, 1843,[8] in part as a result of an aborted British takeover of the Hawaiian kingdom that same year. The takeover lasted five months and was terminated in July 1843 by British Rear Admiral Richard Thomas.[9]

However, during this time period, a French whaling vessel

sailed into Honolulu harbor whose captain, Joseph Marie Le Tellier, was authorized to create new Masonic lodges. The local representative for the French government in Honolulu was Jules Dudoit. Along with fourteen other men, they organized the Lodge le Progres de l'Oceanie. One of the charter members of the lodge was Captain John Meek from Massachusetts.

During the first six years of the lodge's existence, members served to facilitate business contacts as well as social ones. One-third of the thirty-five merchants and storekeepers in Honolulu were Masonic members in the late 1840s. However, the year 1849 brought an enormous change to Hawaii as thousands of gold-seekers traveled in and out of Honolulu. At the meeting on October 8, 1849, Captain Le Tellier remarked on the dwindling attendance at the Masonic meetings.[10]

Alexander Cartwright was accepted for membership in Lodge le Progress de l'Oceanie on December 19, 1849.[11] He was raised (became a Master Mason) on March 1, 1850.[12] Yet March 1 would be the last lodge meeting for another four years, as the lodge was thereafter closed because of low membership and attendance.

Of course, the other sign that Alexander Cartwright wanted to stay in Hawaii was that he immediately developed business prospects. One of the first involved his brother Alfred, who had joined Alexander in Hawaii in December 1849. In February 1850 Alfred formed a partnership with Richard H. Bowlin for general merchandising in Lahaina, located on the west side of the island of Maui, and they began business with financial help from his brother Alexander and Aaron Howe.

Alfred Cartwright and Richard Bowlin's business enterprise included a hotel with a billiard room, bowling alleys, and stores in Lahaina, Kahului, and Kula. However, it was not a success, and quite possibly it created some bad feelings between the Cartwright brothers. A year and a half or so later, in December 1851, Aaron B. Howe and Alexander J. Cartwright were complainants against defendants Richard H. Bowlin, Alfred D. Cartwright, and Gerrit P. Judd (as minister of finance). The ruling was in favor of the complainants for the sum of $7,961.11. Since Alfred and his partners didn't have the money, a sale was held on January 19, 1852, to auction off the businesses on Maui.[13]

Though Alfred was having trouble getting firmly established in Hawaii, Alexander was not. As noted, in partnership with Aaron Howe, Cartwright began shipping produce to the mainland in the summer of 1850, and this business would prove to be just as lucrative as it had initially promised.

Ancient Hawaiians may have revered Pele, the goddess of fire, but mid-nineteenth-century Honolulu society fought fire with buckets of water. Along with American ways, Hawaii also incorporated in its growing plantation towns the highly combustible style of wooden buildings and furnishings of America's western frontier. Since the only sources for interior lighting were candles and lanterns (electricity was not introduced in Honolulu until 1888), fires were inevitable, and they resulted in a steady loss of homes and businesses.

In his *Personal Reminiscences*, William C. Parke wrote about the formation of the early fire department in Honolulu. Sometime shortly after December 1849, Parke persuaded the minister of the interior to purchase an old Number Nine engine. The old engine had been aboard a brig that had driven ashore in a gale and become damaged, though her cargo, including the fire engine, had been saved. After purchasing it, Parke called a meeting of citizens who formed a "Fire Company," which elected him as chief engineer. Parke went on to say that after the legislature passed a law "which placed the Fire Department on good footing, and at the request of the first fire company, Mr. A. J. Cartwright was elected chief engineer."[14]

Thus, Cartwright became Honolulu's first *official* fire chief. According to the *Hawaiian Gazette*, Engine Company Number 1 existed before 1850 (along with a small Chinese engine company), but the company was disbanded in February 1850, "having for some time being poorly supported."[15] This called for action on part of the government and King Kamehameha III. Later that year, on December 27, 1850, the king and his privy council passed a law that organized the fire department.[16] Under that law, Alexander J. Cartwright was commissioned chief engineer. His commission was signed by Governor Kekuanaoa on February 3, 1851. While the present-day Honolulu Fire Department considers Parke its first fire chief,[17] Parke was in charge before the king organized a fire department by law, with Cartwright as its chief.

In June 1850, William C. Parke was appointed by the king to be the marshal of the Hawaiian Islands. Parke's commission included overseeing one hundred men in the police force, which was in dire need of better organization. Parke obviously had his hands full when he released control of the fire department to Cartwright.

Cartwright served as Honolulu's chief engineer until June 30, 1859, but he also served again, as Honolulu's fourth fire chief,

THE ALLURE OF PARADISE

from July 1, 1862, to June 30, 1863.[18] Clearly, the longer Cartwright stayed in Hawaii, the more he was deepening his involvement, by now eagerly putting to use the skills and knowledge he'd developed as a volunteer firefighter in New York. During his first reign as fire chief, he was only away from his position one time, from April 1852 to July 1852, when he traveled to San Francisco and back for business. R. A. S. Wood Esq. was appointed Chief Engineer during Cartwright's absence.[19]

In the very earliest days, the only equipment they had was a hand engine owned by a Chinese firm, Sam Sing and Company, and a homemade canvas hose. By August 1851, a second-hand engine was purchased through Brewer and Company. Its cost was defrayed by public subscription, and Engine Company No. 1 was formed in anticipation of its arrival.[20]

Reportedly, King Kamehameha III took an immense interest in the department. When the alarm went off, the monarch shed his coat, rolled up his sleeves, and helped right alongside Cartwright and the other volunteers.[21]

Alexander Cartwright had been away from his family in New York since early 1849. If, when he reached California, he had had every intention of returning to New York, after over a year in Hawaii, he had changed his mind. Instead, in 1851, he asked his family to come join him to begin an entirely new life in this island paradise.

Eliza Cartwright and their three children—Dewitt, now age eight; Mary, age six; and baby daughter Kate Lee, age two—landed in Honolulu (from San Francisco) on November 13, 1851, aboard the American ship *Eliza Warwick*.[22] However, this long-

awaited reunion after nearly three years apart was marred by
a terrible tragedy: the death of Kate Lee, whom Alexander was
meeting for the first time.

On November 16, three days after arriving in Honolulu, Kate
Lee died at home of a short and severe illness.[23] Her little grave
became the first in the Cartwright family plot at Nu'uanu Cemetery (now Oahu Cemetery). Her marble gravestone was engraved
with the words "Sacred to the memory of Kate Lee, Daughter of
Alex J. and Eliza A. Cartwright, Born in New York, October 5,
1849, Died in Honolulu, November 16, 1851. Aged 2 years and
1 month. Of such is the kingdom of Heaven."

Despite her grief, Mrs. Cartwright took the time on November 21, 1851, to write a thank you note to the captain of the ship
that brought them to Honolulu. It was published in *The Polynesian* the following day: "passengers on board the Eliza Warwick
. . . avail themselves of this medium to return to Capt. Horace
H. Watson, Jr., their most sincere thanks for unwearied attention to their comfort and kind and gentlemanly consideration
for their welfare during the voyage.[24]

Though Kate Lee was alive in Honolulu for only three days,
it was apparently long enough for her and her sister, Mary, to
pose with their father for a photograph (see photo section).

Though the timeline is unclear, Cartwright had at least three
residences in Honolulu during his lifetime. One was located
at the corner of Fort and Chaplain streets, now Fort Street Mall
in the business district.[25] Another residence was at Alakea and
Beretania streets,[26] and yet another was at Kalia and Saratoga
roads,[27] now Fort DeRussy. It was this latter location where
Cartwright died.

Three weeks after his youngest daughter's death, on December 8, 1851, Cartwright was at the home of Captain John Meek for a meeting of Master Masons to discuss forming a new Masonic lodge.[28] At the meeting, the seven members who were on the roster when Lodge le Progress de l'Oceanie had closed were joined by six other interested men.

The discussion that night was led by Lemuel Lyon (whose marriage announcement to Hannah Carter had been printed right above Kate Lee's death notice in *The Polynesian* weeks earlier). The Masonic brothers resolved that a petition be addressed to the Most Worshipful Grand Lodge of California that a charter be granted to the petitioners for a Master Mason's Lodge in Honolulu. Lyon was recommended to the Grand Lodge as Master, with John Meek as Senior Warden and Charles W. Vincent as Junior Warden.[29] All agreed that the word *Hawaiian* should be used in the name of the lodge, and John Meek offered that for meetings, they could use the room previously occupied by the brethren of the Lodge le Progres de l'Oceanie. It was then that Hawaiian Lodge UD (under dispensation) was given a name and provided a home.

Dispensation was granted on January 12, 1852, and the first regular meeting was held February 19, 1852, at which the officers were elected: Lemuel Lyon, Master; John Meek, Senior Warden; Charles W. Vincent, Junior Warden; Joseph Irwin, Treasurer; A. J. Cartwright, Secretary; William Wond, Senior Deacon; and F. W. Thompson, Junior Deacon. On May 5, 1852, the Grand Lodge of California granted the charter to Hawaiian Lodge, so that it officially became Hawaiian Lodge No. 21, Free and Accepted Masons.[30]

This was the first lodge created beyond the territorial limits of the United States by the Grand Lodge of California. As the Masons of the Hawaiian Lodge grew to prominence in Hawaiian society, they attracted the attention and interest of Hawaiian royalty, and the relationships this fostered would play a significant role in future events. The first Hawaiian royal to become involved was Prince Lot Kamehameha, nephew of the king. In June 1853, at the age of twenty-three, Lot was initiated as an Entered Apprentice Mason by the Hawaiian Lodge.[31]

This was only the beginning for Alexander Cartwright, who would become one of Honolulu's most active and established American citizens of the nineteenth century. In these and other organizations and roles, Cartwright would come to be a leader in Honolulu society, one who was intimately connected both to Hawaiian royalty and to the American business community, which would, in time, come to see the monarchy as an obstruction to their growing economic interests.

FIVE

An American in Kamehameha's Kingdom

In the 1850s Alexander Cartwright firmly established himself in Honolulu's social, business, and government circles. There was hardly a club or organization of any influence of which he was not a member, oftentimes serving one or more terms as a club officer. As a prominent Honolulu resident, he attracted public notice, and he also would occasionally make his own opinions about controversial or significant events known. These incidents provide us with deeper glimpses into Alexander Cartwright: his thoughts, personality, and manner.

In addition to the Masonic Hawaiian Lodge, one of the most important organizations for Americans in Honolulu society was the American Club, which was formed in 1856 with about two hundred members. Dr. R. W. Wood was president, and Alexander Cartwright was secretary. Announcements for the club advertised that it provided amusement and recreation for the enjoyment of its members. Their clubhouse was a rented space, and it was furnished with papers and periodicals from all parts of the world.[1]

Like the Masonic lodge, the American Club was another important forum where business and political connections were formed. As secretary, Cartwright was in charge of correspondence for the club. On February 26, 1857, he wrote Prince Lot Kamehameha a letter thanking him for the artillery that was used to salute George Washington on the anniversary of his birth.[2] The sentiment was undoubtedly sincere, but there was some irony in the letter nonetheless, as the Hawaiian monarchy in 1857 had cooled considerably to all things American, particularly to those Americans who just a few years ago had been advocating loudly for Hawai'i's annexation.

After Britain's failed takeover of Hawaii in 1843, King Kamehameha III remained wary of foreign intervention. But of the three nations vying for maritime interest in Hawaii—France, Britain, and the United States—the king most feared France and Britain.[3] Within a decade, Kamehameha III was seeking the power of America as protection against colonization. In 1854 he authorized Robert Wyllie, his minister of foreign affairs, to start negotiations with the American consul David Lawrence Gregg for annexation to the United States.[4] Significantly, both Wyllie and Gregg were fellow Freemasons.

During that year, a final draft of a formal treaty to annex Hawaii to the United States was completed by King Kamehameha III and Gregg, under the instructions of U.S. secretary of state

William Marcy. However, Kamehameha III died in 1854 before it could be signed, and the annexation movement, driven in large part by missionaries and American businessmen, was soon curtailed. One of Kamehameha's nephews, Prince Alexander, became King Kamehameha IV in 1855, and he immediately scrapped the annexation plan.[5]

Kamehameha IV would become known and beloved by Hawaiians because of his reform-minded efforts to protect the Hawaiian people and to maintain Hawaiian sovereignty as an independent nation. He and his brother, Prince Lot (who would eventually succeed him to the throne in 1863), displayed an anti-American attitude. This was clearly a reaction to the long-standing political and cultural meddling of the missionaries, and it also probably arose from the simple fact that the largest foreign population in Hawaii was now American. Yet for the brothers, an early experience of racism and discrimination while traveling in the United States may have had the most profound effect regarding their negative opinion of Americans. As teens, Alexander and Lot traveled to France, Great Britain, and the United States. Upon leaving Washington DC, a train conductor tried to put Prince Alexander off the train because of his color.[6]

The 1850s annexation movement itself was full of ambiguity and differing opinions, even among advocates, who most definitely included Alexander Cartwright. For example, what began as a group of men angry about smallpox ravaging Honolulu in 1853 evolved into an issue of annexation. Calling themselves the Committee of Thirteen, they wanted the king to dismiss the Royal Commissioners of Health, Gerrit Judd and Richard

Armstrong, for their negligence in not vaccinating the community against smallpox.

Apparently in an effort to win back his reputation, Judd submitted an offer to the king from his wealthy New York acquaintance Alfred G. Benson to purchase the islands for $5 million. Though Judd had had possession of the offer since 1852, he gave it to the king only in the last days of his career. This did not mollify the Committee of Thirteen—who were strong annexationists, many of whom expressed contempt for the Hawaiian monarchy—and they wanted Judd gone nonetheless.

In 1853 the Democrat and expansionist Franklin Pierce was elected as the American president; many Americans living in Honolulu were fellow Manifest Destiny men. They saw the recent developments in Honolulu as a means of bringing forth their desired outcome for the Hawaiian Islands. Separately from the Committee of Thirteen, nineteen residents, including Alexander Cartwright, signed a petition in support of annexation, which was laid before the king in privy council on August 24, 1853.[7] In fact, Cartwright was once quoted as saying, "I still think New York is the only city in the world and I am still an American citizen and not a whitewashed Kanaka and all the office and all the wealth of the island would not tempt me ever to forswear my allegiance to Uncle Sam."[8] However, all talk of annexation quieted down when the king died the following year.

Both Alexander Cartwright's business and his family grew in the 1850s. Cartwright and Aaron Howe dissolved their partnership by December 1851, and Howe continued his auction business.[9] Afterward, Alexander Cartwright became a general shipping agent and commission merchant (one who buys and sells goods for others on a commission basis), and by all indications, he made quite a good living at it.

Alexander Cartwright's brother Alfred tried his hand at another business venture in Honolulu. This attempt had a more practical application than his previous one: Alfred opened the first feed store in Honolulu in November 1859. It was located on Fort Street and sold such goods as oats, hay, barley, rice, wheat, flour, potatoes, and onions. Alfred operated the store until well into the 1860s before he and his family moved to Oakland, California, in 1869.

While some have said that Alexander Cartwright never left the islands again after first landing there in 1849, this is not entirely true. He never lived anywhere else, but according to ship manifest records, he sailed to San Francisco in 1850 and 1852. In April 1852, Cartwright boarded the ship *Zoe* for San Francisco and returned on the ship *Isabella* in July for his merchant and shipping business.[10]

Contained within the Cartwright family private collection are several typed transcriptions of letters written by A. J. Cartwright Jr. to California, Oregon, Massachusetts, Connecticut, New York, and England regarding orders for or shipment of merchandise. Some items desired for import were pants, jackets, and boots, while one item sold for export was Kona coffee. These business letters date from 1855 to the early 1860s, and they indicate the growing success and breadth of his business.[11]

One original letter was written by Cartwright to Arthur Ebbets in San Francisco in 1856. It is in reference to a fire engine that would be shipped via the *Frances Palmer* to Hawaii.[12]

A. M. Ebbets, Esq.

San Francisco, Calif.

Dear Sir,

Your favor of 23rd April received and I should have answered it sooner had not illness have prevented. I regret that you could not have availed of the kind offer of G. B. Post Co. but trust that ere this reaches you, the Machine and all its appurtenances will be on her way to this place. We were quite disappointed in not receiving her per *Frances Palmer*, but suppose of course the delay was unavoidable. Did Mr. Perrin give you the name for her, as you say nothing about it. I am afraid he has neglected it. If so, please have the proper letters made and forward first opportunity. Her name is to be *Kamehameha*.

Yours ever,

A. J. Cartwright[13]

Alexander and Eliza Cartwright also gave birth to two more children in Honolulu: Bruce was born in 1853 and Alexander III in 1855. Both boys grew up in Honolulu and married there, too. In 1878 Alexander Cartwright III married Princess Theresa Owana Laanui, who was a direct descendent to a brother of Kamehameha the Great. She and Alexander III had two daughters, Daisy Napulahaokalani and Eva Kuwailanimamao. Alexander III and Princess Theresa divorced in 1883; Theresa would later marry Robert Wilcox, who in 1889 would become a Hawaiian hero for trying to restore the monarchy after it was overthrown (see chapter 10). Meanwhile, the same year he divorced, Alexander III moved to San Francisco and married Susan

Florence McDonald. Alexander and Susan had two daughters—
Ruth Joy and Mary Muriel. Mary Muriel married Elliott Ever-
ett Check, and it was through her estate that the handwritten
transcription of Cartwright's gold rush journal was donated to
the Bishop Museum in Honolulu (the actual wording in her
will is that it is the "original of the diary of Alexander Joy Cartwright, Jr").[14]

Cartwright's son Bruce married Mary Louise Wells in 1881,
and they had two children, Bruce Jr. and Kathleen DeWitt. Bruce
Jr. married Claire Williams, and they had three children, William, Coleman, and Bruce III (who was stillborn). Claire died
in 1919 and Bruce Jr. later married Alyce, a widow with a young
daughter, Virginia. It was Bruce Jr. who wrote to the National
Baseball Hall of Fame in 1935 about his grandfather and his
place in baseball history.

A very telling incident concerning Alexander Cartwright occurred in 1857 in connection with a royal scandal that erupted
in January of that year. Though Cartwright was by all accounts
friendly and sympathetic to the royal family, in this one incident
he very strongly and loudly took the side of an American businessman over the royal family and in the process put himself
at odds with the monarchy and created an adversary out of the
American diplomatic commissioner David Lawrence Gregg.

Gregg was given the American diplomatic commission to
the Hawaiian kingdom in 1853. In late December 1855, Gregg
wrote (in the daily log that he kept) that he was asked by Robert
Wyllie to help arbitrate a financial matter between Wyllie and
Godfrey Rhodes. Cartwright was also asked to help "referee"

the matter, and Gregg and Cartwright worked on the case together amicably for the following year, a process that also included dining together and playing cards.[15] Their association with one another turned cold, one might even say bitter, in the aftermath of a scandal concerning Princess Victoria, who was the sister of King Kamehameha IV and Prince Lot.

One evening in January 1857, Prince Lot was entertaining a few friends for dinner at the palace. His brother, the king, was there, and the guests included a Honolulu auctioneer and married man, Marcus Monsarrat. Toward the end of the evening Monsarrat's absence was noticed, and the king inquired as to his whereabouts. A servant told the king that Monsarrat was in Victoria's room.

Upon trying to enter their sister's bedroom, the king and his brother found the door locked. They demanded that the door be opened, and when there was no reply, the brothers broke down the door to find Monsarrat arranging his pants in the same room with their sister. The king threatened to kill Monsarrat, who confessed he deserved to be shot. The brothers demanded that he leave the kingdom and never return.

Though Monsarrat departed from the kingdom the following week, he returned in May 1857. When the king heard of Monsarrat's return, he consulted Gregg. The king wanted to arrest Monsarrat and forcibly banish him forever from Hawaii, but before doing so, he wanted to hear Gregg's views about the issue. Gregg told the king that according to the Hawaiian constitution, the king had the authority to banish Monsarrat, and Gregg's personal opinion was that it was the king's decision to make.

The king decided to have Monsarrat arrested and insisted that he leave the kingdom forever. This prompted loud protests from members of the American community, including Monsarrat's wife and in-laws. But one of the most vociferous protests regarding the king's decision came from Alexander Cartwright.

The rumor in Honolulu was that Gregg had declared himself the king's advisor. Cartwright confronted Gregg about the rumor, and Gregg said he was entirely convinced of the propriety of the king's course of action. Cartwright retorted that he was surprised to find an American commissioner taking such ground and added further that he would henceforth deny the American name and separate himself from the American Club, and would participate no more in 4th of July and 22nd of February celebrations.

Gregg's response to Cartwright's declarations and denunciations was that it bore no consequence on the king's rights, both moral and constitutional, whether Cartwright remained American or not.

Cartwright responded that he did not mean to be disrespectful but that he felt strongly that constitutional rights had been invaded. Then Gregg asked what punishment Cartwright thought Monsarrat should receive. Cartwright replied that Monsarrat should be treated like anyone else and brought up by the police court and fined for adultery.

Gregg then asked Cartwright: "Apply the offence, for illustration to yourself, and your own family. Would a fine of $30 satisfy your wounded feeling and honor?"

Gregg reports that Cartwright replied, "O no, but that is a different case."[16]

There, the conversation ended, but the following night, a

number of men called on Gregg at his home. Among them was Cartwright. According to Gregg, Cartwright had become anxious to remove the impressions created by his comments. Cartwright said that he had expressed himself too strongly and that his feelings must be understood in a "Pickwickian sense," as he would not want to denounce the land of his birth. (The term *Pickwickian* comes from a series of stories written by Charles Dickens in 1837, and it means "not to be taken literally.") Gregg said he took the occasion to strongly speak his views to Cartwright and the other men about the Monsarrat matter. Gregg stated, "Cartwright winced a little, but he preserved his good temper, and appeared to be impressed with the necessity of backing down from his former high positions."[17]

Later, on June 3, 1857, Gregg wrote in his diary that Captain Thomas Spencer and his wife came to call at his home. Spencer passed along what he had heard Cartwright saying about the Monsarrat matter. Apparently, Cartwright had declared the American commissioner had turned "damned Kanaka" (a derogatory ethnic slur meaning "unsophisticated in modern ways") and could not be considered a true representative of American feeling.[18] The following month, Gregg was told about another statement that Cartwright made publicly; he was heard to have said that "it was damned strange that the American Commissioner should advocate Monsarrat's banishment for being seduced by a damned black bitch of a whore, and at the same time set himself to work to secure a damned runaway felon's admission to the Hawaiian bar." Gregg's reaction to hearing this news was to write in his diary, "If Cartwright wished to make a war between us, he should have it. I would not submit quietly to his abuse, but would defend myself with lawful weapons to the last."[19]

The "runaway felon" Cartwright referred to was a sailor in port named George Bailey who was arrested for attempted larceny. Bailey was publicly whipped as punishment, and he approached Gregg to assist him in redressing the grievance. Gregg insisted that Bailey did not get a fair trial and that his punishment was not a legal one. Even if Bailey had been guilty, Hawaiian law only required a fine and imprisonment. While Gregg continued to argue the case for Bailey to receive compensation from the Hawaiian government, Bailey left Honolulu without informing anyone.[20] Thus, as Cartwright characterized it, he was a "runaway felon."

Needless to say, from that time on, Gregg and Cartwright were adversaries, as Gregg's diary makes abundantly clear in this and other incidents in which he and Cartwright interacted.

Gregg and Cartwright were Masonic brethren, but Masonic membership did not guarantee agreement or even goodwill. In fact, Honolulu's Masonic fraternity experienced a fractious split in the mid-1850s. For unknown reasons, the Lodge Le Progres was reactivated in 1854 following authorization from Paris,[21] and six members of the Hawaiian Lodge demitted (resigned) to restart the new lodge. Most of the demitting brethren had belonged to the original French lodge, including John Meek, but nevertheless, Hawaiian Lodge members were puzzled at the withdrawal.

During this time, the Hawaiian Lodge member Lemuel Lyon left Honolulu to settle in Stockton, California. Not long after, he became the first Worshipful Master of Morning Star Lodge in 1855. Eventually, he moved north to Independence, Oregon, and began Lyon Lodge No. 29 in 1857; its charter was granted in 1860.[22] He resided there for the rest of his life, yet no correspondence with his former Honolulu Masonic brethren was uncovered indicating whether his departure was because of the split.

When the Lodge Le Progres began accepting new initiates in 1855, some Hawaiian Lodge members requested that the Grand Lodge of California make a decision on the "legitimacy" of the reactivated French lodge.[23] The Grand Lodge of California responded with an interdiction banning the members of Hawaiian Lodge from having any association or communication with Lodge le Progres. Then, when it was discovered that members of the Hawaiian Lodge were questioning the legitimacy of Le Progres, John Meek—who was now a member of Le Progres and who also owned the hall where both lodges met—raised the rent for the Hawaiian Lodge. He then threatened to refuse to rent to them at all.[24]

The conflict between the lodges continued through 1857. Part of the controversy pertained to which lodge would benefit by association with the Hawaiian monarchs. The rivalry escalated when friends of the royal princes left the Hawaiian Lodge and joined Lodge Le Progres. The dispute took an even worse turn when King Kamehameha IV joined Lodge Le Progres on January 14, 1857. Though the Hawaiian Lodge members excused Prince Lot from punishment for visiting Lodge Le Progres to witness his brother (the king) being initiated as an Entered Apprentice, Lot and five others were still judged guilty of "un-Masonic behavior" and for violating the interdiction.[25]

Abraham Fornander, then secretary of Hawaiian Lodge, wrote that this division caused "moral and material injury" for two years. In fact, Masons were typically encouraged to attend meetings of other lodges, especially if witnessing the initiation of a respected monarch into the order. Despite this, one person stood out as holding firm to the position that the members who visited Le Progres should be punished. According to Masonic records, Alexander Cartwright insisted on their guilt and on expulsion as the only appropriate action.[26]

It's not entirely clear why Cartwright was so upset. On the face of it, he complained that Le Progres had not yet been confirmed as legitimate, so he seemed opposed to any actions that might be seen to grant legitimacy. And yet he had originally been a Le Progres member himself, so one might imagine that he would be sympathetic to its reformation. It could be that his opposition was really based in resentment because the royal family members received what he considered special treatment, or because Le Progres almost immediately became the favored lodge of the Hawaiian monarchy. In any case, Cartwright remained unwavering in his opposition.

In 1859 the Supreme Council of France received an invitation from Lodge Le Progres to review their documents concerning legitimacy, and they found that the French lodge was in conformity with its regulations (as Le Progres had claimed all along). And yet Cartwright still argued against it, declaring that the Supreme Council of France "was a body not recognized in Masonry below the 18th degree."[27]

The Hawaiian Lodge formally rejected Cartwright's position and reauthorized contact with Lodge Le Progres after being authorized to do so by the California Grand Lodge. In an echo of his response in the Monsarrat incident, Cartwright announced his resignation from the lodge.[28] However, as with his threat to renounce his American citizenship, he apparently reconsidered and remained a member. Yet, Prince Lot was among ten members who then withdrew from the Hawaiian Lodge, most likely owing to the public expressions of their supposed guilt.

Any public person who takes strong stands on controversial issues—major or minor—will have detractors, and Cartwright had his. A century and a half later, it can be hard to recreate the full complexity of issues from the documentation that remains. And when what remains is unflattering, we should be mindful that what we are getting is biased; it's not the "whole story." Still, it is interesting to hear what Cartwright's detractors had to say.

Apparently, as the incidents just discussed make clear, Cartwright freely and boisterously shared his opinions on politics and the events of the day, and his feelings were sharp, his judgments sometimes harsh. David Lawrence Gregg, who had ample opportunity to observe Cartwright but was no friend to him, had this to say on January 7, 1858:

> Cartwright seems to be regarded as an active agent in opposing the government at the Election on Monday. It is not strange. He is a Know-nothing politically, morally, and intellectually; or in other words he is a man of obtuse perceptions, perverted sentiments, and narrow understanding. Such men would be beneath contempt

if there were not many like them, always ready to act the ruffian in support of passion, prejudice or malice.

Dr. Robinson is the co-adjutor of Cartwright, and probably his chief adviser. He is a man of more education better address, and greater tact, yet not more to be depended on or more honorable. The two were Monsarrat's chief advisers, and their defeat in that matter has doubtless prompted them to revenge, at this time. Their efforts are quite as likely to be availing as those of the fly which lighted on the horns of the ox, and buzzed![29]

The election referred to by Gregg was an election of government and legislative representatives, and Gregg clearly thought that Cartwright's indignant reaction in the Monsarrat incident a year earlier was fueling his "opposition." Perhaps, or it could be that it was only Gregg who was holding onto the emotions of the Monsarrat incident.

What is equally interesting about this, on a larger historical note, is that whatever Gregg's feelings for Cartwright, the debates themselves didn't seem to undermine what was for Hawaii a relatively new democratic process. Gregg writes in his diary on the day of the election: "In all the early part of the day there was a great flourish of opposition to those considered government candidates, but towards the evening it was considered as likely to be unavailing. Still there was a spirited contest, and every thing bore the appearance of an American election."[30]

To be singled out is, in its own sometimes backhanded way, a sign of respect. In the 1850s, Cartwright was increasingly financially successful and politically influential, and he was largely opinionated. This made him the target of gossip. Honolulu was then a city, but it was small enough that socially it often felt like a village: everyone knew everyone else, and frequently they knew their business, too.

An interesting little booklet was written, printed, and thought to be distributed to each doorway in town in 1857. Its title was "The Honolulu Merchants' Looking Glass—To see themselves as others see them." The booklet's preface stated that the anonymous author's intention was to enable the people described within its pages to see their own faults as he has seen his own. Decades later, it was thought to have *possibly* been written by a "Widdifield" and published by P. S. Wilcox, who is also named in the little booklet.

Thirty-one merchants are named in this booklet, and among them are Alexander J. Cartwright and his brother Alfred. Another is G. P. Judd, though any accusations the community had against him are defended by the author of this "looking glass." Though most in the booklet received a mild scolding, if any, Alexander Cartwright is greatly assaulted.

Excerpts from the booklet describe him possessing "a better faculty of pulling wool over shipmasters' eyes than any other man in the community; judging from his way of making money." It also states that he is seen as "very vindictive, and does not scruple of anything when there is money to be made," and that "according to his own confession, must be rich. Is fond of display, courts popularity, and has a weakness for females."[31] Alfred, on the other hand, is portrayed initially as a failure in business in

Lahaina, yet it is noted later that he was "sharp in a trade" after opening a feed store.[32]

What are we to make of this? Perhaps nothing more than that Alexander Cartwright made some enemies, one of which slandered him. We can only speculate as to what Cartwright himself thought of this portrait, for we can hardly doubt that it was not brought to his attention.

Despite rifts and disagreements—between Masonic brethren or between American businessmen and the royal family—Honolulu was a tight-knit community, and its members joined together to improve their city and to help each other in need. In 1859 Queen Emma and King Kamehameha IV founded Queen's Hospital.[33] The king first proposed building a new hospital in his opening speech to the Hawaiian legislature in 1855, but money was not allocated until 1859. The royal couple pledged their own money, and they personally raised funds for the hospital to be built. In the end, the coral stone building cost $14,728.92.

At the start of construction, laying the new hospital's cornerstone was the first public Masonic ceremony on the islands. On June 17, 1860, members of both Masonic lodges, Le Progres and Hawaiian Lodge, acted together for the first time to assist in the cornerstone ceremony. Together, King Alexander Kamehameha IV, the past Master of Lodge Le Progress, and Alexander Cartwright, as Junior Grand Warden of Hawaiian Lodge, officiated the ceremony.[34] Twelve years later, Cartwright and a different king would together perform a cornerstone ceremony for another building.

King Alexander Kamehameha IV and Queen Emma had one

son, Prince Albert, born in 1858—the last child ever born to a monarch of Hawaii. The little prince died in 1862 at the age of four. The king thought that he was responsible for his son's death: he had punished Albert by giving him a cold shower because Albert wanted something he could not have. This made young Albert's already ailing health even worse. The following year Kamehameha IV died of chronic asthma at the age of twenty-nine, and in 1863, his brother Prince Lot became King Kamehameha V, the new ruler of the Hawaiian nation.

SIX

America's National Pastime in Hawaii

When the Civil War began in 1861, the reverberations were felt across the continent and even in Hawaii, where Americans such as Cartwright anxiously followed the course of the conflict. In addition to the politics of the times, research has shown that the Civil War did a great deal for the popularity and spread of baseball. It is also interesting to note that three Union generals in that war would play a part in baseball history.

Abner Doubleday, buried in Arlington National Cemetery in Washington DC, was stationed at Fort Sumter in Charleston, South Carolina, in 1861 and is attributed with firing the Union's first shot in the battle that opened the Civil War.[1] Most notably, however, Doubleday is known for his role in baseball history— or the lack thereof. The myth that he "invented" baseball in 1839 was debunked when it was discovered that Doubleday was enrolled at West Point in 1839.[2] Yet the Doubleday myth continues to this day, with many in the general public still thinking Doubleday invented baseball.

Two other Union generals, Rutherford B. Hayes and James M. Comly, earned places in baseball history. Hayes went on to become the nineteenth president of the United States, and he appointed Comly to be the U.S. minister to the Hawaiian Islands in 1877. During a formal reception at Iolani Palace, Comly was presented to the king. Comly extended his assurance to the king for "harmony and good feeling" between their two countries. Comly provided a fitting example of this regarding Hawaii's contribution to aid America during the Civil War: "the people of the Hawaiian Islands contributed a sum almost equal to that of some of the States at home. I cannot forget this substantial evidence of the regard of this people, for I had the honor to be one of the soldiers in that war. The Treaty of Reciprocity was a fit sequel to such evidences of friendly feeling as this."[3]

Because of the appointment of Comly, an unexpected link would be discovered regarding baseball, Cartwright, and Comly (which will be explored fully in chapter 8).

When Protestant missionaries began arriving in Hawaii in the 1820s, they had three main goals: to establish the Christian religion, to provide a Western education, and to introduce printing. Missionaries put the Hawaiian language on paper and taught the natives to read and write English. Native customs and practices, such as the hula and surfing, were discouraged. In their place, missionaries introduced their own customs and practices, including games.

The missionaries also built churches and schools. The Reverend Hiram Bingham received 100 acres from Queen Ka'ahumanu in 1829 on which to build a new school in Honolulu. The land was called Ka Punahou or "the new spring." Punahou School was established in 1841 for the purpose of educating children of missionaries; its doors later opened to all in 1851.[4] In 1859 the school's name officially became Oahu College. During 1918, however, the school was sectioned into elementary school (grades 1–6), junior academy (grades 7–9), and senior academy (grades 10–12). Then, in 1934, the school's name was changed back to Punahou School. The school's first principal in 1841, Daniel Dole, was an enthusiast of "bat-and-ball-games," and the school later became significant to the playing of baseball in Honolulu and Hawaii.[5]

Based on evidence that will be discussed later, it seems clear that many similar ball games that preceded the development of baseball (as played by the Knickerbockers) arrived in Hawaii with the missionaries and became quite popular among children and in the schools.

The point at which baseball in Honolulu began using the rules of the New York game is not exactly known, because no rule books survive. The descriptions of bat-and-ball games before the 1860s are minimal, and what there is seems to confirm that until the mid-1860s, baseball in Hawaii more resembled different versions of bat-and-ball games.

However, 1866 stands out as a significant year for baseball in Hawaii, as several significant developments seem to have occurred at nearly the same time. In chapter 14, we will look more closely at what role Alexander Cartwright may have played in them. One development is that, in the fall term of 1866, Punahou School established its first Punahou School Baseball Club.

In addition, an official league was created in 1866, which was composed of the Pacifics and the Pioneers. The regulations of the California National Baseball Convention were adopted at the first league meeting held on June 1, 1866.[6] Future meetings were held at various firehouses, notably Honolulu Engine Company No. 1. While there is no documentation of Cartwright's participation in the league, it is plausible that Cartwright involved himself in the league at least to the extent of hosting league meetings at this firehouse.

Then, after 1866, the popularity of baseball increased rapidly on the islands. The newspapers began reporting games and announcing lineups, and the players were a veritable "who's who" of missionary descendants, young men who would later rise to political and economic influence and power. These included William D. Alexander, Erdman Baldwin, Charles Baldwin, James Castle, William R. Castle, Clarence Cooke, Willie Damon, Charles Gulick, Allan Wickes Judd, Charles Judd, Willie Kinney, Freddie Smith, Lorrin A. Thurston, Robert Thurston, and Harry M. Whitney Jr.[7]

As reported in the *Hawaiian Gazette*, the league's first nine-inning match game occurred on August 24, 1867, at three o'clock, with a "large concourse of people gathered on the grounds to witness the sport." The game was played at Punahou School, with the Pacifics beating the Pioneers 11–9.[8]

Documentation of Alexander Cartwright's involvement in baseball in Hawaii is slim, but it is clear that his children were avid participants while in school. Cartwright's two Hawaiian-born children, Alex III and Bruce, were students at Punahou from 1864 to 1869. Their siblings DeWitt and Mary (who were born in New York) also attended Punahou. During their school years at Punahou, the Cartwright children spent after-school time with their friends attending parties, picnics, and the like. Girls sometimes made molasses candy or pored over the latest fashion book. Boys, including Alex III, would sometimes scuffle over a girl but then end up shaking hands. The Cartwrights also had a large Newfoundland dog named Dash.[9]

Upon finishing at Punahou, Alex III and Bruce went to school in California. In August 1869 Bruce sailed with his aunt (Alfred's wife) to San Francisco, and the following month Alex III sailed with his mother and Uncle Alfred to San Francisco. Eventually Alex III and Bruce returned and played baseball at Punahou as alumni. The *Punahou Reporter* announced on May 14, 1872, that it "expects the Cartwright brothers to resume their ball playing when they return from school in the United States." The team they played for was the Whangdoodle Base Ball Club, composed of Punahou students and graduates. Other baseball clubs formed over the years included the Wideawakes, Oceanics, Mariners, and Kachiachs.

Alexander III, also known as "Allie," was reported as captain of the Whangdoodle club in 1873, according to the Punahou tally book.[10] In 1875, Allie was noted as the Whangdoodle second baseman.[11] Meanwhile, the same year, a rival team, the Athletes, had a left fielder who would eventually play a central role in Hawaiian history two decades later: Lorrin Thurston.

The Knickerbocker Base Ball Club of New York was still playing in the 1860s. Apparently, the game had also finally become
respectable enough for women to watch. In 1867, the Knickerbockers designated the last Thursday of the month as Ladies
Day, when wives, daughters, and girlfriends were welcomed to
attend the ball games.

Alexander Cartwright was still in touch with some of his fellow Knickerbockers, and he certainly must have known of the
growing popularity of the game. That his baseball memories
were dear to him, and that he had continued to play the game
in some fashion over the years, is clear from a letter he wrote
on April 6, 1865. This letter also provides Cartwright's very gentlemanly accounting of his own fortunes, as well as his opinion
on the Civil War, and it was written in response to a letter from
a former Knickerbocker friend in New York, Charles DeBost.

> Dear Charlie:
>
> I received your kind letter of August 29, 1864, though as
> yet I have not seen our mutual friend James Huntling,
> dear old fellow is he not, and so is Henry his brother.
> Gentlemen of nature's making, both of them, and I con-
> gratulate you on having the friendship of either one, or
> both.
>
> What pleasant memories arise, as I read your dear,
> good letter, dear old Fraley, Neibuhr, and Charlie Bir-
> ney, Harry Anthony, Walter Avery, Tucker, Davis, Dun-
> can Curry, Eugene Plunkett, Dr. Adams, Onderdonk, and
> that genial gentleman, Colonel Lee, (to whom I am un-
> der so many obligations) and his son Ben, not forgetting
> good old Charlie; with your grounds and lofty handling,

and that particular knack you had of striking the balls. Dear old Knickerbockers, I hope the Club is still kept up, and that I shall some day meet again with them on the pleasant fields of Hoboken. Charlie, I have in my possession the original ball with which we used to play on Murray Hill. Many is the pleasant chase I have had after it on Mountain and Prairie, and many an equally pleasant one on the sunny plains of "Hawaii'nei," here in Honolulu my pleasant Island Home—sometimes I have thought of sending it home to be played for by the Clubs, but I cannot bear to part with it, it is so linked in with cherished home memories, it is truly one of my family lares.[12]

Some time since I wrote to Dr. Adams, but have received no answer. Please ask him if he received my letter and once on a time I heard that a lithograph of the old members of the Knickerbockers was to be published. Was it ever done, or if not is it not possible still to have it done. It would be interesting as a memorial of the first Base Ball club of N.Y. Truly the first, for the old New York Club never had a regular organization. I will give $100 or $200 if necessary toward its publication: My Mother (residing in Brooklyn) has my portrait, as I used to be. I will soon send you a carte de visite as I am and I tell you Charlie that (as they say in California) I am not the man I was in '49. Though I am still hale and hearty, I feel the want of exercise and/or bracing climate. I have resided here now over 15 years and have not been off this Island for the last 12 years. I am so fearfully sea sick when I go on the water, that it deters me from traveling.

You are kind enough to ask about my fortunes, though

by no means rich, I am independent and occupy an excellent position in society. I have every reason to be satisfied and grateful, and I am. I have a few spare thousands in Uncle Abraham's bosom (6% Bonds, Gold) my health is excellent and always has been—my children as good as most, and my wife is too good for me. Why should I not be content—but above all this Charlie boy "I am sound on the goose."[13]

God bless the Union, Uncle Abe, Sherman, Grant, Farragut, Poste, each and all, soldiers and sailors from the drummer boy to the Major General, from the powder monkey to the Vice Admiral God bless all who are for the Union and as old Cuttle says, "scatter his enemies and make 'em fall."

I wish you would write to me again and ask Fraley Neibuhr, Dr. Adams and others to do so—please send photographs of all old friends that are obtainable.

I hope the sudden fall of Gold will not affect your business, unless it is favorable.

Apr. 25th—News of Capture of Richmond, surrender of Lee and Company received—Hurrah for us!

Good bye Charlie. God bless you. I send "Aloha" to you and any Sandwich Islander you meet will translate that for you.

Yours always,
Alexr. J. Cartwright

P.S. Anything for me left at Carrington and Company Broadway will reach me sure.[14]

1. Alexander J. Cartwright Jr. Courtesy
of the Cartwright Family Collection.

2. Eliza Cartwright.
Courtesy of the Cartwright
Family Collection.

3. Eliza Cartwright in
later years. Courtesy of
Hawaii State Archives.

4. Alexander J. Cartwright Jr. wearing Masonic apron.
Courtesy of the Cartwright Family Collection.

5. Alexander J. Cartwright Jr. wearing fire department helmet and holding a presentation fire horn. Courtesy of the Cartwright Family Collection.

6. DeWitt Robinson Cartwright.
Courtesy of Hawaii State Archives.

7. Alexander J. Cartwright Jr. and daughters, undated.
Kate Lee Cartwright is sitting on her father's lap with
her sister Mary standing beside them. Courtesy of the
Cartwright Family Collection.

8. Mary G. Cartwright. Courtesy of
H. L. Chase/Bishop Museum Archives.

9. Bruce Cartwright Sr. Courtesy of
Williams/Bishop Museum Archives.

10. A. J. Cartwright III, with rifle and dog.
Courtesy of Hawaii State Archives.

11. A. J. Cartwright III. Courtesy of Bishop Museum Archives.

12. Honolulu Library and Reading Room. Courtesy of Hawaii State Archives.

13. The Judiciary Building, or Aliiolani Hale, was originally intended to be a royal residence for King Kamehameha V. The king himself, along with Alexander Cartwright, laid the first cornerstone for the building in early 1872. Courtesy of the author.

14. Hawaiian Lodge No. 21 at the corner of
Fort and Queen streets, 1880. Courtesy of
Bishop Museum Archives.

15. Honolulu Engine Company No. 1.
Courtesy of the Cartwright Family
Collection.

16. Queen's Hospital, 1870s. Courtesy of Ray Jerome/
Bishop Museum Archives.

17. View of Honolulu from Kawaihao Church tower, 1853.
Courtesy of Hugo Stangewald/Bishop Museum Archives.

18. The ship *Alameda* at the Honolulu dock, 1888.
From Palmer, *Athletic Sports in America.*

19. King Kalakaua (*far left*) on the Iolani Palace grounds, 1888.
From Palmer, *Athletic Sports in America.*

20. Lithograph of Luau for Spalding's baseball players, 1888. From Palmer, *Athletic Sports in America.*

21. Oceanic Baseball Team. Lorrin Thurston is standing second from right. Courtesy of Hawaii State Archives.

22. Baseball game at Makiki Park,
ca. 1890. Courtesy of Bishop
Museum Archives.

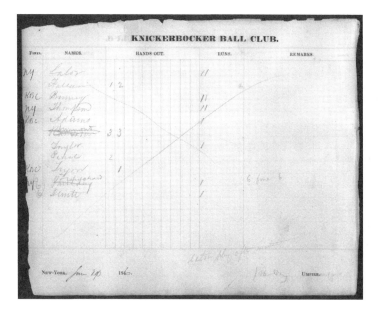

23. Knickerbocker Base Ball Club "Extra Play" on June 19, 1846, with J. Paulding as umpire. Courtesy of Albert Spalding Baseball Collection, Manuscripts and Archives Division, New York Public Library, Astor, Lennox, and Tilden Foundations.

24. Fourth Avenue and Twenty-seventh Street, New York, 1860. Courtesy of the author.

25. Cartwright Day signed photograph from those who played baseball at Doubleday Field on August 26, 1939, in Cooperstown NY. Courtesy of Hawaii State Archives.

26. Artist's rendering of Independence Courthouse
Square, 1849–50. Courtesy of Jackson County
Historical Society Archives.

27. Bruce Cartwright Jr. Courtesy
of Bishop Museum Archives.

SEVEN

Cartwright and the Monarchy
in the 1860s and 1870s

Over the course of the 1860s and 1870s, Alexander Cartwright became, if anything, an even more prominent and important member of Honolulu society. His business relationships expanded, and his relationship with Hawaii's rulers grew more intimate and involved. His two Hawaiian-born sons, as we saw in chapter 6, came into their own as they involved themselves in baseball. Cartwright also seemed to perhaps mellow a bit with age, though he did not escape personal tragedy.

In 1863, when Prince Lot ascended the throne and became King Kamehameha V, he continued his brother's attempts to contain American political influence in Hawaii. One of his first and most significant acts was to hold a constitutional convention in 1864. This repealed the 1852 constitution and replaced it with a new one that returned some powers to the monarchy. This was viewed at the time as anti-American.

However, with King Kamehameha V, Alexander Cartwright would develop his closest relationship yet with a Hawaiian monarch. For example, when the king was ready to grant the new constitution, he sent a formal invitation to Cartwright to attend the privy council. Also, King Kamehameha V appointed Cartwright to be consul of Peru. Ultimately, Cartwright served two terms as consul, from 1865 to 1867 and from 1878 to 1879. These appointments involved Cartwright serving as consulate of Peruvian merchants during their visits to Honolulu for the purpose of trade.

King Kamehameha V and Alexander Cartwright were, of course, fellow Freemasons, but Lot had remained only loosely linked to Freemasonry after the embarrassing incident in 1857 when the Hawaiian Lodge had reprimanded him for visiting Le Progres. In 1872, when construction of the new judiciary building was to be inaugurated, the king asked his minister of finance to invite Cartwright, who was Acting Grand Master of the Hawaiian Lodge, to perform a cornerstone ceremony.

Acting G. M. Cartwright

Dear Sir:

It is the desire of His Majesty, the King, that the Cornerstone of the new Government Building be laid with Masonic ceremonies. I therefore request "Fraternity" through you as acting G. M. of Free and Accepted Masons in Honolulu, to take the Necessary measures to carry out that object. I propose Monday the 19 inst., at 11 a.m. as a convenient time for the ceremony.

Believe me with the highest respect,
Yours truly,
Fred W. Hutchinson[1]

On February 19, 1872, the brethren from Hawaiian Lodge and Lodge Le Progres de l'Oceanie joined together in front of Lodge le Progres. William C. Parke, Marshal of the Kingdom, as well as a member of Hawaiian Lodge, led a procession to the site. The king and his staff viewed the ceremony from a stand that had been erected over a portion of the foundation. As the band played "God Save the King," tools were presented to His Majesty King Lot Kamehameha V and Acting Grand Master Alexander Cartwright. Together they spread cement beneath the cornerstone.[2]

During this ceremony, King Kamehameha V also buried a time capsule, which was discovered on December 10, 2005, when radar was used to penetrate the cornerstone in the northeast corner of the Ali'iolani Hale building.[3] Initially, this building held all the government offices, from the legislature to the Hawaii Supreme Court, though today it houses only the Hawaii Supreme Court, a law library, and the judiciary history center.

In Masonic tradition, time capsules are buried within cornerstones, and this particular one is known to contain photos of royal families dating back to Kamehameha the Great and a copy of the constitution of the Hawaiian kingdom, Hawaiian postage stamps, twenty-one Hawaiian and foreign coins, eleven different local newspapers, a calendar, and books, such as a Hawaiian language dictionary. As exciting as this discovery is, the capsule was left undisturbed, since digging it out would destroy the building, which is also now a historic treasure. At the time of this writing, Matt Mattice, the great grandson of Alexander III and Theresa Owana Kaohelelani Laanui (and grandson of Princess Eva Kuwailanimamao Cartwright) works as the

Executive Director of the King Kamehameha V Judiciary History Center. His office is located in the very spot where the building cornerstone rests.

During the late 1860s and 1870s, there were few important Honolulu personages Cartwright didn't seem to have dealings with through his involvement in civic and business groups. Cartwright became a member of the American Seamen's Institute, which his brother Alfred and Dr. G. P. Judd helped to found with the assistance of the U.S. consulate Thomas Wilson in 1867.[4]

Cartwright was at one time the president of the Union Iron Works, and he served as president of the American Relief Fund Association in 1868, the same year his brother Alfred was treasurer.[5] Their accounts were reported annually in the *Pacific Commercial Advertiser* and the *Hawaiian Gazette*. Cartwright was also, as one might expect, a long-standing member of the chamber of commerce (which first formed in 1850); he was the chamber secretary in 1871 when the chamber's petition for incorporation was granted by King Kamehameha V in privy council.[6] Matters of this nature often brought Cartwright in touch with the king. In the late 1870s, Cartwright also served as secretary and treasurer for the stockholders of the Waimanalo Sugar Company.[7]

Another great illustration of the close-knit nature of Honolulu society, and of Cartwright's intimate standing in it, occurred in August 1858, when he allowed Charles Reed Bishop and William A. Aldrich to open the Bank of Bishop & Company in a corner of his office in the Makee & Anthon Building.[8] The bank began with nothing more than a safe, and during the first year, Bishop and Aldrich made up the entire staff. They received coins from all over the world: Spanish coppers and silver pieces, French gold coins, English sovereigns, and coins from Peru, Chile, Italy, India, and China.[9]

Charles Reed Bishop would become a major figure in Hawaii; he helped develop the state's economic institutions and played an active role in government. He served the royals in a variety of positions: as a member of the house of nobles, privy council, and the collector of general customs; he also helped organize the Royal Hawaiian Agricultural Society, of which Cartwright was at one time treasurer.[10] After Bishop's wife, Bernice Pauahi Bishop, died in 1884, Bishop eventually retired from Hawaiian life and moved to California.[11] However, before he did, he founded the world-famous Bishop Museum in 1889 in honor of his late wife, the last descendant of the royal Kamehameha family.

In March 1866 the steamer *Ajax* brought a thirty-one-year-old reporter for the *Sacramento Union* to Honolulu. His name was Samuel Clemens, though a few years later he would become better known by his pen name, Mark Twain. Clemens had joined his St. Louis Masonic lodge five years earlier, and he attended Masonic functions when he traveled. After witnessing the month-long mourning rituals for the deceased Princess Victoria, sister of King Kamehameha V, Clemens ventured into observing the monthly ritual at the meeting of Hawaiian Lodge No. 21. Though no record of this meeting has been uncovered, it seems highly probable that Cartwright and Clemens would have met on this occasion.

Cartwright had his own remarks published in the *Hawaiian*

Gazette on June 2, 1866, extending condolences to the king and his family on the loss of Princess Victoria. Cartwright added his wishes for the king's lasting health, so that he might long continue to reign over a happy and grateful people. With this condolence, Cartwright seems even a little contrite, as if he is perhaps trying to make amends for his harsh words concerning the king's sister during the 1857 Monsarrat scandal. In closing, Cartwright called himself "his Excellency's most humble and obedient servant."

Samuel Clemens, years later, would often speak and write about his Hawaiian experiences. The speech he gave at Delmonico's Restaurant in 1889 celebrating the return of Spalding's Chicago White Stockings from their world tour (which is excerpted in the introduction to this work), would become one of the most well-known speeches related to the history of baseball, as well as to Hawaii.

As was common in the nineteenth century, Alexander Cartwright was an avid letter writer, and from his letters we can gather a vivid and intimate portrait of him and his relationships with friends and family. One letter, for instance, reveals a beloved hobby: coin collecting. Referred by a mutual friend, Cartwright wrote to a coin dealer in San Francisco in September 1878: "As I am just now in receipt of a large number of coins from Europe and the U.S., East, I am beginning to realize that I am becoming rather extravagant in the pursuit of this hobby."[12]

In a letter to his sister Kate on August 18, 1874, Cartwright speaks about his wife, Eliza, visiting Alfred and family in Oakland, reporting that all is well there. He then turns his attention to his marriage, saying, "we have been together through good and evil for 32 years and have had as pleasant a life as most people." Then, in the next sentence, he lists his enjoyments in life: "good dinners, good wines, good society, good books, and good looking women."[13]

Indeed, because of his distance from the American mainland, particularly New York, one gets the sense that Cartwright relied on letter writing more than most. He was clearly grateful for any communication, and his letters often expressed longing to be with loved ones and promises to visit them. Letters were his lifeline his entire life; the telephone would not arrive in Hawaii until the 1880s, and calls between New York and Hawaii would not be possible until well into the following century.

He sent a particularly revealing letter to his mother, Esther, on July 16, 1862, in which he updates her on his life and family in Hawaii at the time. In it, we hear Cartwright as father, husband, son, and even patriot:

Dear, Dear Mother

It is a long time since I wrote you, but I daily and nightly think of you, and I can truly say that you are ever present to me, as I have in my parlour, as handsome a picture of you as can be procured in any part of the world. I should like much to have a copy (Ambrotype or Photograph) of Father's picture. I could have it copied in San Francisco so as to match yours and Mary's.

Alfred has been sick for some few weeks, but is now about again and is improving in health fast. He is very attentive to his business and is doing well, Rebecca and

Mary are all well, as to myself I am always well, thank
Heaven. I do not know whether I have any better constitution than the rest of us, but I have been well perfectly
for over thirteen years, perhaps it is because I never take
medicine. Tea and toast, exercise and sleep, being my
sole remedies when I feel a little headache or other ill. I
have not lost a day from business (with the exception of
one week) since I have been on the Sandwich Islands,
and notwithstanding some severe losses and pull backs, I
am safely ahead of the world.

Eliza is well as is also DeWitt, Mary, Bruce, Alex. Jr.
They are all good children, and I hope will be a credit to
the name they bear. DeWitt has caused me a good deal
of trouble and anxiety, but he has I hope seen the folly of
his ways and I feel assured he will be yet a good and able
man. The other children are excellent dispositions and
are good, intelligent, obedient children. Mary is as accomplished and we think as handsome a young lady as
there is here. Bruce is a great bookworm and Alick Jr. is
a pet.

Dear Mother I wish you would send me all the partic-
ulars of the Burlock family you can. I mean births, marriages, and deaths also occupations and anything else of
interest concerning them. I am engaged in my leisure
hours in getting up a Genealogical chart of the family,
perhaps, Aunt Mary or Uncle Tom would also write me
concerning it.

I should like to be at home fighting the battles of the
Union, it would be Quixotic for me to leave here however,

as there are so many thousands ready and willing to fight who cannot be employed by the government. God bless the Union and perish all its enemies. I hear that four of the DeForest boys are in the army, all honor to them. I wish to God that I had a son old and strong enough to send. If the Rebellion is not crushed soon I am not sure but what I shall have to come and help the fight, God bless the Union.

Give my love to Ben, Kate, Het, Ann, and also to George and Wash. I should like much to hear from any of them and will answer their letters as soon as received.

> Good bye and God bless you, dear Mother,
> Your Affectionate son
> ALICK[14]

Cartwright's father, Alexander Sr., died in 1855. In an 1858 letter to his mother—in which he addresses her as "so good and kind a mother and one whom I so much love and venerate"—Cartwright indicates the high esteem and deep connection he also felt for his father, which he expressed by creating yet another namesake and naming his own son after him: "Alexander J. Cartwright Jr. I have so named to perpetuate the name of my own dear Father (now in Heaven) and I need not assure you that it will be my chief care so to educate him, as that he may imitate the virtue of his Grand Father."[15]

In a December 21, 1865, letter to his brother Benjamin, an attorney on Wall Street, Cartwright writes about his desire to appoint Ben as power of attorney, authorizing him to act in all things relating to the estate of their deceased father. He relies on Ben to have good judgment in all things pertaining to the welfare of their mother and their youngest sister, Ann, who was widowed with children. He closes his letter: "I know it is not your custom to answer letters, you will please in this instance depart from your custom and answer this at your earliest convenience."[16] In this letter, we see Cartwright struggling to be at such a distance, and perhaps struggling with his brother. Since Cartwright never went back to visit his family in New York, they may indeed have felt estranged from him, regardless of the many letters they received.

On January 20, 1868, Cartwright wrote to his eldest son, DeWitt, who was then twenty-four. The letter is addressed to Suffield, Connecticut, and from the wording, it appears DeWitt may have been visiting friends and relatives, including his grandmother. Cartwright asks his son to cut his trip short and come home: "your dear sister Mary has been ill with fever over nine weeks and is still unable to leave her bed. God only knows if she will ever recover, but we trust in his goodness and mercy and feel assured that He doeth all things well."[17]

Though her health would continue to trouble her, Mary must have recovered sufficiently for her and her husband of two years, Adolf G. Maitland, to travel to San Jose, California, some months later. On August 29, 1868, while Mary was in California, Cartwright wrote to tell her that her mother was suffering from "night attacks," or difficulty breathing and palpitations of the heart. Cartwright asked Mary to return home, saying he would pay her expenses from San Jose to Honolulu and back if only she would remain home for a few weeks.[18] Subsequent letters do not refer to Mary's return to Honolulu, but overall, these letters make clear the emotional strains of distance Cartwright was feeling.

On May 27, 1869, in the tone of a stern parent, Cartwright wrote to his son-in-law, who was in San Francisco at the time, that he would not lend him any more money. His letter reads, "It is impossible for me to comply to your request for a further loan of $300. I have just paid $329.50 to redeem my daughter's jewelry from pawn, and I do not feel able to spare any more. I regret that you have gone into stock gambling, as you certainly were not in the position to do so with any chance of success. I also regret that you should have lost your money and incurred more debt, but I know of but one way to remedy the evil, and that is to get employment as soon as possible." He closes the letter, "The family are all well and Mary is beginning to gain her old health and strength."[19]

However, this assessment may have been more hopeful than realistic, for a week later, on June 4, 1869, Mary died of scarlet fever at the age of twenty-four at the home of her parents.[20] Then, less than a year later, on March 21, 1870, Cartwright's eldest son, DeWitt, died in Honolulu at age twenty-six.[21] DeWitt never married and had no children, and the cause of his death isn't known, though the family history reports poisoning. No death records survived except those accounts written in newspapers for Mary, DeWitt, and their younger sister Kate Lee, who died in infancy in 1851.

The deaths of his first three children were obviously heartbreaking losses for Cartwright. Yet from all accounts in newspapers, various organizations, business transactions, and social events, he remained very busy. It could be that this was how he dealt with his tremendous grief and mourning, by allowing his busyness to keep him moving forward mentally and emotionally.

Then, in 1871, Cartwright's mother passed away. In a letter to his brother-in-law, Washington Durbrow of New York City, dated March 11, 1872, Cartwright wrote to settle matters of the estate regarding his father and mother. Considering the personal tragedies he had experienced in recent years, Cartwright sounds lighthearted and relaxed. His description of their monthly birthday dinners (which include King Kamehameha V and the Hawaii governor at the time, a former clerk of Cartwright's) evokes a poignant warmth and intimacy that Cartwright's public persona often seems to lack:

Dear Wash,

I note your remarks about climate in New York. I have read about it before, as to my getting used to it, "Not for Joe." I am a "Tropic Bird," and could not stand a Northern Winter. I may take a run home some day when they put direct steamers (such as the one that came down this trip) on the line between here and Frisco, but not to stay. Honolulu will be my home until the end, and after all why not. One place is just as good as another to die in. I have lived here for 23 years. My only surviving children Bruce and Alick were born here. My three darlings lie in our quiet little Nuuanu Valley. I have many more friends here and as a general thing have a good quiet time. Remote as we are from the Great World, we are still a part of it. We have every comfort and many luxuries . . . once a

92

month go to a first class dinner. We have a Birthday Club of twelve members, one for each month of the year. H.M. Kamehameha V Honorary President—our dinners are all given at Waikiki about one mile from town. We make a holiday of it, and spend the entire day there. The place itself belongs to the Governor John O. Dominis (a former fellow clerk of mine) who is one of our number. We call it Saints Rest. Be you well assured that our dinners are good ones and that we have here also a good time. Honolulu is very healthy. No small pox, no cholera, no epidemic fever, very quiet, very dull and very slow doubtless, is Hawaii nei, but I love it dearly.

And now enough about Hawaii. I will draw this to a close. Eliza and myself enjoy good health, by this mail we heard from Bruce and Alick. They are both well and so I hear is Alfred and his family. Al has got into employment that seems to agree with him and has I hear purchased a very cozy little home for himself at Oakland. I think he enjoys better health in California than he did here.

Give my best love and kindest remembrance to Het, Kate, Ben, and the rest of us and write to me as often as your inclination prompts or your time will permit.

Yours as Ever,

Alick

P.S. Excuse the slovenly style of this as I write with considerable difficulty. Yesterday my saddle turned just as I mounted my horse, and 205 came to the ground on the opposite side with a thud that shook the Earth. Nothing broke, nothing injured, but just a wee spot or so and a twisted wrist. Will be alright in a few days.[22]

A few months later, on April 17, 1872, Cartwright turned fifty-two years old; yet the Birthday Club met for dinner at Saints Rest on April 25. Mrs. Cartwright cooked chicken and made mince pie and gingerbread. Alexander received a silver cup as a birthday gift.[23] Cartwright's celebration would be the Birthday Club's penultimate gathering. The Birthday Club's last dinner together was May 2, 1872, when they celebrated Fred Banning's thirty-ninth birthday. The Honorary President of the Birthday Club, King Lot Kamehameha V, was later attacked with dropsy (related to congestive heart failure in many cases). The club postponed its meetings because of the king's illness. About six months later, King Kamehameha V died on December 11, 1872, the day of his forty-second birthday.[24] The Birthday Club never met again.

As the first Native Hawaiian to become a Freemason, King Lot Kamehameha V was given a Masonic funeral ceremony. In the ceremony, conducted by both Hawaiian Lodge and Lodge le Progres de l'Oceanie, the king was laid to rest at the Royal Mausoleum on January 7, 1873.[25] The Masonic apron, which he had received as an Entered Apprentice, was placed on the coffin. As a symbol, the apron represents hard work and protection. It also symbolizes the fraternal bond.

Before the king died, he asked Bernice Pauahi Bishop (who had married Charles Reed Bishop in 1850) to succeed him on the throne. Bernice was the last living direct descendent of the Kamehameha line, but she turned the offer down.[26] Under the Hawaiian Kingdom's constitution, if the king did not appoint a successor, a new king would be appointed by the legislature. An election was held for who would be the next monarch. There were several candidates for the Hawaiian throne, including two high-ranking chiefs, William C. Lunalilo and David Kalakaua. Lunalilo was more popular, but Kalakaua was the immediate cousin of the deceased king. In the end, Lunalilo took the throne, promising to amend the constitution to give the people a greater voice in the government. However, Lunalilo passed away a year later, on February 3, 1874.

Kalakaua announced his candidacy for the throne the following day. His main opponent this time was Queen Emma, the widow of King Kamehameha IV, and this time Kalakaua was the candidate who enjoyed more popular support, from both the Hawaiian nobility and citizens. The legislature met on February 12, 1874, and appointed Kalakaua as the new king, by a vote of thirty-nine to six.

However, as members of the legislature left the courthouse to tell Kalakaua of his victory, a mob of Queen Emma's supporters attacked them. The mob forced its way into the court building, beat several Native Hawaiian legislators, and threw one legislator out of a window, killing him. Kalakaua asked marines from American and British warships to help put down the mob, and peace was restored by that evening.

Queen Emma did not like Kalakaua. She saw him as an arrogant pretender, using paid genealogists to give substance to his flawed pedigree.[27] After Kalakaua was named king, she broke off all relations with Kapiolani, the king's wife. The women had been close until this time.

Nevertheless, in 1874, King Kalakaua—who would become

known as the "Merry Monarch" because of his love of Hawaiian culture, the arts, and good times in general—and Queen Kapiolani moved into Iolani Palace, where rulers of Hawaii had lived since 1846. The United States Minister at the time, Henry Pierce, called Kalakaua "ambitious, flighty and unstable. Very energetic; but lacks prudence and good sense."[28] This assessment was not far from the mark, as Kalakaua's legacy is mixed. He enacted the 1876 Reciprocity Act (when it was ratified by the United States), which allowed the United States to use Pearl Harbor in exchange for duty-free trade arrangements. Yet the costs for maintaining the king, the royal family, and military more than tripled during his reign.[29]

The king's extravagances included $40,000 for bands and flags, $15,000 for celebrating the king's birthday, and nearly $23,000 for coronation costs. However, the two-week coronation ceremonies, which took place nine years after the fact, actually rose closer to $50,000. The two crowns he bought for himself and his queen cost $10,000 each.[30] The coronation pavilion, built for the occasion, still stands on the grounds of Iolani Palace.

In any event, life in Hawaii soon returned to a more normal rhythm, and two subsequent events shed light on the degree to which baseball was, and was not, becoming an integral part of life on the islands. During his reign, King Kamehameha V had established King Kamehameha Day to honor his grandfather (Kamehameha the Great). In 1875, this was celebrated on June 6, and it included numerous sporting events, such as marathons, bicycle races, and horse races, which were a particular favorite of King Kalakaua. But in 1875, a new competition was added, baseball, which was commemorated by a game between the Hawaiian infantry and cavalry.[31] Then, six days later, King Kalakaua watched a contest between the Athletes and the Pensacolas. This particular game lasted over three hours and ended with a score of 38–33 in favor of the Athletes.[32] On a side note, girls also began playing baseball in Hawaii in 1875, when Julie Judd and Carrie Castle, both missionary descendents, played baseball at Punahou School that year.[33]

On July 4, 1876, America celebrated its centennial. This was an enormous event across the nation, and it was also a big deal in Hawaii. Of the ten committees that formed to put together the Hawaiian festivities, Cartwright was on the finance committee, which raised nearly $1,000 for the occasion.[34] At the top of the donor list was U.S. minister Henry Pierce, giving $100. Second on the list was Cartwright, also giving $100.[35]

Special committees included music, fireworks, dancing, and games. The hymn "America" (also known as "My Country, 'tis of Thee") was sung by a choir, and so was "The Star Spangled Banner." Fireworks were at eight o'clock at the head of Emma Street, and dancing finished the day's festivities until 10 o'clock.[36]

However, while the day's games included climbing a greased pole, catching a greased pig, a sack race, and foot races, one game that was not recorded as being included was baseball. This seems odd, since baseball was by then quite popular both nationwide and in Hawaii; plus, Cartwright was on the finance committee, and he certainly could have seen that it was included. Perhaps at the time, it was felt that watching someone catch a greased pig would be more exciting than watching someone catch a baseball. In any case, beginning in 1877, baseball would be included in the Hawaiian Fourth of July celebration and remain a staple from then on.

Cartwright was an avid reader, and as he did with so many of his interests, he channeled it into a civic activity, one that today sheds an interesting light on Cartwright's personal politics. In 1879, Alexander Cartwright became one of the founders of the Honolulu Library and Reading Room.[37] The sponsors originally named this the "Workingmen's Library," but they eventually changed it because they felt that it needed a broader name to signify its true purpose. In the local newspaper, the *Commercial Pacific Advertiser*, the editor J. H. Black wrote, "The library is not intended to be run for the benefit of any class, party, nationality, or sect."

On March 9, 1879, Cartwright wrote his brother Alfred in San Francisco about the debate among the founders over who should be allowed into the new library: "Over at the K. P. Hall the other night we had a meeting about the establishment of the new Temperance and Reading Room Association. . . . The idea keeps the blessed ladies out and the children. What makes us old geezers think we are the only ones to be spiritually and morally uplifted by a public library in this city?"[38]

Cartwright mentions that Queen Emma and Princess Bernice Pauahi Bishop wanted to contribute toward the effort but that they would be barred from the organization by the proposed bylaws. Cartwright seems genuinely upset, though he maintains a wry sense of humor about it: "I am mad 'cause I want the ladies. . . . Besides we could keep them busy dusting books, keeping a pot of tea boiling and who says 'the women haven't got enough brains to read?'"[39]

Dr. F. W. Hutchison and several others agreed with Cartwright and saw no reason to close the door to the ladies. However, one man wondered, if they let the gentlewomen in, what would keep the prostitutes out? After all, the not-so-gentle workingmen would be utilizing the library as well as the gentlemen. What finally shifted the tide in favor of the ladies was a surprising turnabout by Dr. Rodgers. He was initially opposed, but then his wife said that she would like to join the library, and so he reversed his vote and the constitution was changed to make women eligible.[40]

Once the ladies were allowed to join, they got to work raising funds to further the programs of the Hall and Library Reading Room Association. By the meeting of March 15, enough donated furniture, books, and periodicals had been received to open the reading room formally. King Kalakaua was elected as the first honorary member, and he and the queen attended the opening.[41]

Alexander Cartwright was involved with the library for the rest of his life; he was president from 1886 to 1892. The reading room librarian, Mary Burbank, wrote in 1927, "Mr. Cartwright's name led the list of the first Board of Directors in 1879, and [he] remained on the board as long as he lived, giving most generously of books."[42] Cartwright was a constant reader, and he would frequently donate his own books after he read them.

In addition to a new public library, Honolulu instituted a new Musical Hall Association in March 1880. Cartwright was one of the trustees for the association. The brick building could seat approximately five hundred people, including two private boxes for the king and royal family. Cartwright was one of the holders of the $25,000 capital stock, his share being one of five hundred shares at $50 each.[43]

Cartwright also took part in an eventful ceremony in 1879 concerning his Masonic lodge. The cornerstone for the first Masonic Hall was laid on January 4, 1879. Cartwright was the only survivor among the original members of Hawaiian Lodge No. 21. It stood on the corner of Fort and Queen streets, and Cartwright was granted a special dispensation from the Grand Lodge in San Francisco, California, to represent the Grand Master in conducting the ceremonies. The building was complete by September of that year and dedicated by brethren from both Lodge Le Progres and Hawaiian Lodge No. 21.[44]

EIGHT

Annexation and the Hawaiian League

James Munroe Stuart Comly, a former Civil War general, was appointed as U.S. Minister to the Hawaiian Islands in 1877 by his close friend from the war, President Rutherford B. Hayes.[1] After the Civil War, Comly had become editor and part proprietor of the *Ohio State Journal* in Columbus, Ohio. Through his newspaper, Comly promoted Hayes's successful presidential bid in 1876. Yet politics were not the only field of interest that Comly promoted in his newspaper.

In 1866 there were three baseball clubs in Columbus, Ohio. They were formed by returning Civil War veterans who had learned to play the game during the war.[2] As the first president of the Capital Base Ball Club and editor of the local newspaper, Comly published notices of meetings, practice sessions, and matches, and he followed up with game accounts and box scores.[3]

Eleven years later, his political appointment in Hawaii brought him face to face with Alexander J. Cartwright, and the two would come to know one another well. Unfortunately, no diary or journal written by Comly during or about his assignment in Honolulu has survived. Lacking other sources, we do not know whether Comly and Cartwright ever talked baseball, or what views they exchanged concerning increasingly volatile Hawaiian politics.

In any case, Comly began his appointment on a very positive and welcoming note. On September 25, 1877, at Iolani Palace, Comly was formally introduced as the new U.S. "Minister Resident" by the outgoing U.S. minister Henry Pierce, and Comly rose to address King Kalakaua:

> I have the honor to present my credentials to your Majesty, as Minister Resident of the United States to the Hawaiian Islands. In following a predecessor who has so long and faithfully represented the United States Government at this Court, it is only a fit recognition of his character for me to say, that I hope for the good fortune to succeed to a share of the regard won by him from your Majesty's Government and people. It is with cordial and sincere pleasure, also, in compliance with my instructions, that I assure your Majesty of the earnest desire of the Government I have the honor to represent, to continue and augment the harmony and good feeling which have characterized the relations between the two countries from the earliest times down to the present. Among the illustrations of this good feeling, pardon me for recalling the generous contributions of the Hawaiian

people to the fund of the Sanitary Commission, during
the late unhappy war in my own country. To this fund
the people of the Hawaiian Islands contributed a sum
almost equal to that of some of the States at home. I
cannot forget this substantial evidence of the regard of
this people, for I had the honor to be one of the soldiers
in that war. The Treaty of Reciprocity was a fit sequel to
such evidences of friendly feeling as this.

In conclusion, I beg to tender to your Majesty the
respectful regard due to a King who governs wisely for
the benefit of his people. I hope and pray for the health
and happiness of your Majesty, and for prosperity to the
beautiful land the Lord has set you to reign over.[4]

Throughout the first couple years of his assignment in Honolulu, no doubt Comly and his family enjoyed their new tropical surroundings and became involved in the community. Mrs.
Comly and their daughter Susie, along with Mrs. Cartwright,
took part in the "Spirit of the Fair" in May 1880, which was a
fundraiser for the Honolulu Library and Reading Room.[5] The
fair was held in the library rooms on Fort Street and netted
$2,400. However, "friendly feeling" evaporated quickly that year
for James Comly.

During King Kalakaua's rule, the king was often criticized
for his extravagance and profligate spending, and for the way
he handled his cabinet. If one of his proposals failed to be ratified, he would sometimes dismiss uncooperative cabinet members and immediately appoint others who were more sympathetic, despite dubious qualifications. One such controversial

appointee was Celso Caesar Moreno, an Italian who was natu-ralized as a Hawaiian citizen on the day of his appointment as minister of foreign affairs in August 1880.

Hawaiian supporters of Moreno felt that he was their salva-tion and expected him to eliminate foreigners from high po-sitions and replace them with true Hawaiians to whom the land belonged. The opposition to Moreno claimed that his ap-pointment was inconsistent with the principles of the Hawai-ian government as a constitutional monarchy as established by the Kamehamehas. U.S. minister James Comly reported to his home office that he heard talk that included the abdication of the king, the crowning of Queen Emma, annexation of Hawaii by the United States, and even the lynching of Moreno.[6] Five days after Moreno was appointed, Comly met with King Kalakaua to discuss the situation. During the week of August 15, 1880, meetings took place for the purpose of public opinion and busi-ness matters regarding the king's appointment of Moreno. On Wednesday of that week, a group of twenty-five gentlemen had gathered, at which point Alexander Cartwright stepped in and announced that Mr. C. C. Moreno had resigned, and that this resignation had been accepted.[7] This did not mollify the busi-nessmen, who demanded that other cabinet appointees also be dismissed. Soon thereafter, despite attempts by Comly to per-suade them not to, the businessmen petitioned the king to this effect. It is not clear if Cartwright argued for or against the pe-tition, but Comly wrote to the Department of State, "a little tact would have given the King time to 'feel good in,' and then the people might have had their way. But these Old Puritans don't know any half-way between damnation and election."[8]

In August of 1886, Moreno sent an open letter to King Kalakaua. The several-page letter, mostly attacking the politics
of Hawaii and particular men in high position (including Kalakaua), was also a bill for payment of services. After Moreno's
dismissal, Kalakaua entrusted Moreno to accompany three Hawaiian youths for the purpose of educating them in Germany
and Italy. Kalakaua planned for these young men to become future leaders in Hawaii. One of them was Robert W. Wilcox, who
would later be a hero to the Hawaiian people during a counterrevolution. Yet for Moreno, political life in Hawaii was over, and
he was now asking for his salary to be paid for the ten months
of expenses he had incurred supporting the Hawaiian youths.[9]
It was a sign of what was coming that a man who was favored
by Hawaiians couldn't hold his post for even a week.

In 1881 King Kalakaua made history by being the first king to
visit the United States and the first to travel the globe. He spent
nine months visiting such countries as Japan, China, India,
Egypt, Italy, Spain, and Great Britain. While in the United States
he was honored at a state dinner given by President Grant, he
addressed a joint session of Congress, and he successfully ne-
gotiated an extension of the reciprocity treaty, which allowed
Hawaiian sugar into the United States duty free.[10] As a result,
Hawaii's sugar industry boomed, and the kingdom enjoyed a
period of economic prosperity.

As King Kalakaua traveled, he studied immigration, attempted
to improve Hawaii foreign relations, and studied how other
monarchs ruled.[11] Of all of his accomplishments during his

reign, Kalakaua's most constructive and lasting legacy was the restoration of Native Hawaiian culture and customs. In opposition to the missionaries, he encouraged the transcription of Hawaiian oral traditions and supported public performances of the hula.[12]

Kalakaua was attempting to advance his kingdom by combining what he saw as modern progress with traditional Hawaiian ideals. And yet, the reciprocity treaties he signed with the United States, while providing Hawaii with economic opportunity at a surface level, also opened the door to an ever-growing American involvement and investment, thus fostering U.S. desire to control the country to protect its interests.

In December 1881, not long after King Kalakaua returned to Hawaii, U.S. Secretary of State James G. Blaine wrote to James M. Comly to argue the benefits of annexing Hawaii as part of the United States. These were not altogether new arguments, but they were being made more forcefully at higher levels. And indeed, it was a very curious justification Blaine put forth: recognizing that Native Hawaiians were not participating sufficiently in Hawaii's increasing wealth and industrialization (in what he saw as an inevitable ethnological decline in the presence of inferred superior Americans), annexation was necessary to secure better workers to improve plantation productivity. These better workers, meanwhile, were artfully fantasized—not slaves, but "thinking, intelligent" laborers induced to come by opportunity. Last, and most important (and perhaps unnecessarily), he asked Comly to plant the seeds of annexation and colonization in the thoughts of local American businessmen:

106

Mr. Blaine to Mr. Comly.

[Confidential.]

DEPARTMENT OF STATE,

Washington, December 1, 1881.

JAMES M. COMLY, Esq., Honolulu:

. . . The decline of the native Hawaiian element in the presence of newer and sturdier growths must be accepted as an inevitable fact, in view of the teachings of ethnological history. And as retrogression in the development of the Islands can not be admitted without serious detriment to American interests in the North Pacific, the problem of a replenishment of the vital forces of Hawaii presents itself for intelligent solution in an American sense—not in an Asiatic or a British sense.

There is little doubt that were the Hawaiian Islands, by annexation or district protection, a part of the territory of the Union, their fertile resources for the growth of rice and sugar would not only be controlled by American capital, but so profitable a field of labor would attract intelligent workers thither from the United States.

A purely American form of colonization in such a case would meet all the phases of the problem. Within our borders could be found the capital, the intelligence, the activity, and the necessary labor trained in the rice swamps and cane fields of the Southern States, and it may be well to consider how, even in the chosen alternative of maintaining Hawaiian independence, these prosperous elements could be induces [sic] to go from our

shores to the islands, not like the coolies, practically en-
slaved, not as human machines, but as thinking, intelligent, working factors in the advancement of the material
interests of the islands. An examination and report will
be valuable if showing the proportion of occupied rice
and sugar lands to the unoccupied and undeveloped territory, the capacities of production, the peculiarities of climate, the wages of labor, and the cost of living. It will also
be well for you in conversation with the leading men of
Hawaii to turn their thoughts discreetly in the direction
of inviting American colonization there. I desire, therefore, that you will give this subject due attention . . .

JAMES G. BLAINE[13]

One organization that Blaine might have hoped to interest in
colonization was the Planter Labor and Supply Company (later
renamed the Hawaiian Sugar Planters' Association), which was
formed on March 20, 1882, and organized into eight committees.[14] The association was created for the advancement, improvement, and protection of the sugar industry, and it had committees
devoted to labor, cultivation, machinery, legislation, reciprocity,
transportation, and manufacture of Sugar. There was also an executive committee. Alexander Cartwright was a member of the
Reciprocity Committee, along with Sanford Dole.[15]

The new association had its roots in the then-defunct Royal
Hawaiian Agricultural Society, which became inactive after 1856.
A decade later, an attempt to reform a similar society, with Cartwright as treasurer, had failed. The impetus for the new association was the 1876 Treaty of Reciprocity between the United

States and the Kingdom of Hawaii. Through the treaty, the United States received a coaling station at Pearl Harbor, and Hawaii's sugar planters received duty-free entry into U.S. markets for their sugar. The Planter Labor and Supply Company resurrected many of the programs of the original Royal Hawaiian Agricultural Society in the 1850s.

Only four months after this sugar planters' association was formed, many of the group's members would gather again, this time to say good-bye to James Comly, whose assignment as U.S. minister to Hawaii was ending. A farewell dinner took place on August 24, 1882, at the Hawaiian Hotel.[16] The grounds were decorated with colored lanterns that hung from the trees, fountains bubbled, and music played. The "president of the evening," Alexander J. Cartwright, escorted the guests into the dining hall. There, a large American flag (as yet with only thirty-eight stars) was draped over the head of the table. Wreaths of evergreens were hung about the lamps and walls and radiated a mountainous scent through the room.

The tables were garnished not only with silver, glass, and china, but with many kinds of flowers and fruit. Placards at each place setting announced who would dine where, and these guests included Charles Bishop, Sanford Dole, William Parke, William Castle, Samuel Damon, Bruce Cartwright, and the new U.S. minister to succeed James Comly, Rollin Daggett.

At the center of the head table sat Alexander Cartwright. On his right was James Comly and at his left was Rollin Daggett. For an hour and a half the diners ate and laughed as they listened to music by the Royal Hawaiian Band, which was conducted by Heinrich Wilhelm Berger (also known as Henry Berger). At half past nine, Cartwright stood to address the crowd. He announced that it was time to introduce the speakers and to commence with toasts.

As each distinguished speaker rose, made a toast, and addressed a few remarks, applause occasionally rang out. When Sanford Dole spoke, several times he drew applause. Like Blaine, he made the case for annexation (without naming it), but he didn't speak generally about the minds of workers and increasing productivity. He spoke to the fear in the heart of each gentleman in the room: if they didn't have a say in Hawaii's government, then everything they'd built on the islands could be taken from them and from all "Hawaiian born Americans," that is, their children and grandchildren:

Mr. Chairman and Gentlemen:

. . . I believe that I but reflect the thought that is uppermost in our minds when I say, whatever may be the nominal character of the government that its constitutional and representative features have as a matter of fact ceased to exist. This is a very serious matter for Hawaiian born Americans living here as well as other residents. By industry and enterprise, they have built up houses and acquired property. All they have is here. They have been and are loyal to the law rather than to persons, yet they are not wanted in the administration of government and the making of laws. It may be said that they are few in number and of little consequence in Hawaiian affairs. I say that although they are comparatively few in number, they are a good nucleus from which they will grow a controlling and lasting influence in these Islands. Their descendants will form a constantly increasing force moved by the political instincts of the Anglo-Saxon.[17]

On a more personal note for Alexander Cartwright, 1882 was significant because it marked the final season of the Knickerbocker Base Ball Club. It is currently unknown if Cartwright was made aware that the Knickerbocker era had ended. Afterward, the Knickerbocker records were entrusted to the sportswriter Henry Chadwick. Upon his death in 1908, the books passed to Albert Goodwill Spalding. Upon Spalding's death in 1922, the books were deposited in the New York Public Library, where they reside today.

Cartwright was actually becoming involved in a new athletic group, the Athletic Association of Honolulu, which formed in February 1882 with eighty members.[18] Dr. Frances B. Hutchison was elected president, and Sanford B. Dole was vice president, while on February 6, 1882, Cartwright was inaugurated as a life member into the organization.[19] The nature of the group was announced as follows:

> The Directors of the Athletic Association of Honolulu, met on the evening of Thursday, 9th and again on Thursday evening last, at the residence of Dr. Hutchison. Various details of business were transacted, and arrangements made, the results of which are not yet open to publication. Pending the completion of negotiations for premises, etc, it was determined to make an immediate start in the organization of out-door games, and

today was fixed for that purpose. A game of cricket under the auspices of the Association, will be played on
the drill ground, Makiki, this afternoon, by members
of the Honolulu Cricket Club. Two sets of lawn tennis
material have been politely lent to the Association for
the occasion, and it is hoped that there will be a good
number of Lady members of the Association, both to
encourage the cricketers by their presence and to join
in the game of lawn tennis. Those who wish to join in
the latter game, are requested to bring with them their
own rackets and balls.[20]

Baseball doesn't seem to have been on the roster of the association, nor would it have been, most likely. Cartwright himself
was now nearly sixty-two, and he was perhaps more an honorary member than an active one.

In addition, Cartwright's two Hawaiian-born sons, who had
once been written about for their baseball athletics, Bruce and
Alexander III, were now grown and had lives of their own by
this time. The following year, in 1883, Alexander III and his first
wife, Princess Theresa, divorced. Divorce papers reflect that the
defendant (A. J. Cartwright Jr.) deserted and refused to provide.
Until the latter part of the nineteenth century, custody of children was awarded to the father. Since it was not in the best interest of the children to award custody to their father, and it was
not yet customary to grant custody of children to their mother,
the court made an alternative decision. A note at the bottom
of the divorce decree states, "And it is further ordered that the
custody of the two minor children in the Complaint named be

awarded to Alexander J. Cartwright Senior provided however that the mother (the Plaintiff) shall have frequent opportunities to visit them."[21]

When the elder Cartwright passed away, his granddaughter Daisy was thirteen years old, and Eva was eleven. Princess Daisy spent her remaining childhood and early adult years in San Francisco, apparently with her father. Princess Eva was adopted by her great aunt Elizabeth Pratt in Hawaii. After she grew up, Eva married Dwight Styne. She is buried a few yards away from her grandfather in the Oahu Cemetery burial plot of the Franklin Seaver Pratt family. Franklin Pratt was married to Eva's great aunt Elizabeth.

Not long after he ascended the throne, King Kalakaua decided he needed a more luxurious home, and he had a new Iolani Palace built at a cost of $350,000. The cornerstone for the palace was laid on December 31, 1879, with full Masonic rites;[22] Cartwright was present during the ceremony. In December 1882 the new Iolani Palace was finished: it was outfitted with indoor plumbing and gas chandeliers (which were replaced by electric lighting five years later). The king also installed a new communications system that included the recently invented telephone.[23] Later, in 1886, Cartwright would own ten shares of stock in the Mutual Telephone Company.

In addition, Cartwright became involved in the first Stock and Bond Exchange in Honolulu. A group of gentlemen first met on July 20, 1883. Alexander Cartwright was elected president. The newspaper reported that this association was for bona fide

transactions only and that stock gambling or "washed" transactions was strictly prohibited.

At the end of 1882, on Wednesday, December 27, King Kalakaua hosted a banquet that was the new palace's first official
social function. The guest list, about 120, consisted of Masonic
brethren from both Lodge le Progres de l'Oceanie and the Hawaiian Lodge.

Music was provided by the Royal Hawaiian Military Band,
under conductor Henry Berger—the same band that had entertained during Comly's farewell banquet. Today known as the
Royal Hawaiian Band, this band has entertained the people of
Hawaii ever since and still plays at civic functions.

David Dayton, the orator of Lodge le Progres de l'Oceanie,
called the brethren to order for the first toast of the evening:

> Worshipful Masters, Wardens and Brethren—It being
> obligatory on members of Lodge le Progres to drink sev-
> eral toasts on this occasion, before doing so, I will in-
> form you that the cornerstone of this edifice, the Pal-
> ace, was laid by the Masonic fraternity on December 31,
> 1879, by request of His Majesty Kalakaua, King of the
> Hawaiian Islands. And now, my brethren, His Majesty
> King of the Hawaiian Islands, and Past Master of Lodge
> le Progres de l'Oceanie, has become our host, honor-
> ing us with the first festival in this edifice. My breth-
> ren, I will invite you to charge your glasses and drink
> the first regular toast of the evening, "His Majesty the
> King and the Royal Family."

This toast was followed by several more, as was typical of

Masonic functions, and the last toast of the evening was concluded in part with the following:

> It is that portion of the charge wherein the novitiate is taught that Freemasonry is so esteemed as an honorable order that even monarchs have, at times, exchanged the scepter for the trowel to join in our mysteries and aid in our labors. To this fact is due in no small degree the prosperity in Hawaii of an order that bears upon its active roles the name of one whom we greet tonight as Sovereign, as host, and as brother.[24]

Around midnight, the brethren then joined hands and, accompanied by the Royal Hawaiian Military Band, sang "Auld Lang Syne." From the perspective of today, it is hard to square this genuinely warm scene with the banquet only four months earlier bidding farewell to Comly. Many of the same guests, including Cartwright, attended both. One evening celebrated and honored the Hawaiian monarchy and its new Iolani Palace, and by all indications sincerely. The other honored Americans and rumbled with talk of annexation. It is quite probable, in fact, that some of the participants themselves were having a hard time squaring their conflicting feelings and desires. In any case, it was the first and the last Masonic function to be held strictly for the Craft at Iolani Palace.[25]

Given the evidence of events (and despite the fact that there are as yet no known writings from this period by Cartwright himself regarding annexation), it can hardly be doubted that Alexander Cartwright was conflicted. By the 1880s, he had enjoyed a long, friendly, and at times seemingly intimate relationship with the Hawaiian monarchy, one that involved both social and civic events as well as business dealings. For instance, a year after the inauguration of the new Iolani Palace, in December 1883, Alexander Cartwright and Charles Judd were appointed as "lawful attorneys" regarding financial matters for three royal siblings and their spouses: King Kalakaua and his wife Queen Kapiolani, the king's sister Liliuokalani and her husband John Dominis, and the king's sister Likelike and her husband Archibald Cleghorn. After the death of their brother, William Leleiohoku, the king and his sisters had inherited some land, and regarding it, Cartwright and Judd were given power of attorney to "lease and collect the rents, and to sell and convey for such price as they may think fit."[26]

This wasn't Cartwright's only financial involvement with the royal family. Beginning in 1874, he became the financial advisor for Queen Emma, the widow of King Kamehameha IV, and he was in charge of her estate as power of attorney. Though Queen Emma never ruled her beloved kingdom, she remained active and pursued noteworthy causes throughout her life.

Apparently, the queen was not always very thrifty with her money and accumulated some debt. In a letter dated September 30, 1874, Cartwright laid out a plan for Queen Emma to pay her debts and for her "to liquidate liabilities by personal sacrifices and most stringent economy."[27] Queen Emma also appointed him executor and trustee in 1884 of her will.[28] James Monsarrat (the eldest son of Marcus Monsarrat) was her legal advisor and drew up the will.

Emma died the following year on April 25, 1885. In her will, she listed a number of recipients who would obtain particular assets from her estate upon her death. In addition to land or money bequeathed to various individuals, money for scholarships was awarded to St. Andrew's Priory, and all of her books were given to the Honolulu Library and Reading Room Association. The remaining items included a number of tracts and parcels of land on Kauai and Oahu that were bequeathed to Alexander J. Cartwright and his heirs. However, the proceeds derived from the sale of any lands were to be divided half to Queen's Hospital and the remaining half in trust for her cousin Albert K. Kunuiakea.

Ultimately, all the evidence seems to indicate that Alexander Cartwright and Queen Emma became good friends, as further seen in the gift of a gold watch Emma gave to Cartwright on his birthday in 1880. The inscription on it reads, "Emma Kaleleonalani, Alexander Joy Cartwright, April 17, 1880."[29] Emma had taken the name Kaleleonalani, meaning "flight of heavenly chiefs," after the loss of her son and husband.

Despite his close relationship with the royal family, Cartwright was first and foremost an American and a businessman, and each year his investment in Hawaii grew. For instance, in 1885, an advertisement announced the "Great Land Colonization Scheme." Property of 115,750 acres on the island of Oahu was offered for sale to a joint stock company called the Hawaiian Colonization Land & Trust Company. The 10,000 acres proposed for colonization were located on the northwestern shore of Pearl Harbor, extending up a gradual slope of the Waianae foothills to an elevation of about a thousand feet.[30]

The owners of these estates and promoters of the company were James Campbell (president), John Paty (vice president), M.

Dickson, J. G. Spencer, and B. F. Dillingham. Among the names of individuals who consented to be nominated for directors were included Sanford B. Dole and Alexander J. Cartwright.[31]

In January 1887, King Kalakaua announced that Queen Kapiolani would travel to London to attend the Golden Jubilee of Queen Victoria. Princess Liliuokalani, who spoke perfect English, accompanied her. The queen's first stop was San Francisco and the Bay Area, where she was warmly welcomed at churches and schools.

One school she visited was Mills College, near Oakland, to see the Hawaiian girls enrolled there. Her husband had been honored at a tea at Mills College in 1881. Queen Kapiolani was received by Susan Mills, who escorted her to a reception at which the girls sang her several songs. Mrs. Mills had been the matron at Punahou School in Hawaii when her husband was serving as president in the early 1860s.[32]

While in San Francisco, the queen visited the firehouse at City Hall on Kearny Street; she was shown the modern firefighting equipment and how the horses were harnessed. In 1886 in Honolulu, a fire had stopped just a few blocks from Iolani Palace, and sparks had landed on the palace roof. Her husband, King Kalakaua, himself a volunteer fireman, had helped battle the blaze.[33]

The threat of fire was a foremost concern throughout the nineteenth century. After the great Chicago Fire of 1871, the people of Honolulu had been moved to donate money for relief efforts under the direction of Alexander Cartwright.[34]

As the queen toured San Francisco and visited London, King

118

Kalakaua was attempting to put out a very different kind of fire. He spoke before the opening session of the 1887 Hawaiian Legislature, presenting news that he no doubt hoped would appease both foreign businessmen and Hawaiians worried over the threat of foreign intervention:

> I take great pleasure in informing you that the Treaty of Reciprocity with the United States of America has been definitely extended for seven years upon the same terms as those in the original treaty, with the addition of a clause granting to national vessels of the United States the exclusive privilege of entering Pearl River Harbor and establishing there a coaling and repair station. This has been done after mature deliberation and the interchange between my Government and that of the United States of an interpretation of the said clause whereby it is agreed and understood that it does not cede any territory or part with or impair any right of sovereignty or jurisdiction on the part of the Hawaiian Kingdom and that such privilege is coterminous with the treaty.
>
> I regard this as one of the most important events of my reign, and I sincerely believe that it will re-establish the commercial progress and prosperity which began with the Reciprocity Treaty.[35]

This extension of the Treaty of Reciprocity would be too little, too late. In July 1887, while the queen was still in England, a group of American and European businessmen, with the aid of an armed militia, took control of the Hawaiian government.

They presented King Kalakaua with a new constitution (written by Lorrin A. Thurston) and forced him to accept it.

This so-called Reform Constitution became known as the Bayonet Constitution because the king was forced to sign it at gunpoint, with a bayonet at his throat. The new constitution stripped the monarchy of much of its authority, and it extended voting rights to American and European males in Hawaii (in addition to Hawaiian males), so long as they met certain economic and literacy requirements.

Some of the men involved in the Bayonet Constitution were part of a secret society called the Hawaiian League, which was made up of members of Hawaii's political Reform Party who were in favor of annexation to the United States.[36] There is clear documentation that Alexander Cartwright and his two grown sons, Bruce and Alexander, were members of the Hawaiian League.[37]

The Hawaiian League's armed militia was known as the Honolulu Rifles. The Honolulu Rifles were originally established in 1846 as a volunteer militia pledged to serve the Hawaiian government. Indeed, a list of subscribers to the Honolulu Rifles from 1857 (now in the Hawaiian State Archives) includes Alexander Cartwright's name, in addition to many other well-known Americans in Honolulu at the time, with King Kamehameha IV heading the list.[38]

However, as the Hawaiian League grew, the Honolulu Rifles became a vigilante group with only a minor allegiance to the government. By 1887 its primary allegiance was to the secret Hawaiian League, whose only allegiance was to itself. This was made clear by an oath that was found tucked inside a pocket of a notebook among Lorrin Thurston's possessions:

> I do solemnly promise upon my honor, that I will keep secret the existence and purposes of this League. That I will not, in my position of a member of any military organization, oppose or oppress the whole citizens of this Kingdom that I will stand by and support my military superiors in their necessary efforts to protect the white community of this Kingdom against any arbitrary or oppressive action of the government, which may threaten the lives, liberty or prosperity of the people, and will at all hazards protect and defend the members of the League who may be jeopardized in its service.[39]

At the time, members of the Hawaiian League had differing opinions on the best course of action. All favored annexation by the United States, but some felt that the monarchy, with modified powers, could be allowed to continue, while more radical members wanted the monarchy overthrown. One member even proposed assassinating the king. In 1887 the Hawaiian League decided that they would not attempt to overthrow the government; they would allow the king to remain on the throne, but they would limit his power with the new constitution. Only if he refused this arrangement would they consider killing him.

After the Bayonet Constitution, the political Reform Party remained split over how annexation should occur: the radical side, led by Lorrin Thurston, still wanted to overthrow the monarchy, while the moderate side, led by Sanford Dole, wanted to keep a modified monarchy.[40]

As yet, no evidence has been uncovered to indicate which side of this debate Cartwright was on, or the specific role he played in July 1887 when the Bayonet Constitution was forced on the king. However, one thing is certain: he was in favor of the U.S. annexation of Hawaii, and he supported the Hawaiian League. He was outspoken regarding his pride in his American citizenship and in America itself, and his political and commercial connections as an American businessman were consistent with those who favored U.S. intervention in the name of profit and personal security.

Cartwright's ties to the monarchy being what they were, he must have had torn emotions, but there was some contradictory behavior that occurred among his cohorts. As Tom Coffman, the author of *Nation Within*, has said, "There was a lot of two-faced behavior going on; with one face professing warm aloha for the Hawaiians while the other face advocated taking over and dismembering their country. Dole was the ultimate practitioner of that behavior."[41]

Several months after the Bayonet Constitution, members of the Hawaiian League secretly approached King Kalakaua's sister Liliuokalani and proposed that she take over the monarchy from her brother. She declined. On January 18, 1888, Liliuokalani wrote in her diary that she would have considered taking the throne, but only if her brother willingly abdicated it. Some speculate this request was an attempt to use Liliuokalani as a pawn to undermine the monarchy rather than as a way to continue the monarchy with a more acceptable ruler.

For the next several years, into the early 1890s, the political ramifications of the new constitution caused increasing tensions

in Honolulu and throughout Hawaii. But to successfully overthrow the monarchy, the radical wing of the Reform Party needed
a government ally. Lorrin Thurston found his ally in John L.
Stevens, who replaced George W. Merrill as U.S. minister resident. Stevens was appointed by secretary of state James Blaine.
Stevens and Blaine were close friends, and Stevens openly declared himself an advocate of annexation.

NINE

Spalding Comes to Hawaii

From the beginning, baseball has always functioned as a delightful distraction from the problems and conflicts of everyday life, and this was certainly true in Honolulu in November 1888. For a day, Hawaii residents could put aside politics and give themselves over to the excitement of professional baseball. Albert Spalding's 1888–89 world tour, which included the Chicago White Stockings and an All-American team, was coming to Honolulu to host an exhibition. It was this world tour—in which Spalding and his players visited Hawaii, Australia, Ceylon, Egypt, Italy, France, and England—that ended with a celebratory homecoming dinner at Delmonico's restaurant in New York in 1889, and at which Mark Twain gave his famous speech.

As fate, perhaps, would have it, the visit didn't go according to plan. Spalding and his players were due to arrive on Saturday, November 24, and they were scheduled to play an exhibition game at one o'clock in the afternoon the same day. Unfortunately, their ship was delayed, and it didn't arrive until 5:30 on Sunday morning, November 25.[1]

However, unaware of the delay, the great majority of Honolulu residents—anxiously anticipating the arrival of Spalding and his ball players—began to assemble at the wharf as early as four o'clock in the morning on Saturday, and they waited there until one o'clock, which was the time that the game was to commence. Even the royal band played tunes from six o'clock in the morning until noon. As the afternoon wore on, however, the crowd gave up waiting and went home.

Then, at daybreak on Sunday morning, the ship *Alameda* was sighted off Diamond Head. Word spread quickly, and soon thousands were again gathered at the wharf. The musicians scrambled out of bed and returned to play their welcoming melodies. A large number of Americans were in the crowd, but some were as eager to learn the result of the recent U.S. presidential election as they were to welcome the baseball players.

As the *Hawaiian Gazette* reported the following day:

BASEBALL TOURISTS!

The Royal Mail steamer Alameda after disappointing everyone on Saturday by her non-arrival, was signaled off Diamond Head at half-past five o'clock Sunday morning. . . . As the steamer lay off the bell buoy waiting for the pilot, telescopes and opera glasses were brought into requisition for the purpose of interpretation of the various signals displayed by the steamer as to the result of the Presidential election. The Hawaiian flag was noticed flying from the foremast and as it had

125

been arranged by Mr. G. E. Boardman before leaving
San Francisco with the Honorable H. A. Widemann,
that it should be hoisted there in case of the election of
Harrison, shouts of "It's Cleveland" were soon turned
into those of "It's Harrison." . . .

The deck of the steamer as she drew near the dock
was lined with passengers, among them several well
known island people and the Spalding baseball tourists. The Hawaiian band was on the wharf and played
several appropriate selections as a welcome to the tourists. Mr. George W. Smith had previously boarded the
steamer and presented a number of our residents to
Mr. A. G. Spalding, (who by the way, is a cousin of Mr.
Smith's), the manager of the ball teams and an enthusiastic baseball man himself.

Carriages decorated with flags were in readiness and
conveyed the baseball party to the Hawaiian Hotel, where
shortly afterwards they partook of breakfast.

At 10:30 o'clock the baseball party and their friends,
accompanied by His Excellency George W. Merrill, U.S.
Minister Resident, formed a line of twos in front of the
Hotel, and marched to the Palace, led by the band, and
preceded by a number of ladies in carriages. At the Palace Mr. J. W. Robertson, Vice-Chamberlain, presented
Mr. Merrill to His Majesty. Mr. Merrill presented Mr.
Spalding, and Mr. Spalding presented the following ladies and gentlemen . . .[2]

It's interesting to note that, as will be described in chapter
11, George W. Smith, whom the article mentions as making

the introductions of Honolulu residents to his cousin, Albert Spalding, would some twenty years later write to Spalding asking what "facts" he had concerning Alexander Cartwright and baseball's founding.

George Smith's introductions were typically Hawaiian in flavor: Large floral bouquets that were prepared for the anticipated arrival the day before were now presented to the ladies of the party. Floral leis or wreaths were draped over the gentlemen's necks. A number of carriages then took the visitors to the Royal Hawaiian Hotel, where a bulletin board stated that the queen would give a luau in honor of the guests at half past five.[3]

The hotel corridors became crowded with citizens eager to greet the ballplayers. Among those noted by the newspaper were John A. Cummins, Samuel Parker, U. S. Minister George W. Merrill, C. U. Arnold, Attorney General C. W. Ashford, W. N. Green, and scores of others.[4] From the hotel, the baseball visitors headed to Iolani Palace, where they met King Kalakaua. Upon entering the palace, the guests were introduced to the Committee of Reception, Council of State, ministers, and other dignitaries. Of the ballplayers, two of the most notable were future Hall of Famers A. C. "Cap" Anson, who was first baseman for the Chicago Cubs, and John Montgomery Ward, who was shortstop for the New York Giants.[5]

The guests were brought to the throne room, whose prominence was evidenced by a velvety carpet beneath their feet. Spalding was the first to be introduced to the king by the U.S. minister, and then all the parties were presented individually, each member having his or her name called aloud as the king recognized their presence with a courtly bow.[6]

After some time was spent in seeing the rooms inside the palace, the entire party headed back to the hotel. There, the question became: Would they be able to play baseball? It was now Sunday, and the Hawaiian "blue laws," originally enacted by New England missionaries in 1820, prevented the playing of ball games on Sunday. That morning, a petition had been quickly drawn up asking that an exception be made and that Spalding hold his exhibition game anyway. Though in circulation for only an hour or two, the petition gathered over a thousand signatures.

At the hotel, Mr. Cummins handed the petition to Spalding, and he made a speech requesting that Spalding play the exhibition; Cummins guaranteed that all fines for violating the blue laws would be paid by the wealthy citizens eager to see the game played. Spalding replied that he would take the matter into consideration for ten minutes, during which time Spalding apparently consulted with an attorney.[7]

Spalding was told that, although the attorney general wanted him to play baseball, as did a majority of the citizens, if he attempted to play, some of the missionaries would procure warrants and make trouble. Under the circumstances, Spalding decided not to play.

Upon returning to the crowd, Spalding replied that his men would love to have given an exhibition game that day, but at the outset of their trip, it was decided to honor any regulations in the countries they visited. Thus, they would not play on Sunday, and in order to keep to their schedule, they had to depart that night. At this announcement, an outcry of disappointment rose from the waiting crowd. Of Honolulu's 40,000 inhabitants, almost a quarter had already gathered at the ballpark expecting a game. A new grandstand capable of seating 800 people had been expressly built for this occasion.[8]

For the remainder of their day-long visit, the American baseball tourists broke up into smaller parties to see what they could of Honolulu and its surroundings. Many community members personally escorted them around. Later that evening, they came together on the grounds of Queen Kapiolani's private retreat to participate in a native feast provided by King Kalakaua. In addition to the out-of-town guests, a large number of Honolulu folks attended.[9]

The Kawaihau Quintet Club furnished vocal music. The king sat at the center of a long table with Spalding's mother beside him on the right and Attorney General C. W. Ashford on his left. Before sitting down, Mr. Spalding proposed a toast to the king and his loyal subjects.

Afterward, one of the ball players wrote in his diary about the feast, "Behind us, Native girls armed with long palm leaf fans guarded us from the myriads of mosquitoes and insects which kept continually hovering about."[10]

The baseball tourists were taken afterward to the wharf, where a large number had assembled, as well as the Hawaiian Band. By ten o'clock that evening, Spalding and his entourage were back aboard the *Alameda*. The reporter for the *Hawaiian Gazette* remarked, "The deck of the steamer presented a gay scene, as most of the departing passengers were covered with leis . . . the band playing *Auld Lang Syne*."[11] The band also played the

"Star Spangled Banner" and "God Save the Queen" and closed with the Hawaiian national anthem. Those on the dock could hear the baseball players sing along with the choruses until they went past the lighthouse.[12]

Where was Alexander Cartwright among all the hoopla? It's hard to say. Cartwright is not specifically mentioned in any newspaper article or historical documents concerning Spalding's Honolulu visit, either as a participant or merely as being in attendance. It is highly likely that he *was* there, though no official record was made at the time of Spalding meeting or interacting with Cartwright in Honolulu.

The most that Spalding himself said about Cartwright was that he was in the crowd. Or, as Spalding put it in his 1911 book *America's National Game*: "Alexander J. Cartwright, among many other thousands, was one of the devotees of Base Ball disappointed by reason of the failure of the steamer 'Alameda' to make scheduled time, on the occasion of the visit of the 'All America' and Chicago teams to Honolulu, on their world tour in 1888–9."[13]

Beyond this, Spalding does not mention having a conversation with Cartwright, or even of meeting Cartwright specifically, though this statement may indicate both. Nor is there any letter or direct evidence from Cartwright that he met Spalding or participated in this notable and widely reported baseball celebration.

Afterward, and until his death, the only other documentation of Cartwright's involvement in baseball concerned the Hawaiian Base Ball Association. In 1890 the association was chartered by Lorrin Thurston.[14] The capital stock of the organization was

$5,000 divided into five hundred shares, which were valued at $10 each. Cartwright purchased five shares.[15]

Chapter 14 looks more closely at Alexander Cartwright's connections to baseball in Hawaii, but this information, along with the rest presented in part 1, seems to bring to a close the story of Alexander Cartwright's involvement in the sport.

TEN

The Death of Cartwright,
a King, and a Kingdom

The 1887 Bayonet Constitution reduced King Kalakaua to nothing more than a figurehead, in addition to which the Reform government declared the king bankrupt and ordered him to pay his personal debts. As a result, King Kalakaua closed the palace and moved to his summer home at Kailua-Kona on the Big Island of Hawaii, where he took up coffee cultivation.[1] In March 1888, the *Hawaiian Gazette* called coffee "one of the future most important industries of the kingdom."[2]

However, a counterrevolution against the Reform government was building, led by Robert Wilcox. Half-Hawaiian and half-American, Wilcox had been selected by Kalakaua for special military training in Italy. On July 30, 1889, Wilcox and an armed group marched to the palace to force the Reform Cabinet to return the king to his proper status.[3] Oddly enough, Kalakaua was not there. He'd instead heard a rumor that Wilcox was there to assassinate him and put his sister on the throne, so he had earlier left with his personal guards.[4]

Sharpshooters in surrounding buildings and volunteer forces retaliated, leading to a short-lived fight on palace grounds. Seven insurgents were killed and a dozen wounded, and the rebels were arrested. Wilcox wasn't charged with treason but on a conspiracy charge, and he was eventually acquitted as being "under orders of the king."[5] Afterward, Wilcox became a hero to Hawaiians.

By 1890, the internal divisions within the Reform Party were causing it to split, and in the spring, Thurston's Reformers lost an election to the National Party (also known as the National Reform Party), led by Robert Wilcox. On May 21, 1890, King Kalakaua addressed the open assembly. He spoke with confidence and gave commendations to his cabinet; then, the legislative body demanded a new cabinet, one appointed by the king. Afterward, Kalakaua wrote his friend Charles Spencer that he was finally in power to appoint him to the position of minister of interior—replacing Lorrin Thurston.[6]

Mindful, perhaps, of his tentative hold on power, Kalakaua created a new cabinet consisting of members from both the National and the Reform parties. Next, Kalakaua planned to revise the Bayonet Constitution, particularly so that voting would be restricted to Hawaiian subjects rather than be open to all residents.[7] Amid this optimistic turn of political events, Kalakaua decided to take a trip to the United States.

Doctors thought it would do him good if he had a change of climate, so Kalakaua decided to go to San Francisco; he designated his sister Liliuokalani as regent during his absence. Liliuokalani (in her book *Hawaii's Story by Hawaii's Queen*) wrote that when her brother came to see her three days before his departure to the United States, she did all she could to dissuade him from going. It did no good. In November 1890, King Kalakaua sailed to California on what would be a fateful trip.

Kalakaua's agenda wasn't merely to improve his physical health. In San Francisco, he intended to speak with Henry A. P. Carter, the Hawaiian minister to the United States and Europe, about the McKinley Tariff Bill, which was then before the U.S. Congress. The McKinley bill would deny Hawaiian sugar planters the advantage that they enjoyed in the American market and would, in essence, repudiate the 1876 Reciprocity Treaty. Kalakaua feared that if the Reciprocity Treaty were invalidated, then this might invalidate the United States' promise to respect the independence of the Hawaiian nation.

Both King Kalakaua and the Hawaii sugar barons opposed the McKinley bill, and Kalakaua wanted to voice his opposition and see what Carter could do to stop it. If the bill passed, he worried that the Hawaiian League might foment another revolution, this time toppling the Hawaiian monarchy. Then, the United States, which had formally shied away from talk of annexing Hawaii, might change its mind. Kalakaua was right to worry.[8]

While in San Francisco, King David Kalakaua witnessed a professional baseball game. On December 20, 1890, two teams made up of major league and California League players took part in a benefit game between the All-Californias and the Picked Nine. The game, the first ever in the United States in the presence of royalty, was played before a crowd of four thousand at the Haight Street Grounds to raise money for Christmas gifts for the poor.

As reported in the *San Francisco Examiner* the next day, "His Majesty, Kalakaua, King of Hawaii, occupying a private box handsomely decorated with the white and blue of his own Island Kingdom, the red, white and blue of America and the evergreen and holly of Christmastide, watched with animated interest the playing of the great charity game in aid of the *Examiner* fund for the purchase of toys for the homeless and sick and abandoned children of San Francisco."[9]

King Kalakaua and his party arrived by train from Monterey. Not quite half an inning had begun when the king's arrival was announced and the band struck up the Hawaiian national anthem, written by the king himself, "Hawaii Ponoi." As the king entered the grandstand, the crowd stood up and cheered. The king's response to his enthusiastic reception was to say, "If my coming here today will be the means of making even one poor orphan happy on Christmas Day, I shall feel more than repaid for the coming." Kalakaua also expressed his great admiration for the game, saying that he had seen it played a little by the clubs in his own kingdom. In the king's honor, the Picked Nine wore uniform patches of Hawaii's royal colors. Unfortunately, his team lost.

King David Kalakaua died exactly one month later at the age of fifty-four on January 20, 1891, in the Palace Hotel in San Francisco.[10] United States Navy Admiral George Brown was at his bedside, along with Claus Spreckels and Charles Bishop. The cause of death was given as Bright's disease, related to a condition of the kidneys. The king's final words were, "Tell my people I tried." Curiously, for nearly ten days before his death, an Edison phonograph had been placed at his bedside. A representative of the phonograph company told the king that a recording of his voice might aid in publicizing the instrument and provide a personal message to his people.

Finally, the king decided to record a message. Speaking in the Hawaiian language, his words were translated as "Greetings to you. Greetings to you. We will very likely hereafter go to Hawaii, to Honolulu. There you will tell my people what you have heard me say here."[11] The king then fell back against his pillows in exhaustion; the machine was left in his suite in hopes that he would record more, but it was not to be.[12]

Large crowds gathered in the streets of San Francisco as the king's casket was carried to the *S.S. Charleston*, which would take him to Hawaii. In Honolulu, the people were expecting the king's arrival and were ready to celebrate his return. Liliuokalani had sent invitations for a ball at the palace. Diamond Head Charlie (or Charles Petersen, the lighthouse keeper) was the first to spot the ship approaching. He saw the ship's flags flying at half-mast, and knew what this meant. As the ship neared, the waiting Hawaiians saw it was draped in black. Groans of mourning replaced the anticipated shouts of celebration even before the ship was tied to the dock.[13]

Liliuokalani, sister of the deceased monarch, succeeded to the throne. Under intense pressure from her inherited cabinet, she took an oath to uphold the Bayonet Constitution, though she despised it.

A few weeks later, Alfred Cartwright died in Oakland, California, on February 6, 1891, at the age of sixty-nine. He was, even then, caught in the shadow of his more well-known older sibling,

and the Hawaiian newspapers at the time referred to him as
the "brother of A. J. Cartwright."[14] The following year, on July
12, 1892, Alexander Cartwright died at the age of seventy-two.
According to his death certificate, he died of blood poisoning.[15]
The story handed down through the family is that a boil on his
neck had become infected.

The *Hawaiian Gazette* printed a lengthy obituary on July 19,
1892. Part of it appeared in a column announcing his death,
and yet another part was more of a biography of his life and accomplishments. His death announcement read as though he
were royalty himself:

> No man in this city was better known here and through-
> out the Kingdom than the deceased, and no one was
> looked up to with greater respect for those sterling quali-
> ties which go to make a kind husband and father, a valu-
> able and useful citizen and an upright and successful
> businessman than Alexander J. Cartwright. Many a one
> can recall instances where he has received assistance fi-
> nancially, or by advice more valuable than money, that
> has served to make him remembered as a friend indeed,
> and his death will be felt and his presence missed in a
> much larger sphere than his family circle. But perhaps
> his most conspicuous trait was his sterling patriotism—a
> stalwart American of the old Henry Clay school of 1840,
> and this trait endeared him to every American, whether
> Republican or Democrat. He was for many years, or
> until his death, Treasurer of the American Relief As-
> sociation, and as such has aided many of his destitute

countrymen, who needed relief here. In various other associations, where he has long been the moving spirit, his presence will be greatly missed.

Alexander Cartwright was buried in Nuuanu Cemetery (now known as Oahu Cemetery). A letter written by Mrs. Judd, a missionary descendent, to her son regarding Cartwright's funeral, dated July 18, 1892, exists in a private collection:

> Attended Mr. Cartwright's funeral from his Emma St. home. Flowers exquisite, service short, Rev. Mr. [unreadable], singing by a double quartette from Fort St. Church Choir. I played "Abide with me" and "Rock of Ages" selected by Mrs. Cartwright. Only a few selections of scripture not pertaining to a funeral, a brief appropriate prayer. Your father was one of the pall bearers and had to walk all that distance way up in the rain and mud. I drove up by back street, taking Nellie up and sat at 8 home waiting for papa. Quite a long procession, band at cemetery ... In the p.m. we went to see Mrs. Cartwright. Found her very composed—elegant flowers. She wanted to see Aunt Mary. Put her arms about her and kissed. Found out they had been to the same academy in Albany (NY) and knew the same girls—mentioning the names of some of them.[16]

On January 17, 1893—about six months after Alexander Cartwright's death and almost exactly two years after David Kalakaua's death—the Hawaiian monarchy was overthrown. The group of Americans at the center of the coup—led by Lorrin Thurston, who years earlier had played baseball at Punahou School with the Cartwright brothers—asked the United States president, Benjamin Harrison, to annex Hawaii as part of the United States. The president was in favor.

Shortly after the overthrow, Liliuokalani wrote an article that appeared in the *San Francisco Examiner.* In it she stated, "Annexation is not necessary for the ends of peace or of civilization, or of commerce, or of security."[17] In contrast, William McKinley declared, "We need Hawaii just as much and a good deal more than we did California. It is Manifest Destiny."[18]

Following the overthrow of the monarchy, one of Cartwright's comrades in business, Sanford B. Dole, became president of the provisional government.[19] Dole assisted in drafting a Treaty of Annexation to be sent to Washington DC, but before it was approved by the Senate, President Harrison's term ended and Grover Cleveland took office. President Cleveland was a friend of Liliuokalani, and he did not support annexation. Citing a lack of popular Hawaiian support for the revolution, he immediately withdrew the treaty from the Senate, and in December 1893, he demanded that President Dole disband the provisional government and Queen Liliuokalani be reinstated on the throne. Dole refused.

Instead, after a constitutional convention, the Republic of Hawaii was proclaimed on July 4, 1894, with Sanford Dole as president. It wasn't until the U.S. White House changed administrations again, with the Manifest Destiny–minded William McKinley becoming president, that the United States annexed Hawaii in 1898. Hawaii became a U.S. territory in 1900, with

Dole serving as the territorial governor from 1900 to 1903. Hawaii became the United States' fiftieth state in 1959.

Sanford Dole died in 1926 at the age of eighty-two in the same town in which he was born, Honolulu. His father, Daniel Dole, was the founder and first principal of Punahou School. Because Dole's mother, Emily, died four days after his birth, Sanford was raised by Hawaiian nurses, who sang and chanted to him in Hawaiian. This led Sanford Dole to once say of himself, "I am of American blood but Hawaiian milk."

Though he was not born in Hawaii, the same was very much true of Alexander Cartwright. When he was twenty-nine, he left New York and America, and though he made a few journeys back to California, in his heart he never returned. It was fitting that like Dole, Cartwright died in Hawaii, in the land where he bloomed and whose future he helped shape. By the end, New York and baseball seemed nearly footnotes in Cartwright's life, which instead had been devoted to "Hawaii nei," the islands he so dearly loved.

PART 2

THE MYTHOGRAPHY OF A MAN

ELEVEN

"Dear Old Knickerbockers"

Alexander Cartwright spent most of his life in Hawaii, and it could be argued that he had as significant an impact on the islands as he had on baseball, but that's not how he's most remembered. Instead, he is the "Father of Modern Baseball," and it is Hawaii that has become but a footnote to his life.

However, compared with what we know about him in Hawaii, we know relatively little about Cartwright's involvement in baseball. Or at least, we know very little from primary sources, or from Cartwright himself. Significant portions of Alexander Cartwright's legacy are based on the evidence of secondhand stories, and even these are sometimes conflicting. It is to the nature of Cartwright's baseball legacy, and of those sources, that we now turn.

Regarding Cartwright's baseball legacy, part 2 attempts to answer a series of central questions: Were the Knickerbockers the first organized ball club, and were they founded by Alexander

Cartwright? Did the Knickerbockers and Cartwright play in the first true "match game"? Did Cartwright create or establish any of the rules that the Knickerbockers used (which were officially adopted when the league was established in the 1850s)? Did Cartwright "seed" the game across the country when he traveled west during the California Gold Rush in 1849? And did he introduce baseball to Hawaii?

This chapter will tackle the first three questions: Were the Knickerbockers the first club, who organized them, and did they play the first match game? It's tempting to quip that these questions ask not "who's on first" but who *was* first? Beginnings can be hard to determine. It is well documented that, long before the nineteenth century, there were numerous informal games using bats and balls, and there were plenty of teams and contests. So we are looking to pinpoint within this moving stream the moment that one of these games and contests became organized in a way that we recognize as baseball today.

In fact, there is a published, firsthand account of the creation of baseball in New York that predates the Knickerbockers by about eight years. William Wheaton was interviewed for an article that appeared in San Francisco's *The Daily Examiner* in 1887. The title of the article was "How Baseball Began— A Member of the Gotham Club of Fifty Years Ago Tells about It." Here is almost all of Wheaton's tale, which calls into question nearly every claim made for Cartwright. Wheaton begins by saying that in 1836, he had just passed the bar exam and become a lawyer, and that he was "very fond of physical exercise." He continues:

In fact, we all were in those days, and we sought it wherever it could be found. Myself and intimates, young
merchants, lawyers, and physicians found cricket too
slow and lazy a game. Three-cornered cat was a boy's
game, and did well enough for slight youngsters, but it
was a dangerous game for powerful men, because the
ball was made of a hard rubber center, tightly wrapped
with yarn, and in the hands of a strong-armed man it
was a terrible missile, and sometimes had fatal results
when it came in contact with a delicate part of the player's anatomy.

We had to have a good outdoor game, and as the
games then in vogue didn't suit us, we decided to re-
model three-cornered cat and make a new game. We first
organized what we called the Gotham Baseball Club.
This was the first ball organization in the United States,
and it was completed in 1837. Among the members were
Dr. John Miller, a popular physician of that day; John
Murphy, a well-known hotel-keeper, and James Lee,
President of the New York Chamber of Commerce.

The first step we took in making baseball was to abol-
ish the rule of throwing the ball at the runner and ordered that it should be thrown to the baseman instead,
who had to touch the runner with it before he reached
the base. During the regime of three-cornered cat there
were no regular bases, but only such permanent objects
as a bedded boulder or an old stump, and often the diamond looked strangely like an irregular polygon. We
laid out the ground at Madison square in the form of

an accurate diamond, with home-plate and sand bags for bases. You must remember that what is now called Madison Square, opposite the Fifth Avenue Hotel, in the thirties was out in the country, far from the city limits. We had no shortstop, and often played with only six or seven men on a side. The scorer kept the game in a book we had made for that purpose, and it was he who decided all disputed points. The modern umpire and his tribulations were unknown to us . . .

After the Gotham club had been in existence a few months, it was found necessary to reduce the rules of the new game to writing. This work fell to my hands, and the code I then formulated is substantially that in use today. We abandoned the old rule of putting out on the first bound and confined it to fly catching. The Gothams played a game of ball with the Star Cricket Club of Brooklyn, and beat the Englishmen out of sight, of course. That game and the return were the only matches ever played by the first baseball club.

The new game quickly became very popular with New Yorkers, and the numbers of the club soon swelled beyond the fastidious notions of some of us, and we decided to withdraw and found a new organization, which we called the Knickerbocker. For a playground we chose the Elysian Fields of Hoboken, just across the Hudson River. And those fields were truly Elysian to us in those days. There was a broad, firm, greensward, fringed with fine shady trees, where we could recline during intervals, when waiting for a strike, and take a refreshing rest.

We played no exhibition or match games, but often our families would come over and look on with much enjoyment. Then we used to have dinner in the middle of the day, and twice a week we would spend the whole afternoon in ball play. We were all mature men and in business, but we didn't have too much of it as they do nowadays. There was none of that hurry and worry so characteristic of the present New York. We enjoyed life and didn't wear out so fast. In the old game when a man struck out those of his side who happened to be on the bases had to come in and lose that chance of making a run. We changed that and made the rule which holds good now.[1]

William Wheaton was one of the founding members of the Knickerbocker Base Ball Club in 1845, becoming the club's first vice president. He also served on the Knickerbockers' first Committee on By-Laws (along with William Tucker). His story is filled with credible details that accurately reflect other accounts of the city and of games being played at the time. As someone who was present when the Knickerbockers formed, we could presume that he should know how it happened.

No firsthand account of the formation of the Knickerbockers by Alexander Cartwright was found by this author. The earliest historical reference found that traces the beginning of the Knickerbocker Base Ball Club is from the *Dime Base-Ball Player*, published by Irwin P. Beadle and Company of New York in 1860. This compendium of the game included elementary instructions about the "American Game of Ball" written by Henry Chadwick. Within it, Chadwick states, "There was a Club called the

New York Club, which existed before the Knickerbocker, but we shall not be far wrong if we award to the latter club the honor of being the pioneer of the present game of Base Ball." Another early and elaborate description of the club was written in 1866 by Charles Peverelly in his book *American Pastimes.* Since Peverelly was not himself one of the New York ball players, where did he get *his* information? We don't know this either, since he did not name his source.

Based on Chadwick's writings in *Beadle's Dime Base-Ball Player,* Peverelly likely spoke to Henry Chadwick, an Englishman who would become a sports journalism pioneer and inventor of baseball's statistics (and who is described further in chapter 15); Peverelly may have also talked with Duncan Curry, the first Knickerbocker president. We may never know his exact source, but Peverelly's text is the most thorough and descriptive account of the formation of the Knickerbocker Base Ball Club. As with Wheaton's, it is full of credible general details:

> During the years of 1842 and '43, a number of gentlemen, fond of the game, casually assembled on a plot of ground in Twenty-Seventh Street—the one now occupied by the Harlem Railroad Depot, bringing with them their bats, balls, etc. It was customary for two or three players enough to make a match. The march of improvement made a "change of base" necessary, and the following year they met at the next most convenient place, the north slope of Murray Hill, between the railroad cut and Third Avenue. Among the prominent players were Col. James Lee, Dr. Ransom, Abraham Tucker,

James Fisher, and W. Vail, the latter better known in later years of the Gotham Club, as "Stay-where-you-am-Wail." In the spring of 1845 Mr. Alex Cartwright, who had become an enthusiast in the game, one day upon the field proposed a regular organization, promising to obtain several recruits. His proposal was acceded to, and Messrs. W. R. Wheaton, Cartwright, D. F. Curry, E. R. Dupignac, Jr., and W. H. Tucker, formed themselves into a board of recruiting officers, and soon obtained names enough to make a respectable show. At a preliminary meeting, it was suggested that as it was apparent they would soon be driven from Murray Hill, some suitable place should be obtained in New Jersey, where their stay could be permanent; accordingly, a day or two afterwards, enough to make a game assembled at Barclay Street ferry, crossed over, marched up the road, prospecting for ground on each side, until they reached the Elysian Fields, where they "settled." Thus it occurred that a party of gentlemen formed an organization, combining together health, recreation, and social enjoyment, which was the nucleus of the now great American game of Base Ball, so popular in all parts of the United States, than which there is none more manly or more health giving.

The parent Knickerbockers claim for themselves the original organization, from the succeeding clubs derived their rules of playing, and which was always ready to foster, encourage, and promote the pleasure of all who were desirous of enjoying the game. Its members have from its inception been composed mostly of those sedentary habits required recreation, and its respectability has ever been undoubted. The same standard still exists, and no person can obtain admission in the club merely for his capacity as a player; he must also have the reputation of a gentleman; and hence arises one of the causes of its not being what is called a match-playing club.

The organization bears the date the 23d of September, 1845. Its first officers were: President, Duncan F. Curry; Vice-President, Wm. R. Wheaton; Secretary and Treasurer, Wm. H. Tucker.[2]

There are some striking similarities and equally striking differences in Wheaton's and Peverelly's accounts. But one thing seems sure: September 23, 1845, became known afterward as the day organized baseball was born. For instance, in 1888, the October 3 edition of the *Baltimore Daily News* announced that the previous Sunday marked the forty-third anniversary of baseball in America. That coincides precisely with the date of September 23, 1845, which surely means that contemporaries of the time revered this day as the significant founding moment of baseball.

But was it? Both Wheaton and Peverelly seem to agree that a loose confederation of men were playing some version of the game, until someone (Peverelly says Cartwright) decided to get more organized. At this point, they moved their playing to Elysian Fields in Hoboken, New Jersey. Wheaton does not date

these events, but they match Peverelly overall. Besides not naming Cartwright, the most important discrepancy is that Wheaton
claims to have founded the first club and written its rules. Why
have Wheaton and his Gotham Club been overlooked?

The New York Club that Wheaton mentioned was also known
as the Gotham Club as well as the New York Nine. It is specu-
lated that the Gotham Club adopted the "New York" name upon
moving to Elysian Fields, also home of the New York Cricket
Club. The fact that some members of the New York Club got
together to form the Knickerbocker club is also reflected in
writings by the Knickerbockers' second president, Daniel L.
Adams. However, Adams dismissed the New York Club as lacking organization.[3]

Adams was quoted saying this in the February 29, 1896, edition of the *Sporting News*, in an article entitled, "Dr. D. L. ADAMS;
Memoirs of the Father of Base Ball; He Resides in New Haven
and Retains an Interest in the Game." Adams then recounted
a story very similar to Wheaton's: he described how he began
to play baseball in 1839 with a number of other young medical
men. He spoke of the New York Base Ball Club and that it had
no very definite organization, and that some of the younger
members of that club got together and formed the Knickerbocker Base Ball Club.

In addition to Adams, Alexander Cartwright is documented
as mentioning the earlier New York Club, and with the same dis-
missive appraisal. In 1865, Cartwright wrote a letter to former
fellow Knickerbocker Charles DeBost (this letter is reprinted in
chapter 6). Cartwright asked DeBost about a lithograph of the
Knickerbockers. Conveying pride in his former team, Cartwright

said of the lithograph, "it would be interesting as a memorial of the first Base Ball Club of N.Y. Truly the first, for the old New York Club never had a regular organization."[4]

Though Cartwright and Adams didn't really recognize the New York Base Ball Club as a "regular organization," it did get mentioned in the *New York Herald* on November 11, 1845, as celebrating its second anniversary on the grounds of Elysian Fields. Afterward, the club members ate dinner at McCarty's and were honored by the presence of representatives from the Union Star Cricket Club, the Knickerbocker clubs, senior and junior, and other gentlemen of note.

Yet another club was mentioned by the *New York Herald* as it reported on November 2, 1843, that the members of the New York Magnolia Ball Club would meet at Elysian Fields, Hoboken, and that play would commence at one o'clock. A surviving artifact from 1844 of the Magnolia Ball Club was recently discovered that depicts the New York game being played on an elaborately designed ticket for an annual ball that was intended as a keepsake for the event.[5]

What does this tell us about the New York Base Ball Club (and that of the Magnolia Ball Club)? Were they "real" clubs with rules and organization? Wheaton felt that the New York Club was a legitimate organization, but then of course, he might be biased toward the club that would give him the credit. Adams and Cartwright don't think so, but then of course, they might be biased toward the club that would give them the credit.

What we do know is that both William Wheaton and William Tucker had dual membership in the New York Club and the Knickerbocker club early on. Before aligning themselves solely with the Knickerbocker club, they "tried out" the new rules between their original New York Club and the Brooklyn Club.[6] The *New York Herald* reported their games, wins, and losses, including any corrections to errors made in initial reporting. Steadily, members of the New York Club began appearing more and more in the lineups for the Knickerbockers.

Having the results of games reported in the newspaper would seem to indicate a level of play and organization that would qualify the New York Club as a real baseball club. Does this mean the Knickerbockers were not the "first" true baseball club? Perhaps, depending on one's interpretation. How organized is organized, and how many current rules needed to have been in place to qualify as "baseball"? Without more evidence, it's impossible to definitively determine these things today. However, without question, the Knickerbockers became the more popular club, and this occurred quite possibly because they were more self-consciously organized: they held meetings, elected officers, and had committees.

So, who formed the Knickerbockers? All the accounts just mentioned agree that there was a clear moment when they were formed. Who were those "fastidious" team members Wheaton mentions, those who argued that the Gotham Club needed better organization, and so formed a new club with a new name? Was it a group of men—including perhaps Daniel Adams, Duncan Curry, Alexander Cartwright, and others—or was it in fact just a single "fastidious" person?

From what we know of Cartwright's personality, certain traits about him can be surmised. He was the kind of man who enjoyed creating organizations, and also taking a significant part in them. He was a stickler for the rules, and he was one who forcefully asserted his opinion. It's easy to imagine that Cartwright was one of the "fastidious" team members that Wheaton referenced.

Another very important history of baseball's founding is provided by Albert G. Spalding in his 1911 book *America's National Game*. In it, Spalding credits Cartwright alone with the idea of forming the Knickerbockers (as Peverelly does in his book *American Pastimes*). After the book was published, Spalding had a copy sent to Bruce Cartwright Jr. (Alexander's grandson), and Bruce Jr. sent the following acknowledgement: "I have read the book with great interest and it is my opinion that no better history of Baseball could have been written and I thank you and Mr. Spaulding [sic] again for sending us a copy."[7]

While Spalding wrote an interesting book, this passage from chapter four is likely what won Bruce Jr.'s praise:

To Alexander J. Cartwright, beyond doubt, belongs the honor of having been the first to move in the direction of securing an organization of Base Ball players. It is of record that in the spring of 1845 Mr. Cartwright, being present and participating in a practice game of ball, proposed to others the formal association of themselves together as a Base Ball club. His suggestion met approval, and a self-constituted committee, consisting of Alexander J. Cartwright, D. F. Curry, E. R. Dupignac Jr., W. H. Tucker and W. R. Wheaton, at once set about securing signatures of those who were desirous of belonging to such an organization. The result of the efforts of this committee was the gaining of a nucleus for what soon became the famous Knickerbocker Base Ball Club, of New York, the first recorded association of Base Ball players in the world. The organization was perfected September 23, 1845.[8]

Spalding says that Cartwright's patrimony of baseball is "beyond doubt" and a matter "of record." He doesn't, however, list what these records are. Wheaton's account was published in 1887, but perhaps Spalding never saw this; similarly, Adams's account (in a story that called Adams the "Father of Base Ball") was published in 1896 but also might have escaped Spalding's notice. He certainly read Peverelly's account, but was he simply repeating Peverelly's claim for Cartwright without thorough research?

Interestingly enough, Spalding had a cousin, George W. Smith, who was a well-known druggist in Honolulu (and who participated in the ceremonies during Spalding's 1888 visit to Honolulu for his baseball world tour[9]). Smith would have known of or met Alexander Cartwright in some capacity; we have no evidence of this, but it seems reasonable, considering Cartwright's standing in Honolulu society as well as the opportunity that Spalding's 1888 world tour would have provided (which is described in chapter 9). After *America's National Game* was published, Smith wrote to his cousin Albert. We don't have Smith's letter, but we have Spalding's reply, and it makes clear that Smith asked his cousin about Cartwright and the source for his cousin's claims. Spalding's letter, which exists in a private collection, has an unreadable date in the 1900s. Spalding wrote in response to Smith:

My Dear Smith:

Replying to your communication of the 19th of February, in which you ask for historical facts connecting Alexander Joy Cartwright with the early beginnings of our national game, I regret that I cannot supply your friend with fuller information than is found in the records of the old Knickerbocker Club in my possession.

That Mr. Cartwright was one of the founders of that first organized base ball club, there can be no doubt. Not only does his name appear frequently in records of the social side of the organization, but at the very beginning of the club's history Mr. Cartwright was in evidence at every practice game. I have on my desk as I write this letter the old Knickerbocker Score Book of Games played in 1845, and the name of Cartwright, with more than the average number of runs to its [his] credit appears at each succeeding game. That he was a very active spirit in guiding the counsels of the great original club, is also most apparent. Beyond this statement of fact, I find nothing in these records that would interest your friend. Further research would simply multiply the number of practice games in which he participated and the number of meetings at which his voice was heard in earnest espousal of the game's best interests. Hoping this will be quite satisfactory, and with the assurance of my appreciation of the honor to him of having been identified with that grand old organization, believe me.

Yours Most Truly,

A. G. Spalding[10]

This letter indicates a few interesting things. One is that Spalding clearly did do some research. However, he seems to acknowledge that the original Knickerbocker club records are his primary source for his claims regarding Cartwright. Further, these records establish Cartwright as "one of the founders" (as well as an above-average hitter), but not, perhaps, as *the* founder. It would help, of course, to know what question Smith asked, and why he asked it. Did Smith have a reason to doubt Spalding's claim or was he merely curious to know more? Given Spalding's openness in the letter, it seems likely that if he had other sources for Cartwright, he would have named them, but he says just the opposite. He claims to have no "fuller information" and dismisses the need for further research, presumably into the records he had in his possession, claiming that they would only yield more of the same.

All the available documentation seems to agree that Cartwright was one of the founders of the Knickerbockers, and that he was an involved and important member of the club while he was in New York. Peverelly does not list Cartwright as one of the original club officers in 1845, but Cartwright was an officer the next three years.

According to Peverelly, May 5, 1846, marked the second formal meeting of the Knickerbockers, held at McCarty's Hotel at Elysian Fields. The officers elected for that year were Duncan F. Curry as president, Daniel L. Adams as vice president, William H. Tucker as treasurer, and Alexander J. Cartwright as secretary.[11] In April 1847, at McLean's Hotel in New York, Daniel L. Adams was elected president, Alexander J. Cartwright was elected vice president, Alexander H. Drummond was elected secretary, and Charles H. Birney was elected as the treasurer. In 1848, the last year that Cartwright would involve himself as a Knickerbocker, Daniel L. Adams was elected president, Alexander J. Cartwright was vice president, Eugene Plunkett was secretary, Fraley C. Niebuhr was treasurer, and Alexander H. Drummond and Benjamin C. Lee were directors.

To give a sense of who and how many men were involved, the names of the remaining 1848 Knickerbockers are as follows: Edward A. Bibby, Charles H. Birney, Benjamin K. Brotherson, George A. Brown, Ebenezer R. Dupignac, Edward A. Ebbets, A. T. Gourlie, Peter S. Henderson, George Ireland, F. U. Johnstone, James Moncrief, Henry T. Morgan, A. C. Morrill, J. Murphy, Walter Oakley, Henry M. Onderdonk, Edward W. Talman, William L. Talman, A. P. Taylor, A. D. Thompson, William H. Tucker, George C. Waller, William H. Wetervelt, and honorary members James Lee, Esq., and Abraham G. Tucker, Esq.

Again, establishing that Alexander Cartwright was "one of the founders" is quite different from saying he was "the" founder, the sole father of modern baseball. More than one man seems eligible to claim this title, or more rightly, *there is a core group of men who share it.* However, there is still more evidence to consider before reaching a conclusion about Cartwright, and we will consider this founding moment of the Knickerbocker Base Ball Club further in chapter 12, when we look at the formation of the rules.

Now, we reach the last question of this chapter: Did the Knickerbockers play the first true match game of baseball, and did Cartwright play in it? There are doubts regarding both.

The Spalding Collection at the New York Public Library holds the score books for the Knickerbocker Base Ball Club. Within that collection, torn stubs of pages that once existed are all that remain for the famed June 19, 1846, match game at Elysian Fields between the Knickerbockers and the New York Club. This is, by all accounts, the first match game the Knickerbockers played (see Duncan Curry's description of the game earlier in this chapter).

However, before these pages of the Knickerbocker score book were mysteriously removed, they were copied for reprinting in the 1953 book *The Umpire Story* by James M. Kahn. In this book, the game score sheets appear in black and white. Cartwright is not in the lineup for the game, and no one signed the umpire signature line.

However, on the same day, there was an "extra play" game, and (at the time of this writing) the pages for this game *do* still exist in the Knickerbocker score book. On this page, faintly written in pencil, is the date of June 20, 1846, yet a darker marking of "19" is written over the number 20. Also lightly written on the umpire's signature line is the name "J. Paulding." And yet, for the game that Paulding umpired, Cartwright's name is also *not* in the lineup.[12]

In Duncan Curry's description of this match, he does not mention who played; thus, given the state of the evidence, we simply do not know if Cartwright was there that day.

But was this even the first match game? In his account, William Wheaton claims that his New York Club played the first match game against a Brooklyn club, and there is documentation that possibly supports this. In October 1845, the *New York*

Herald announced a match game between the New York Base
Ball Club and the Brooklyn Club: "The New York Base Ball Club
will play a match of baseball against the Brooklyn Club tomor-
row afternoon at 2 o'clock, at the Elysian Field, Hoboken."[13]

As Wheaton indicates, these teams were made up primarily
of cricketers who had converted to baseball, but some historians
consider this event on October 21, 1845, as the date of the first
match game of baseball at Elysian Fields.[14] Possibly the reason
this game's significance has been ignored is because the *New
York Herald* printed the announcement a day late. Therefore,
the players and their friends were likely the only ones present
at Elysian Fields for the game.

Last of all, a very early reference to playing "base ball" in New
York was found in the *National Advocate* of 1823. Though the
words *organized association* appear in the brief article, there is
no mention of any team names. Much about the article leaves
one to wonder, but we at least know that some form of "base
ball" was played then.[15]

TWELVE

"Baseball on Murray Hill"

Who came up with the rules of baseball? This simple question doesn't have a simple answer. It would be ideal to be able to credit one man and one moment, but the game that became baseball, as is the case with most sports, evolved over time (and it still sometimes changes). The question is really: Can the creation of those early baseball rules be attributed to certain individuals and particular moments?

I will not attempt to trace the development of baseball from its earliest roots. Instead, I'll focus on the specific claims made for the Knickerbockers and Cartwright—that, as his plaque in the Hall of Fame states, Cartwright "set bases 90 feet apart, established 9 innings as game and 9 players as team." Early baseball had many more rules, some just as essential, but these particular rules, also known as the "Cartwright rules," are key to our investigation: they are central to Cartwright's Hall of Fame legacy and also to our conception of "modern baseball."

In *American Pastimes,* Charles Peverelly listed William R. Wheaton and William H. Tucker as the only Knickerbocker members on the Committee on By-Laws when the club was created in 1845. Perhaps Cartwright and other Knickerbockers were on this committee, but the records do not say. Also, though the surviving Knickerbocker score books date as far back as 1845, the oldest surviving *Knickerbocker Base Ball Club By-laws and Rules* are from 1848. Unfortunately, this surviving pamphlet in printed form does not reference an earlier printed or handwritten version, and it does not assign authorship to any particular person for establishing the first set of organized rules, either in 1845 or 1848. The 1848 pamphlet *does* list the committee members "to revise constitution and By-Laws" for that year. These were: D. L. Adams, A. J. Cartwright, Eugene Plunkett, J. P. Mumford, and Duncan F. Curry.[1]

Thus, the Knickerbockers themselves did not officially identify an author for the game they played. This doesn't mean there wasn't one, but it means that we must turn to the accounts of players and contemporaries to learn what we can. There is no known written account by Cartwright himself in which he specifically claims to have authored the "Cartwright rules."

Peverelly further wrote that succeeding clubs derived their rules of play from the Knickerbockers. These clubs were noted by Peverelly as the Gothams, Eagles, and Empires. Once the Knickerbockers developed their particular rules, Peverelly says, others adopted them, including ball clubs that had played long before the Knickerbockers existed.

Instead of citing the 1845 Knickerbocker rules from Peverelly's *American Pastimes,* I will here list the 1845 Knickerbocker rules as they appeared in *Beadle's Dime Base-Ball Player* of 1860:

FIRST RULES OF BASE BALL.

SECTION 1. The bases shall be from "Home" to second base 42 paces; from first to third base 42 paces equidistant.

SECTION 2. The game to consist of 21 counts or aces, but at the conclusion an equal number of hands must be played.

SECTION 3. The ball must be pitched and not thrown for the bat.

SECTION 4. A ball knocked outside the range of the first or third base is foul.

SECTION 5. Three balls being struck at and missed, and the last one caught, is a hand out; if not caught, is considered fair, and the striker bound to run.

SECTION 6. A ball being struck or tipped, and caught either flying or on the first bound, is a hand out.

SECTION 7. A player, running the bases, shall be out, if the ball is in the hands of an adversary on the base, as the runner is touched by it before he makes his base— it being understood, however, that in no instance is a ball to be thrown *at him.*

SECTION 8. A player running, who shall prevent an adversary from catching or getting the ball before making his base, is a hand out.

SECTION 9. If two hands are already out, a player running home at the time a ball is struck, can not make an ace if the striker is caught out.

SECTION 10. Three hands out, all out.

SECTION 11. Players must take their strike in regular turn.

SECTION 12. No ace or base can be made on a foul strike.

SECTION 13. A runner can not be put out in making one base, when a baulk is made by the pitcher.

SECTION 14. But one base allowed when the ball bounds out of the field when struck.[2]

The closest we have to a direct description by Alexander Cartwright of what he did to create baseball's rules is a published reminiscence by his grandson Bruce Cartwright Jr. This appeared in a magazine article curiously published in the May 1947 issue of *Paradise of the Pacific*. Written by S. F. Furukawa, the article was printed eight years after Bruce Cartwright Jr.'s death. However, Bruce's interview is in the first person and the present tense, making it seem as if Furukawa spoke with him directly. In addition, Furukawa sent a First Day Cover Envelope (or a commemorative envelope) of Baseball's Centennial to a member of the Cartwright family in 1939. "Baseball's Centennial" was commemorated in 1939, which was the supposed one-hundred-year anniversary of Abner Doubleday inventing baseball in 1839 in Cooperstown, New York, where the National Baseball Hall of Fame was built.[3] On the back of the envelope is printed the "Story of Baseball Diamond," which Furukawa copyrighted.[4]

Furukawa's article in the *Paradise of the Pacific*, "Originator of Organized Baseball," quoted Bruce Jr. as follows:

When I was a small boy it was my great joy to hear

grandpa tell about the early days of baseball in New York and his adventures while crossing the continent. It seems that around 1842 a new game called baseball came to town from upstate. Young men in New York took much fancy to the game, which resembled cricket but provided more fun than the English pastime. My grandfather was a bank clerk then, and he and his friends were among the first to play "town ball" as it was sometimes called. Their rendezvous was a field where the old Madison Square Garden was to be built fifty years later.

The game Abner Doubleday (who became Major General in the Civil War) originated in 1839, is said to have been developed from the old boy's game of One, Two, or Three Old Cats. When it reached Gotham it was crude and primitive, having no written playing rules. Grandpa, having an inventive turn of mind, decided to improve it by framing rules, including the definitions and dimensions of the playing field.

So, one day, Alex and his teammates decided to lay out the diamond. First, he placed a piece of wooden board to represent "home," then walked thirty paces toward first base, designating the point with a sand bag. For each succeeding base he stepped off another thirty paces in a line at right angle to the preceding one, thus forming a square. In the 1845 rules adopted by the Knickerbocker Club, of New York (the first baseball team in America, which my grandfather helped to organize) there is a section which reads: "The bases shall be from home to second base forty-two paces, from first to third base forty-two paces, equidistant." You see, forty-two paces measures approximately one hundred twenty-seven feet and thirty paces measure ninety feet, slightly more or less according to the pacer. Incidentally in those days a team fielded eleven players which later was reduced to nine. But, that's how the baseball diamond came into being.[5]

In addition, Mr. Furukawa asked Bruce if he knew how his grandfather arrived at the idea of making the infield ninety feet square. Bruce replied that he had asked his grandfather that question, and the response his grandfather gave was "thirty paces would be just about right."[6]

This charming story may be true from Bruce's perspective, perhaps if not in the details (many of which conflict with other accounts). To get a fuller picture of how things actually proceeded, we need to consider several other existing accounts of what happened and what they may tell us. It is unfortunate that Bruce didn't elaborate on what other rules his grandfather framed, but since the focus of the article was the creation of the baseball diamond, these may not have been considered important in that moment. However, it is curious that Bruce mentioned Abner Doubleday as the "originator" of baseball. As of 1938, Bruce was in fact actively working to have his grandfather awarded this honor instead.

The first piece of possibly conflicting evidence regarding the claim that the Knickerbockers and Cartwright created these rules is William Wheaton's 1887 account of the New York Club (for the full passage, see chapter 11). Wheaton does not specifically claim to have created the rules himself, but he said that "we laid out the grounds at Madison square in the form of an accurate diamond, with home-plate and sand bags for bases." According to him, the New York Club had no shortstop; only six or seven men played on a side; and there was no umpire. He also said they established making an out with a fly ball (not on a bounce), and that he was assigned the task of writing down all these rules. All this, Wheaton claimed, occurred before the Knickerbockers formed.

The 1845 Knickerbocker rules do not list the number of players per side, but Wheaton acknowledges that the earlier game was less than nine players. The Knickerbockers later also added an umpire. Wheaton doesn't say how many innings there were per game, and the Knickerbocker rules note that three outs ended a side, and that 21 "aces" ended a game. The nine-inning game was thus a later innovation.

Most significantly, Wheaton says the establishment of the baseball diamond occurred before the Knickerbockers were formed, and he claims that he himself initially drafted the rules. If he did, then it makes sense that the Knickerbockers selected Wheaton in 1845 for their initial rules committee, as he'd already had a head start on them. But also, since Cartwright clearly must have been playing baseball on Murray Hill before the formation of the Knickerbockers, he may have been part of the "we" Wheaton refers to who marked off the diamond, though this would then have occurred some years before the Knickerbockers were officially organized. A baseball historian of contemporary times, David Block, has written about baseball's origins in his 2005 book *Baseball before We Knew It: A Search for the Roots of the Game*. In the chapter "How Slick Were the Knicks?" Block discusses a number of the early Knickerbocker rules as well as the diamond-shaped playing field. However, in another chapter of the book, he states that a diamond-shaped base layout appeared in the 1829 book from Boston entitled *The Boy's Own Book*. We are thus left to ask, as in the famed comic routine by Abbott and Costello, "Who's on first?"

Even more confusing than Abbott and Costello in their famous comedic act, a journalist named William Rankin seemingly pitched a curveball when he changed a story in 1908 from one that he had reported on in 1905. In 1877, Rankin interviewed Duncan Curry, the original president in 1845 of the Knickerbocker Base Ball Club.[7] Rankin later provided this interview to Alfred Spink, who quoted it in his 1910 book *The National Game*. In Spink's book, Curry (using rather flowery language) credits Cartwright for many of the Knickerbockers' revised rules:

> Baseball is purely an American game and owes its origin to Mr. Alexander J. Cartwright, who also suggested the organization of a club to play his new game. I do remember the afternoon when Alex Cartwright came up to the ball field with a new scheme for playing ball. The sun shone beautifully; never do I remember noting its beams fall with a more sweet and mellow radiance than on that particular spring day. For several years

it had been our habit to casually assemble on a plot of ground that is now known as Twenty-seventh Street and Fourth Avenue, where the Harlem Railroad Depot afterward stood. We would take our bats and balls with us and play any sort of a game. We had no name in particular for it. Sometimes we batted the ball to one another or sometimes play one o'cat.

On this afternoon I have already mentioned, Cartwright came to the field—the march of improvement had driven us further north and we located on a piece of property on the slope of Murray Hill, between the railroad cut and Third Avenue—with his plans drawn up on a paper. He had arranged for two nines, the ins and outs.

That is, while one set of players were taking their turn at bat the other side was placed in their respective positions on the field. He had laid out a diamond-shaped field, with canvas bags filled with sand or sawdust for bases at three of the points and an iron plate for the home base. He had arranged for a catcher, a pitcher, three basemen, a short fielder, and three outfielders. His plan met with such good natured derision, but he was so persistent in having us try his new game that we finally consented more to humor him than with any thought of it becoming a reality.

At the time none of us had any experience in that style of play and as there were no rules for playing the game, we had to do the best we could under the circumstances, aided by Cartwright's judgment. The man who could pitch the speediest ball with the most accuracy was the one selected to do the pitching. But I am getting ahead of my story. When we saw what a great game Cartwright had given us, and as his suggestion for forming a club to play it met with our approval, we set about to organize a club.[8]

Like Wheaton, Duncan Curry was a central figure in the Knickerbockers, and we can suppose he knew what happened. So why are their stories seemingly at odds on so many important points? If we were to imagine that Cartwright did mark off the diamond (which Wheaton agrees was done by *someone*), then what do we do with the fact that Curry describes a full nine-player-per-side game that lasted nine innings—when Wheaton says they fielded fewer players, and the Knickerbockers' own rules don't specify the number of innings or players?

It is also odd that Curry would say there were "no rules" for playing the game, or even a name for what they were doing, when Cartwright presented his version of baseball apparently fully formed. Ample evidence shows that *baseball* was becoming a common enough term, and that at least by 1837 and the formation of Wheaton's Gotham Club, it was developing into something resembling its modern form (but one that perhaps, per chapter 11, was not yet quite organized enough to matter). Curry's remarks don't square with what we know of the time.

So we have to ask, did Curry—or, more likely, Rankin and Spink—conflate a complex series of events into one "radiant" spring day and a single piece of paper for the sake of making a better story?

This speculation is spurred by further discrepancies in the published versions of Duncan Curry's 1877 interview. William Rankin was a baseball journalist for *The Sporting News* in the 1880s, and in 1886 he wrote a brief history of the origin of baseball, based on what he learned from Duncan Curry during the summer of 1877. This article dealt with the theories surrounding rounders, town ball, and baseball. Rankin also wrote two articles for the *Sporting News*, one in 1905 and one in 1908, based on the same 1877 interview with Duncan Curry. However, the two articles have some strikingly different remembrances.

In the 1905 article, Rankin said he'd asked Curry about the theory he'd heard that Henry Chadwick (the Englishman we will hear more about in chapter 15) was responsible for drafting the first rules for the game and was chiefly responsible for the development of baseball. Rankin quoted Curry as replying, "Thomas Fiddlesticks. He had no more to do with the original rules than you had. William R. Wheaton and William H. Tucker drew up the first set of rules for base ball during the late summer of 1845."[9]

This quote, ascribed to Curry, then, would seem to support Wheaton's version of events, that he (with Tucker) drew up the first rules, and this would explain why the Knickerbockers put them on the first rules committee.

In the 1905 article, Curry also talked about how he had played ball when he was a little boy but that there wasn't a name for the game then. He then described what he remembered about how baseball originated:

> One afternoon, when we had gathered on the lot for
> a game, some one, but I do not recall his name now,

presented a plan drawn upon paper, showing a ball field, with a diamond to play on. Eighteen men could play at one time. There was the catcher, the pitcher, three basemen, a short fielder and three outfielders for each side. The plan caused a great deal of talk as all new ideas generally do, but finally we agreed to try it. That was the origin of base ball and it proved a success from the start.[10]

This is more confusing still. If the person with the paper wasn't Wheaton or Tucker, then why did Curry say they were the ones who "drew up" the first rules? Did he mean that they wrote them down (perhaps since they were on the rules committee) but didn't conjure them up? And here again we have a discrepancy between Wheaton's remembrance of the number of players and this specific listing of a nine-player game.

Like any good journalist, Rankin sought out old-time players who were still alive to corroborate Curry's information. Rankin wrote that he went to ask "Thomas Tassie" to verify who was responsible for drawing up the diagram of the field with the suggestion to organize a club. Tassie claimed that "Mr. Wadsworth" did so, and this is what Rankin reported in 1905.

By the 1908 article, Rankin had changed his story, and credited Curry's quote, so that now Curry named Cartwright as the one who was responsible for baseball. In addition, Curry's quote in Spink's book two years later includes some wording similar to that in Charles Peverelly's 1866 book *American Pastimes*.

So what is happening here? Did William Rankin merge portions of Duncan Curry's 1877 interview with text from Peverelly's

1866 book and give this to Spink? Or did Curry speak to Peverelly and later to Rankin and use the same language each time? And most important, without talking to Curry again, why did Rankin change what Curry said in 1877 to name Cartwright?

In his 1908 article, Rankin said that in the 1905 article he had written that Curry had forgotten the name of the man who had brought his plans to the ball grounds. After the 1905 article was published, however, Rankin came across some other records of his for a New York paper that called into question Mr. Tassie's declaration that Wadsworth was this person. Rankin also found a letter given to him by H. G. Crickmore in 1876. Crickmore was then a sportswriter for the *New York World*. On the back of the letter he had written, "Mr. Alex J. Cartwright, father of base ball."[11]

Rankin stated that this sparked his memory and wrote in the 1908 article that he called on the editor of the *Sunday Mercury*, Mr. Cauldwell, and asked him about "Mr. Wadsworth." Cauldwell stated that the only Wadsworth who played with the Knickerbockers was from Greenwich Village and that he first played with the Gothams. Cauldwell then said to Rankin, "It was Cartwright who organized the old Knickerbocker Club and it would be only natural that he had a game to play or he would not have suggested organizing a club."

Furthermore, Rankin then visited Mr. Van Cott, one of the old Washington Club players and one of the organizers of the old Gotham Club. Van Cott told Rankin that Wadsworth joined the Gotham Club in 1852 and "afterward played with the Knickerbockers": "It was Alex Cartwright who took the plans of base ball, the present game, up to the ball field and was laughed at, but he was so persistent about having his scheme tried that it was finally agreed to do so, and it proved a success from the start. It was Cartwright who suggested organizing a club to play his game."[12]

Rankin also reported in his 1908 article that his final attempt at corroborating all the pieces of information was to go back to visit Mr. Tassie and tell him what Cauldwell and Van Cott said. Tassie then admitted that he must have been mistaken when he said that Mr. Wadsworth was the person who took the plans to the ball ground: "I knew it was some one connected with the Knickerbocker Club, but I was wrong in mentioning Mr. Wadsworth. I know Mr. Cartwright quite well, and I know he did suggest the organization of a club to play the then new game."[13]

Where does all this journalism and detective work leave us? Given the number of recollections, we could make a good case that, at a minimum, Cartwright originally marked the diamond and suggested organizing the club. We have Cartwright's own grandson claiming that this was the story Cartwright himself told, at least among friends and family. Beyond this, though, it is much less clear what rules Cartwright was responsible for. The remembrances we have are not always specific: some (particularly Wheaton's) disagree with others on important points, and those of one person (Curry) change from one published version to the next, indicating that the descriptions may have been manipulated.

The *Sunday Mercury* editor, Mr. Cauldwell, argued that, in essence, it's just common sense that Cartwright must have suggested how to play baseball if he suggested forming a club to play it. But is this assumption correct? There is another way to see the evidence. Perhaps the ball players on Murray Hill already had a pretty good game by 1845; the evidence we have suggests that they did. Perhaps Cartwright's focus wasn't the game itself but the management of their gatherings—they were disorganized, and he wanted a more formal club with established rules and more stringent guidelines for membership. By 1848, in fact, when Cartwright was vice president of the club as well as on the committee for revising the constitution and by-laws, a few of the rules that year included attendance, fines, and collection of dues. Also, they often refer to their gatherings as "exercise." If Cartwright indeed suggested organizing a club, and the Knickerbocker rules are the result, the concern seems to be as much about getting their "exercise" running smoothly and without argument as in codifying baseball as such—as if certain "fastidious" persons (to use Wheaton's phrase again) had tired of pickup matches: with the uncertainty of who would show up, arguments over who was in charge, and the chaos of adding new players who arrived late. So instead, a smaller group of dedicated players broke off, those who were willing to commit to a regular schedule, being on time, playing on a certain-shaped field (allowing their game to be moved to any open space), participating in committees, and establishing a hierarchy of authority. Cartwright's orderly approach to life, evident in the many groups and clubs he formed in Hawaii and the committees in which he held office, makes it seem highly probable that he pressed for organization of the Knickerbocker Club. Unfortunately, again, there are no firsthand accounts of Alexander Cartwright's that have survived or other primary sources uncovered to date to fall back on.

There is one last remembrance to consider concerning who was responsible for developing the rules of the game. Daniel Adams was one of the early New York baseball players. In 1846, he was the Knickerbockers' vice president, becoming president in 1847 and 1848. He was also instrumental in the 1857 and 1858 conventions that established the national baseball association. In the 1896 *Sporting News* article mentioned previously—"Dr. D. L. ADAMS; Memoirs of the Father of Base Ball; He Resides in New Haven and Retains an Interest in the Game"—this "father" of baseball described how baseball's official rules were drawn up:

> The Gotham Club was organized in 1850 and the Eagle in 1852. The playing rules remained very crude up to this time, but in 1853 the three clubs united in a revision of the rules and regulations. At the close of 1856 there were 12 clubs in existence, and it was decided to hold a convention of delegates from all of these for the purpose of establishing a permanent code of rules by which all should be governed. A call was therefore issued, signed by the officers of the Knickerbocker Club as the senior organization, and the result was the assembling of the first convention of base ball players in May, 1857. I was elected presiding officer. In March of the next year the second convention was held, and at this meeting the annual convention was declared a permanent organization, and with the requisite constitution and by-laws became the "National Association of Ball Players."

I was chairman of the Committee on Rules and Regulations from the start and so long as I retained membership. I presented the first draft of rules, prepared after much careful study of the matter, and it was in the main adopted. The distance between bases I fixed at 30 yards—the only previous determination of distance being "the bases shall be from home to second base 42 paces, from first to third base 42 paces equidistant"—which was rather vague. In every meeting of the National Association while a member, I advocated the fly-game—that is, not to allow first-bound catches—but I was always defeated on the vote. The change was made, however, soon after I left, as I predicted in my last speech on the subject before the convention.

The distance from home to pitcher's base I made 45 feet. Many of the old rules, such as those defining a foul, remain substantially the same to-day, while others are changed and, of course, many new ones added. I resigned in 1862, but not before thousands were present to witness matches, and any number of outside players standing ready to take a hand on regular playing days. But we pioneers never expected to see the game so universal as it has now become.[14]

Though it seems a small matter, Adams claims that he was the one who turned the Knickerbockers' "rather vague" rule number one—"The bases shall be from 'home' to second base, forty-two paces; from first to third base, forty-two paces, equidistant"—and made this a firm ninety feet (or thirty yards). Cartwright's

Hall of Fame plaque credits him with establishing this particular distance, and yet even here the credit is more likely shared, if anything: If Cartwright indeed came up with the initial rough measure, this was later standardized and made exact by Daniel Adams.

Was the same true for nine players on a side and the nine-inning game—the other two innovations credited to Cartwright on the Hall of Fame plaque (and in Spink's book), but neither of which are supported by the Knickerbockers' own 1845 rules? The truth is that at the convention in 1857, Louis Fenn Wadsworth was named the Knickerbocker representative on the "Committee to Draft a Code of Laws on the Game of Base Ball, to be Submitted to the Convention." During the convention, Wadsworth made a motion and proposed a nine-inning game. The other Knickerbocker members who were present had initially decided on a seven-inning game, but Wadsworth's recommendation was adopted instead.[15]

So what exactly did Cartwright do? Other than holding office in the club before he traveled west, there is no other documentation uncovered as to what Cartwright accomplished for the Knickerbockers regarding rules and the playing field. Yet Bruce Cartwright Jr. declared his grandfather the "father of organized baseball." Perhaps, with what we know about Alexander Cartwright during his years in Honolulu, he very well could have made the suggestion to officially organize the Knickerbockers. Without primary sources on which to base this theory, it must remain speculation.

THIRTEEN

"On Mountain and Prairie"

What began as a sixteen-page article in the April 14, 1969, edition of *Sports Illustrated* magazine—entitled "Baseball's Johnny Appleseed"—culminated in a 1973 book by the same author, *The Man Who Invented Baseball*. In the article and the book, the *Sports Illustrated* writer Harold Peterson attempted to retrace Cartwright's steps across the country during the California Gold Rush of 1849 and to show how, as he went, Cartwright "seeded" the game of baseball, which he had invented—thus turning what had been a regional game, one confined to the eastern seaboard, into a national game that was played from coast to coast.

Peterson tells of a diary kept by Cartwright of his journey. He stated that "scattered old sources can be found in Hawaii that refer to Alexander Cartwright having taught the game to enthusiastic saloon keepers and miners, to Indians and white settlers along the way and at nearly every frontier town and Army post where his wagon train visited."[1] Unfortunately, Peterson did not cite his sources.

Peterson also stated that a secondary source mentioned that New Yorkers were "laughing as they watched the converts to the game attempt to imitate their own grace and skill with the bat and ball, such as catching the ball with the hands cupped and allowing the hands to 'give' with the catch." Yet another source asserted that "one such match was interrupted by Indian attack," but again, Peterson provided no source.[2]

I have attempted to find Peterson's sources for his article and his book, in Hawaii and elsewhere, mostly without success. As yet, there are no known sources that corroborate what Peterson wrote about what Cartwright did along the gold rush trail. Further, the primary source Peterson used for Cartwright's journey—his diary—is apparently not original, and the transcribed versions that exist conflict with each other. And they conflict precisely over the entries concerning baseball. Once again, another major piece of Cartwright's baseball legacy seems to rely mainly on ambiguous original sources and the secondhand remembrances of others.

In describing the research for his article, Peterson mentioned a very enlightening incident: he says that one of Cartwright's sons, Bruce Cartwright Sr., burned Cartwright's original gold rush diary because it contained information "potentially damaging to prominent people in California and Hawaii." Knowing what we do now about Cartwright's involvement in the Hawaii annexation movement, it's tantalizing to consider that this was the focus of Bruce's concern after his father's death. Of course, we'll never know what happened for sure, but for Bruce Sr. to consider burning some of his father's papers, the information in them likely involved very serious matters of character or politics concerning people who had perhaps grown to national importance, especially in late nineteenth-century Hawaii.

However, Peterson added, Cartwright's other son, Alexander III, copied parts of the gold rush diary that he considered of historical interest before burning the original notes. "But, more unfortunate still," Peterson declared, "few of these concerned baseball, despite the fact that Alexander III was a lover of the game."[3]

In retracing Peterson's research, and in establishing the details of Cartwright's gold rush journey, what gets confusing is that several transcriptions of the original diary exist, and these were created apparently by more than one Cartwright family member. For the *Sports Illustrated* article and his subsequent book, Peterson interviewed Alexander Cartwright's great grandson William Cartwright, who was the son of Bruce Cartwright Jr. Since photocopiers did not then exist, Bruce Jr. typed more than one version or transcription of his grandfather's diary, and William showed one of these to Peterson.

Peterson was also fortunate enough to interview Mary Check, a granddaughter of Alexander Cartwright. Mary was in her seventies at the time and living in San Francisco. Alexander Cartwright died when Mary was six months old, but she said that her mother and father told her many stories about her grandfather.

Mary's father told her that his father talked about how he scrawled out the first rules of baseball in a notebook balanced on his knee, and later of how he fiddled around with baseball a little while in San Francisco. She also delighted in the fact that her grandfather named her. No doubt she was named for his own daughter Mary, who died in 1869 at age twenty-four.

In addition, Mary Check showed Peterson an old notebook that contained the account of her grandfather's journey to California. Mary told Peterson that it was her belief that this notebook was her grandfather's original gold rush diary, "because the start of the trip to Hawaii is in the back." William, however, believed the notebook was more likely the transcribed extracts of the original made by Alexander III, Mary's father.[4]

Upon her death, Mary left the notebook or journal to the Bishop Museum in Honolulu, Hawaii, where it resides today. Despite William's belief about the uncertain authenticity of the journal, Mary's will stated that she believed her journal to be the original:

> I give to the Bishop Museum at Honolulu, Hawaii, the original of the diary of Alexander Joy Cartwright, Jr. as an addition to the Cartwright Family collection of said museum, to be designated and identified as a gift to said collection by me.[5]

We have good reason to believe that Mary was mistaken. For one, the portion at the back of the journal that describes Cartwright's journey from San Francisco to Hawaii actually refers to his 1850 trip as a merchant on the vessel *Sam Russell*.

But also, a handwriting analysis done in 2005 indicates that Mary's diary was not written by Alexander Cartwright. Reed Hayes of Honolulu, famed for proving the infamous Jack the Ripper diary to be a fake, considered many samples of Cartwright's known handwriting (including the famous 1865 letter to the former Knickerbocker Charles DeBost). In all, Hayes had eleven authentic handwriting samples, dating from 1842 to

1873, to compare with the diary. In his final report, Hayes drew the following conclusions:

> The diary writing and Cartwright's handwriting initially appear similar due to writing characteristics typical of the mid to late 19th century when handwriting instruction was more rigid and writers tended to adhere more closely to the "class characteristics" they were taught. However, despite any initial indications of similarity, upon closer examination it becomes clear that Cartwright's handwriting is unique in comparison to the diary writing.
>
> Based on the significant differences noted between the handwritten text of the diary and handwriting attributed to Alexander J. Cartwright, Jr., in addition to notable differences between the "Alexr J. Cartwright Jr." diary inscription and Cartwright's usual signatures, I am of the opinion that Cartwright personally did not author the "Gold Rush Diary."[6]

One very mysterious and obvious error appears on the first page of the diary. The cover page has the words "New York March 1st, 1850." Plus, actual physical aspects of the journal are suspect. The paper and binding itself are too clean to have traveled such a long and dusty way across the country by wagon train. In interviews I conducted, historians in Independence, Missouri, who are familiar with gold rush diaries say that the journal in the Bishop Museum is not the typical size or shape of those that were brought with emigrants on the trails west in 1849.[7] Also, Hayes remarked that the handwriting of the Bishop Museum journal is too consistent, indicating that it was likely written all at once in one sitting rather than as a series of entries penned over many days.[8]

Finally, on the cover of the journal is a label that reads "Williams, Coopers & Co. Export Stationers Account Book Manufacturers 85 West Smithfield, London."[9] At my request, the Guildhall Library in London researched this company and found that the exact title of the company, along with the exact address, did not exist as such during the nineteenth century (or during early twentieth century, for that matter), although they confirmed that companies with similar names and similar addresses existed from 1817 to 1821 and from 1890 to 1895.[10] Therefore, for all these reasons, the journal that resides in the Bishop Museum was almost certainly transcribed by someone other than Alexander Cartwright Jr. And the person most likely to have written it was Mary's father, Alexander III.

However, even this has not yet been determined as fact. Alexander III's handwriting was also analyzed in comparison with that of the diary, as well as that of Bruce Sr. and Jr., and there was not a match for any of them. DeSoto Brown, the archivist and collections manager at the Bishop Museum, states that handwritten items of high importance to families were sometimes transcribed by someone with excellent handwriting. Scribes were sometimes hired in nineteenth-century Honolulu to transcribe important documents. This may be the case for the Cartwright diary. However, one avid collector of Cartwright artifacts in Honolulu believes the handwriting to be authentic to Alexander Cartwright Jr., based on years of reading his handwriting from other collected items.

In the Cartwright family collection, there is more than one typed version of the gold rush journal; all were likely created in the early twentieth century, and all have missing pages. However, typed on one of them beneath the May 19, 1849, entry reads, "Note: This Journal was evidently written from Notes after the journey was completed. B. C. Jr."[11]

This "Journal" that Bruce is likely referring to is the hand-written journal that now resides in the Bishop Museum. The "Notes" are likely what was burned. However, the handwritten version does not match the typed transcriptions that Bruce Jr., Cartwright's grandson, created (one of which William Cartwright presented to Peterson). The reason for this becomes clear when looking over the typed transcriptions possessed by the Cartwright family. On one, Bruce Cartwright Jr. typed that he "completed the narrative drawn from all available sources."[12]

In another place is Bruce Jr.'s notation, "falling back on other sources, letters, memos, etc." In particular, this note referred to the fact that the original journal entries stopped after June 5, 1849. Bruce Cartwright Jr. also noted, "The following memo appears in his journal":

> Our mess stood on arrival in Sacramento as follows: Sacramento California July 1849

Capt. Thomas W. Seely	New York
Capt. Benj. F. Woolsey	Jersey City
Caleb D. Boylston	New York
John W. Shaff	Newark
Alex. J. Cartwright Jr.	New York[13]

In this instance, Bruce's typed transcription of the memo

differs from the handwritten version in the Bishop Museum in that the date is added. The journal in the Bishop Museum does not have the words "California July 1849."

Other discrepancies with dates appear among the typed versions: one states that Cartwright and his party reached Green Valley, California, on August 4, 1849; another typed version says July 4, 1849. In one preface to his family history, Bruce wrote:

> In order to give the reader an idea of what must have happened, the diary of a similar expedition, which followed the same route is drawn from. The dates being estimated. (See Forty-Niners by Archer Butler Hulbert, Little, Brown, and Company, Boston, 1932).[14]

In addition to using letters, memos, and other gold rush diaries to create his typed transcriptions, one of the "other sources" Bruce Jr. also relied on was his own memory. In the typed family history version, Bruce explains this, expounding a bit on his reminiscences of hearing his grandfather talk about his gold rush adventures: "My grandfather told people in Honolulu that he had introduced Base Ball wherever he went and that it immediately became popular and that it was 'comical' to see 'Mountain Men' and Indians playing the game."[15]

Nevertheless, one of the biggest discrepancies between the Bishop Museum journal and Bruce Jr.'s typed version is that the former does not mention baseball at all, while the latter does mention baseball occasionally. It is difficult to know what documented sources Bruce based those added baseball references on. Of all the letters held in private collections and public archives, this author knows of only one in which Alexander

Cartwright makes a passing reference to playing baseball during his gold rush journey: the 1865 letter to Charles DeBost (reprinted in chapter 6), in which Cartwright said, "Many is the pleasant chase I have had after it [the original ball] on Mountain and Prairie." This makes it most likely that Bruce added further details based on his family's oral history, or stories his grandfather told him directly.

The most significant discrepancy among the diaries concerns Cartwright's description of his activities in Independence, Missouri, before starting out with the wagon trains. The Bishop Museum journal does not mention Cartwright playing baseball in Independence, while Bruce Jr.'s typed transcription says that he did, and in an added diary entry, dated April 23, 1849.

According to the widow of William Cartwright, her late husband believed the diary entry to be correct.[16] This was based on the belief that the original diary was given to the Baseball Hall of Fame in 1938, and later lost. Harold Peterson reported to the Cartwright family during his research that the Baseball Hall of Fame did not possess the original. However, according to the Baseball Hall of Fame, they had never had possession of the original.

One other curious piece of information regarding Cartwright's gold rush journey comes from an obscure source. Jack McDonald, a writer for the *San Francisco Call-Bulletin*, wrote about Cartwright and the Knickerbockers for an article in 1947. He contacted another San Francisco newsman, Mike Jay, for more information about Cartwright. Mike Jay was once a reporter in the 1920s in Hawaii, and Jay once commented on Bruce

Cartwright Jr. presenting his grandfather's 1865 letter to Charles DeBost to the State Archives.[17] From his San Francisco office in 1947, Jay produced for McDonald a copy of Cartwright's diary from his desk drawer.[18]

This version of Cartwright's diary referenced baseball in a number of diary entries, but these entries do not appear in the Bishop Museum journal, or in the typed versions created by Bruce Jr. in the possession of the Cartwright family. From Jay's copy, McDonald quotes the following words in his article:

> It is comical to see mountain men, scouts, and Indians trying to learn how to play baseball. During our week's stay here [Boundary, Missouri, outside of Independence] I unpacked the ball we used in forming the Knickerbockers back home and we have had several satisfactory contests. My original copy of the rule book has come in handy and saves arguments.
>
> Tonight we held a council and decided to strike for California by the Santa Fe Trail until we reach the Oregon Trail and then follow that to South Pass and thence north of the Great Salt Lake then through the Sierra Nevadas to California.[19]

The article also states that Cartwright reached Fort Sutter on July 4, 1849, and that he described the journey as "one of great hardship," noting that on his arrival at Fort Sutter, "my original belongings have been reduced to the clothes I have on, my journal [diary], the original baseball, the book of baseball rules, my rifle and ammunition."[20]

Did Harold Peterson see this article, and was this one of his unnamed "old sources" describing Cartwright playing baseball on his journey? While in Hawaii during the 1920s, did Mike Jay write other newspaper stories about Cartwright, ones now lost or never published, based on this journal in his possession— and were these stories Peterson's "old sources"? Mostly, however, where did Jay get a copy of Cartwright's journal to begin with? We do not know.

As noted in part 1, it is unlikely that Cartwright reached Sutter's Mill by July 4, 1849. On that date he would have barely crossed the California border, territory that is now part of Nevada. This alone leads one to believe that Jay possessed another typed version produced by Bruce Jr., one that was expanded to include "all available sources." However, Jay's copy differed from others known to have been produced by Bruce Jr.—but this is another mystery that is likely to remain unsolved. With the original diary burned, there is no way to determine exactly what Alexander Cartwright actually wrote. Cartwright may have played baseball, even to such hilarity, but he likely only told stories about it, if anything, to those in Hawaii. And like Peterson, we would presume that if Cartwright had written about baseball originally, whoever copied those passages would have included them. Further, if we were to suppose instead that Bruce Jr.'s (and Jay's) typed copies reflected the original, then we have to wonder why someone would deliberately remove baseball references from the handwritten diary entries. This seems highly unlikely. So, the most credible explanation is that Cartwright did not originally mention baseball in his diary entries, and that the references that now exist in the typed versions were inserted later by his family members from recollected oral history.

Of course, Cartwright's failure to mention playing baseball in his diary entries does not mean that he did not play. It just means that no written evidence of it has been uncovered.

Finally, if Alexander Cartwright did play baseball on the gold rush trail, particularly as often and with as much fanfare and such a wide variety of participants as Peterson indicates, wouldn't baseball have been noted in other gold rush diaries? Even if these references didn't name Cartwright, any mention might support the claim that Cartwright was spreading the game at every available opportunity.

I have attempted to find baseball references in other gold rush journals: so far, I have not located any. The Oregon-California Trails Association keeps a database of existing diaries and their locations, a Census of Overland Emigrant Documents (COED), which is maintained and updated by a research committee of the same name. I have stayed in contact with Jim Riehl (the head of technical development) and Sallie Riehl (the chair of the COED committee), and as of the time of this writing, both of them declare that they know of no diaries mentioning baseball, despite the thousands of diaries in existence spanning many years, and including the four diaries that remain from the Newark Overland Company: those of Charles Glass Gray, Cyrus Currier, Robert Bond, and Alexander Cartwright.

In addition, I spoke with Kathleen Tuohey, who volunteers in the National Frontier Trails Museum in Independence, Missouri. Tuohey has been involved with the museum since 1990; in that time, she has transcribed seven diaries and read several more. The years of those diaries range from 1849 to 1853. Kathy

Tuohey noted that the diaries tended to have leather bindings with a tab that fit into a slot to close it. The size of most diaries was smaller than a three-by-five-inch index card. The men keeping the diaries wrote about their sore feet and worn-out clothes and boots, and they rarely skipped a day of writing. She also stated that the diaries often mention some form of entertainment, such as music and dancing, but that she does not recall any mentions of games being played.

But, as I ask in chapter 3, was it even feasible to imagine Cartwright teaching and playing baseball, especially during the two weeks he stayed in Independence before heading west by wagon train? To this question, Tuohey remarked, "I think it is very possible, since they [the Newark Overland Company] were so organized. There were many men with him and they were very prepared. These young guys would be bored silly, so it's very plausible."[21]

Plausible, however, does not mean that it happened. In addition, particularly decades after the fact, memories of what one *thought* one heard Cartwright say about his journey may not be completely accurate, and stories might perhaps be embellished (by those involved and those who came after). In saying this, I do not mean to question the motives or remembrances of anyone but merely to note that, as have the stories of Cartwright's creation of baseball's rules, the stories of baseball on the gold rush trail seem to have grown in scale and detail with the passage of time and each new telling.

Given what we know, the most likely scenario is that Cartwright did have his Knickerbocker ball, and he did bring it out occasionally, but most likely for casual amusement rather than with any intention to promote the game of baseball. And quite likely, given the tribulations of the trail and the lack of primary evidence, he did this a whole lot less, and with less effect, than Peterson and others have described. Nicknaming Cartwright the "Johnny Appleseed of Baseball" is likely not entirely accurate. However, there is substantial evidence that baseball was played in San Francisco as early as February 1851.[22]

Though the newspaper account in *San Francisco Alta California* doesn't name the men, some of these "sporting gentlemen" were probably transplanted New Yorkers. Recent research shows that a few former members of the Knickerbocker club of New York traveled to San Francisco during this time, and even a Knickerbocker Association formed as early as January 1851 (though the purpose for the association is not known).

Alexander Cartwright did not stay long in San Francisco before embarking for the Sandwich Islands. Though his brief stay may have been just long enough for him to meet up with a few friends from New York and play a game of baseball, there is no solid evidence that he or any other Knickerbocker brought the New York game to San Francisco and taught it to others there. If evidence for this did exist at one time, it was likely destroyed in the San Francisco earthquake of 1906 and the many fires that resulted.

FOURTEEN

"On the Sunny Plains of Hawaii nei"

In January 1923, three years before Sanford B. Dole died, he attended a graveside tribute to his late friend Alexander Joy Cartwright. The occasion was the arrival of Herb Hunter and his American All-Stars, who stopped in Honolulu while on a tour of Asia.[1] In an article describing the tribute, *The Star-Bulletin* described how Dole briefly sketched Cartwright's baseball career: how Cartwright organized the Knickerbocker Baseball Club of New York, stepped off the first diamond, drew up the first set of rules, and engineered the first game of organized baseball.[2]

Dole went on to describe how Cartwright went west with the gold rush of 1849, spreading the game as he went until he came to Hawaii. "I remember him well—a great big broad shouldered man who had no trouble in quelling a riot single-handed one day on the docks here. Of course his playing days were over when he came to Hawaii, but I recall him many times being called on to settle disputes." Dole ended by saying that it was owing to Cartwright's efforts that baseball became a national game rather than being confined and remaining provincial to the eastern seaboard.[3]

We do not know how much of Dole's speech reflected stories Cartwright told Dole directly, or how much he drew from the accounts told about Cartwright and baseball that had by then circulated. It was no doubt a bit of both. For many years the two men had mixed together closely, and by 1923, Peverelly, Spalding, and Spink had all published their books. And yet, the place where Dole would have had direct firsthand knowledge of Cartwright's participation in baseball was in Hawaii. Dole's father, himself a "baseball" enthusiast, was the first president of the Punahou School, where Cartwright's sons played baseball. And one can imagine that Cartwright and Sanford Dole most likely *did* discuss baseball occasionally (at least, in between political discussions).

Considering this, it's striking that Dole would imply in his tribute that Cartwright did not himself play baseball in Hawaii. When Cartwright arrived in Hawaii, he was only twenty-nine years old. This would not have made him too old to play. Even if Cartwright had quit playing by the time he met Dole, wouldn't Dole have heard, from Cartwright himself, about any Hawaii baseball exploits? And if Cartwright had played baseball after arriving in Hawaii, and in fact had been the first to do so, wouldn't Dole have credited Cartwright with that honor in his 1923 tribute? Are we to believe, according to Dole, that in Hawaii, Cartwright's participation in baseball extended only to settling disputes at games he attended?

This chapter looks at what evidence there is connecting

Alexander Cartwright, baseball, and Hawaii. Did Cartwright, as legend has it, bring baseball to Hawaii, or was he merely a spectator to its arrival and growth in the islands? Inadvertently, Sanford Dole probably struck closest to the truth.

In fact, there is no direct evidence of Alexander Cartwright's participation—in any capacity—in baseball while he lived in Hawaii. An example of what might lead people to think that there is evidence can be found in a 1952 book, *Heroes of Baseball*, that mentions how Cartwright often visited schools throughout the territory of Hawaii explaining baseball with chalk and a blackboard. Yet, the book lists no sources and cannot be corroborated or verified.[4] Most of the time, when the Cartwright name *does* appear in connection with baseball in Hawaii, it concerns his sons, Alexander III and Bruce. However, one of Alexander III's classmates was once quoted in reference to his father. Alexander Cartwright III and Harry M. Whitney Jr. were both students at Punahou School during the 1869–70 academic year (as documented by that year's catalogue). Decades later, in 1926, H. M. Whitney was interviewed for an article about baseball in the *Honolulu Advertiser*. Whitney was quoted as saying about Alexander III's father: "He did a big thing in bringing that sport to the islands in the old days."[5]

Did Whitney know something specifically about Alexander Cartwright, or was he by then just repeating the common assumption? It's hard to say, but Whitney was an active player on what were very active school teams. Whitney played with the Whangdoodle baseball team from 1870 to 1874.[6] His classmate Alexander Cartwright III (also known as "Allie") played with the Whangdoodles, too, in 1875. In 1867, Allie, along with his brothers Bruce and DeWitt (three years before DeWitt Cartwright died), also played cricket.[7] Allie and Bruce were sent to school in California sometime from 1870 to 1872. When they returned by 1873, they joined other Punahou students and alums on the ball field. Allie's position was second baseman, while Bruce kept score. Some of their teammates included Thurston, Monsarrat, and Whitney.[8] In later years, Bruce belonged to a team called the "Married Men."

On September 18, 1875, the *New York Clipper* reported that a championship game was played in Honolulu on August 14, 1875, between the Whangdoodles and the Pacifics. The article stated that the ball clubs belonged to the Hawaiian Amateur Baseball Association formed earlier that spring. The game was played on the Association Grounds on a large plain just west of Honolulu. The article also reported the lineup, which listed "Cartwright" playing second base for the Whangdoodles. The Pacifics beat the Whangdoodles 11–10. Though the article reported on the game, it did not mention that a dispute about the game later occurred. The captain of the Whangdoodles, James B. Castle, appealed to the Judiciary Committee of the Honolulu Amateur Baseball Association. Castle's letter to the committee, written up in an issue of the *Islander* on August 19, 1875, noted three "glaring violations" of the umpire's decisions. The committee responded that they were in agreement and therefore decided that the game was "illegal and irregular" and did not count as a championship contest. The decision split the Whangdoodle club members and a few "prominent members" resigned, according to the *Islander* of September 7, 1875. Two other entire

clubs resigned from the association as well. They were the Athletes and the Pacifics, as mentioned in the *Islander* on August
28, 1875. (Lorrin Thurston played left field for the Athletes that
season.) Efforts to locate the records of the Honolulu (or Hawaiian) Amateur Base Ball Association of 1875 (or any records
of the clubs, for that matter) were unsuccessful.

According to the *Pacific Commercial Advertiser* in 1901, "It was
Punahou College boys who were the first to play baseball in the
Islands."[9] If so, then who brought it to the school?

In April 1860 *The Polynesian* published an article by the name
of "Game of Ball." In the story, the Hawaiian word *makai* is used
to mean "toward the ocean":

> Quite an interesting game of ball came off yesterday af-
> ternoon on the Esplanade between the Punahou Boys
> and the Town Boys. The game was so good; and so good
> when our reporter left the scene of action.
>
> The "boys" of a larger growth, among whom were
> some of the leading merchants and their clerks, had a
> game of good old-fashioned base ball on Sheriff Brown's
> premises, makai, which is said to have afforded much
> amusement both to actors and spectators. Success to
> the "sport."[10]

Unfortunately, there is no mention as to *who* the merchants
were who played "good old-fashioned base ball" that day, or even
an indication of whether this was modern or "Knickerbocker"
baseball or some other variant. In 1860, Alexander Cartwright
would have been forty years old, and probably still young enough
to give chase. But in truth, even if Cartwright had played that day,

and played the New York game, 1860 was eleven years after his arrival in Hawaii. Surely there would be evidence of baseball in Hawaii before then if Cartwright were actively promoting it.

One of the earliest reports of a ball game in Hawaii predates Cartwright's arrival, and predates even the Knickerbockers. In 1840, in a story titled "Sports in Honolulu," *The Polynesian* reported: "One evidence of the increasing civilization of this place, and not the least gratifying, is to see the ardor with which the native youth of both sexes engage in the same old games which used to warm our blood not long since. There's good old bat and ball, just the same as when we ran from the school-house to the 'Common' to exercise our skill that way."[11]

Almost assuredly, "good old bat and ball" does not refer to the modern game of baseball but to one of the other earlier games. Evidence suggests that, as in New York, these games were common in early Hawaii. However, there is someone who claims to have brought "baseball" to Punahou School in 1866, the same year that Punahou School established its first official baseball team (as described in chapter 6).

In March 1924, William R. Castle, the son of the missionary Samuel N. Castle, wrote an article for *The Friend* magazine. William attended Punahou School from 1860 to 1864, then went to Oberlin College in Ohio for two years before returning to Hawaii. Here is what he wrote:

> While a student at Oberlin College in 1864–66, I played baseball as it was then played. It was introduced into Hawaii while I was in Oberlin, and it was called the "new game of baseball." At that time the underhand

toss was the vogue and it was the accepted method of pitching, or, as it was called, tossing, the ball. It always seemed to me a very weak and ineffectual method. Others felt as I did, but accepted it as part of the "new game of baseball." I learned to pitch (toss) in that manner, but detested it.

In the summer of 1866, I returned to Honolulu and found that no one knew how to play baseball, although several had read of the new game and were curious to try it. The only game of ball played in Hawaii at that time was exactly the same as when I had gone away two years before, that is, "two o-cat" or "three o-cat," and I felt that to introduce baseball as I had learned it and as it was played in the United States, would add greatly to the sports of the community. So when the fall term opened at Punahou in September of 1866, I went out there and talked the new game over with the boys and proceeded at once to organize a "Baseball club."

For the use of the new club I got the foundry to cast a home base. It was a circular iron plate, perhaps 14 inches in diameter and 3/4ths of an inch thick with either three or four legs to pin it to the ground, the top being painted white. This club continued to exist for many years and for a long time the Punahou School Baseball Club was the model for baseball throughout the Kingdom of Hawaii. This game with all its variations from the old rambling "two" or "three o-cat" became a favorite. Curiously enough some Hawaiian spectators picked up from what they saw in watching the game, sufficient

knowledge to introduce it throughout the Islands. In
a trip around Hawaii some years later, in the late 60's
or early 70's, as I rode through the town of Waiohinu,
way down at the south end of the island in Kau, I passed
the town park or playground and was much interested
to see a full fledged ball match in progress. All of the
countryside was on hand, deeply and enthusiastically
interested. All sided with one or the other of the con-
tending parties. I waited for half hour or so and saw
some pretty good ball playing, although I was amused
to notice the introduction of some laughable rules regarding the rights of players on bases. For instance, if
two runners got caught on the same base they decided
which of the two was to be put out, although the decision oftentimes resulted in the wildest opposition, up-
roar and excitement. This game, as I saw it, was simply an illustration of what was going on throughout the
country, so I was informed.[12]

In the same article, Castle also recalled speaking with Alexander Cartwright about baseball:

I used to have a good deal of business with Mr. Cartwright and while in his office one day several years after my return he surprised me by saying that he was an
old ball player but added that he hardly recognized the
game "as played now." However, his interest seemed
as keen and alive as ever and I remember seeing him
at Punahou several times, watching the play as it had
been recently introduced. He commented on some new

features or different methods of playing from those he had learned as a New Yorker.[13]

Castle's article is clearly significant. First, his account appears consistent with what we know about when the first baseball club was organized at Punahou School. In fact, decades later in his autobiography, Castle repeated that when he returned from Oberlin College and began playing the game in Hawaii, this was the first time "Baseball" as it was then played in New York and elsewhere on the continent was introduced.[14] If, in fact, he's correct that baseball as it was played in New York hadn't been introduced at the school before his arrival, and if local newspapers are correct that Punahou School introduced modern baseball to Hawaii, then William Castle is likely the one who introduced it. The description of "baseball as it was then played in New York" probably refers to the rules and regulations that were established as a result of the first baseball convention held in 1857 and in subsequent years thereafter.

Castle also said that before that time, boys played "Aipuni." This was the most popular form of ball playing, according to Castle: a single batter and sometimes two batters each stood in front of a stick placed across the road. Each end of the stick rested on a brick or square stone, and the catcher stood directly behind the stick. If he managed to catch a ball that was struck by the batter or batters, he passed it under the stick. If the stick lifted, the striker was out, and three outs made that side out.

Unfortunately, no early baseball rules have been uncovered at either Punahou School or Oberlin College. But even if Punahou School and Castle were not the first to introduce the New

York style of baseball to Hawaii, Castle's account helps shed light on Cartwright. In fact, Castle initially says that baseball was introduced into Hawaii while he was gone, but that when he returned, the game at Punahou School wasn't the modern game, but the old "three old-cat" version. However, Cartwright's sons Alexander III and Bruce attended Punahou beginning in 1864. If Cartwright were actively promoting baseball in Hawaii, wouldn't it have been natural for him or one of his sons to introduce it in Punahou School in 1864 or 1865? This may have occurred, but there is no evidence of it. Perhaps the "introduction of baseball" while Castle was at Oberlin was to the style of play that Cartwright played in the 1840s in New York (which he probably taught his sons), yet certainly not the style of the baseball convention from the latter part of the 1850s. Again, this is only speculation, because no evidence has surfaced. By the 1870s, plenty of documentation shows the Cartwright boys playing baseball, so we know they liked to play.

Castle's remarks give the impression that Alexander Cartwright actually wasn't openly playing or promoting baseball before the 1860s, and this sense is deepened by Castle's description of Cartwright himself. After all, why should Castle have been *surprised* that Cartwright once played baseball? And why did it take "several years" for this revelation to come up between them? By the 1860s, Cartwright was a very prominent member of Honolulu society; if he were promoting baseball, it would have been noticed, certainly by someone who had direct business dealings with him. Further, Castle's recollections seem to indicate that Cartwright's unique connection to baseball must not have been widely known either, which makes it seem that not only wasn't Cartwright playing, he wasn't even talking about baseball very much. Conversely, if Cartwright *was* talking about and promoting baseball before the 1860s, he wasn't doing so on a very grand scale, or he was doing so very informally and infrequently and using an early version of the Knickerbocker game that significantly differed from the way baseball had come to be played after his departure.

Finally, Castle seems fond of Cartwright. He doesn't seem to have written the article to somehow compete with Cartwright or denigrate him. As with Dole, he presents a sympathetic portrait, and it is of a man now nostalgically watching the game as a spectator.

About twenty years after William Castle wrote his article, in the early 1940s, Reverend C. P. Goto wrote a book about the history of Japanese baseball in Hawaii. This book is also significant, as it contains several references to Alexander Cartwright teaching and playing baseball in Hawaii. Most of the book is written in Japanese and is about Japanese ballplayers; however, one section is written in English and entitled, "The Early Baseball in Hawaii."[15] Goto was working on this book during the development and the grand opening of the Baseball Hall of Fame. Much of his research came from the archives of Punahou School in Honolulu, where Cartwright's sons had played the game.

Goto describes 1867 to 1883 as the "Dark Age" of Hawaiian baseball history, claiming that not a single article or a verse describing Hawaiian baseball can be found.[16] However, this is not true. I have found a number of newspaper and other articles from the late 1860s and 1870s that mention baseball in Hawaii, including several articles in the *Pacific Commercial Advertiser* in 1875 that announce and record games. Indeed, one of the star players during 1875 was Allie Cartwright. This is just one troubling aspect of Goto's research, which he conducted in the 1930s. Perhaps Goto was relying on Punahou records alone, but we cannot know why he didn't find additional information about baseball in Hawaii.

As interpreted for me by a retired professor of Japanese, inside the Japanese portion of Goto's book, Charles Siders is described as being an influential teacher of baseball at Punahou School. This also is incorrect. First, Charles Siders was a student, not a teacher, at the school. Second, in 1906, Arthur C. Alexander wrote an article entitled "Baseball at Punahou Thirty-Seven Years Ago." The article appeared that year in *The Oahuan*, as well as in the *Pacific Commercial Advertiser* on July 30, 1906. A. C. Alexander was the editor of *The Oahuan* in 1906 and an alumnus from the Punahou School class of 1883. He and Bruce Cartwright Jr. were in school together at Punahou and later at Yale University as well.

Arthur Alexander wrote his article after finding a tally book of a Punahou baseball club inside his father's attic. Arthur's father was William DeWitt Alexander, president of Punahou School (then called Oahu College) from 1864 to 1871. The tally book for 1872 lists Charles Siders as one of the new players, along with "Mr. Chickering, a teacher (who for what he did for baseball here might almost be called the 'father' of baseball in Honolulu), acting as umpire and catcher for both nines." Among the new players for 1873 was Allie Cartwright.

This article not only refutes Goto's claim regarding Charles Siders but also sows further doubt about Alexander Cartwright. It doesn't make sense that A. C. Alexander, a contemporary of Cartwright's grandson Bruce, would credit "Mr. Chickering" as the "father" of baseball in Honolulu if Alexander Cartwright had been promoting it in the city decades earlier. However, it could be that A. C. Alexander was specifically referring to baseball at Punahou in Honolulu.

In 1948, some portions of Goto's history of baseball in Hawaii were excerpted in a series of five articles in the *Honolulu Star-Bulletin*. For these articles, Richard Gima translated some of the Japanese portions of Goto's book. The first installment states, "In his memoirs, Mr. Cartwright records the game as being played in Honolulu immediately after he arrived here in 1849."[17] This mention of Cartwright's "memoirs" is the most curious and mysterious claim in Goto's research. As far as I have been able to determine, Alexander Cartwright produced no "memoirs," nor is there anywhere but here even a mention of them.

Goto mentions Cartwright a few more times. In one place, in the English portion of the book, Goto states that the late Charles Wilson, father of the postmaster of Honolulu, John Wilson, was taught baseball by Cartwright behind the old court house.[18] Goto does not date this incident, but it could very well be true, as reflected in some things Bruce Cartwright Jr. has said about his grandfather. But other than Goto reporting it here, this is all the proof that exists. According to *Thrum's Almanac and Annual*, the Cartwright Building adjoined the court house.[19]

As has been mentioned, as yet, there is only one piece of documented evidence, though uncorroborated, establishing that Alexander Cartwright himself mentioned playing baseball in Hawaii. This is in his famous letter to former Knickerbocker Charles DeBost in 1865 (reprinted in full in chapter 6). Goto, on the first page of the English section of his book, focuses on this letter. So, too, did Bruce Cartwright Jr. in 1938 in a letter he wrote to his friend Arthur C. Alexander. Alexander is the one who, in 1906, published an article crediting a "Mr. Chickering" as the "father" of baseball in Honolulu.

For reasons that remain unclear, Bruce wrote to A. C. Alexander in 1938, and Bruce underlined the words of the DeBost letter that held the most significance to him:

Dear Arthur:

On April 6th., 1865, my grand-father, Alexander Joy Cartwright Jr., "The Father of Base Ball," wrote to his friend Charles S. DeBorst [sic], one of the old Knickerbocker Base Ball Club of New York (the first base ball club)— a letter press copy of this letter is in the Archives of Hawaii.

He said—"Dear old Knickerbockers. I hope that the Club is still kept up, and that I shall some day visit again with them on the pleasant fields of Hoboken—Charlie, I have in my possession the original ball with which we used to play on Murray Hill. Many is the pleasant chase I have had after it on Mountain and Prairie, and many an equally pleasant one <u>on the sunny plains of 'Hawaii neï', here in Honolulu, my pleasant island home</u> . . ."

I have underlined the sentence proving beyond question that he played base ball in Honolulu before the date of his letter—April 6th. 1865.[20]

This letter alone shows that Alexander Cartwright clearly played with his baseball in Hawaii before 1865. But what does that tell us? All the other evidence that exists (beyond phantom memoirs) seems to demonstrate that before 1866, the "modern game of baseball" was not well known or even played in Honolulu. Several other persons are named as introducing modern baseball and initiating the game. And Cartwright himself was not acknowledged by contemporaries at the time (Sanford Dole's tribute wasn't until 1923) as being a significant player or promoter when he was in Hawaii. Even during Albert Spalding's famous 1888 visit to Honolulu during his world tour, Alexander Cartwright's name is conspicuously absent from the detailed newspaper accounts of the day.

This lack of evidence doesn't mean Cartwright never played baseball in Hawaii, but it does seem to confirm a few things: Cartwright was not a prominent person in the Honolulu baseball scene; he was not declared or documented as an originator of baseball in Hawaii while he was alive; and he was not self-consciously pursuing recognition of his baseball patrimony. Later in his life, as baseball became a beloved national game, one might imagine him stepping forward to participate and claim his deserved share of the spotlight. But he did not. He remained content, it seems, to watch.

Spalding and Cartwright's son, Bruce Sr., acknowledge as much themselves. In Spalding's 1911 book *America's National Game*, he wrote:

His son, Mr. Bruce Cartwright, a prominent citizen of Honolulu, in a personal letter to me, under date March 22, 1909, says: "Although far removed from the field of his former activities, he never forgot Base Ball, and never missed an opportunity of being present whenever the game was played here."[21]

FIFTEEN

Baseball and the "Family Lare"

If Alexander Cartwright didn't seem to pursue the title of "father of modern baseball," and if the evidence for giving him the honorific now seems rather slim and contradictory, then why was he so anointed half a century after his death? To answer this, we have to look at both professional baseball and the national mood in the late nineteenth century.

We hardly give it a thought today, except maybe on the 4th of July, but in the late nineteenth century—over a century after declaring political independence from England—America was still trying to separate from the British culturally. America wanted its own independent identity, its own artistic and cultural traditions, and its own sports. In fact, it steadily became a matter of national pride to prove that baseball had not "evolved" from British children's games but was instead wholly original, a uniquely American national pastime. The most heated aspect of that debate centered on one particular British man who loved baseball, and who in the nineteenth century had in fact been dubbed the "The Father of Baseball."

Henry Chadwick, born in England, migrated to New York in 1837 with his parents and sister. A lover of cricket, he enthusiastically watched the game being played in early New York. However, at Elysian Fields, Chadwick saw a new bat and ball game and became drawn to it.

Writing about baseball in the *New York Clipper* and the *Brooklyn Eagle*, as well as for other local papers, Chadwick did much to promote the game. His love of the game prompted him to join the baseball community by attending meetings of the rules committee in 1858.[1] Not only that, but Chadwick wrote a series of baseball guide booklets from 1860 through 1881 called *Beadle's Dime Base-ball Player*, published by Beadle & Company.[2]

Chadwick also began editing a baseball guide in the early 1880s for a friend of his, A. G. Spalding.[3] Their friendship was tested, however, over their conflicting opinions about the origins of baseball. Chadwick held the view that baseball derived from the English game of rounders, which he had played in his youth. Spalding insisted that baseball originated in America. In the 1905 edition of *Spalding's Official Base Ball Guide*, Spalding himself declares that "the original Knickerbocker Club should be honored and remembered as the founders of our national game." Those he declares as deserving of that honor within the club are "Col. James Lee, Dr. Ransom, Abraham Tucker, James Fisher, W. Vail, Alexander J. Cartwright, Wm. R. Wheaton, Duncan F. Curry, E. R. Dupignac, Wm. H. Tucker and Daniel L. Adams."

In 1905, Spalding appointed a commission to determine

baseball's origins, and he hoped that some of these founding Knickerbockers who were still living or "possibly some of their heirs . . . might shed some light on the early history and especially the origin of baseball" (and, of course, prove his case and win the argument with Chadwick).

The committee's chairman was Abraham Mills, a former ball player from the Civil War era and former president of the National League. Mills was also present during the celebration of the return of Spalding and the ball players in 1889 from their world tour. In fact, Mills was one of the speakers that night who conveyed that "patriotism and research" had established baseball as being of American origin.[4] Other members of the commission included Nicholas Young, Arthur Gorman, Morgan Bulkeley, James Sullivan, Alfred Reach, and George Wright.[5]

Spalding put the call out to anyone in the country who had information on baseball's origin to send it to the committee for evaluation. Hundreds of pages of testimony were received. Mills weighed much of the evidence himself, trying to determine whether baseball had developed or evolved over time, or if the game had a single creator. Before chairing the commission, Mills believed that the Knickerbockers were responsible for creating baseball.[6] However, one letter received by the commission declared that Abner Doubleday made a drawing of the baseball diamond in Cooperstown, New York, in 1839.

Based on this letter, the commission was ready to declare Abner Doubleday as baseball's originator, but one piece of information held them back: this was William Rankin's 1905 article, based on Rankin's 1877 interview with Duncan Curry, in which Rankin quoted Thomas Tassie as naming "Mr. Wadsworth" as the one who had brought the diagram to the playing field and suggested organizing the Knickerbockers (Rankin and his 1905 article are described in chapter 11). Mills also pointed out Curry's important role as the first president for the Knickerbockers, and that Curry participated in drafting the game's first published rules.[7]

Whatever other candidates may have been considered to establish *who* was responsible for originating "American Base Ball," for the committee, it all came down to *when* the most original version of the game was known to be created in America. As it stood, Spalding was most impressed by the claim made on behalf of Abner Doubleday, who was seen drawing "the present diamond-shaped Base Ball field" in 1839, which preceded the formation of the Knickerbockers.

A. G. Mills wrote the final decision on December 30, 1907. In spite of his early convictions, and that of Spalding, regarding the Knickerbockers, Mills declared that Abner Doubleday, a former Civil War general, devised the game of baseball in Cooperstown, New York, in 1839. He affirmed that this was "according to the best evidence obtainable to date," which rested entirely on one letter sent by Abner Graves.[8]

The commission's findings sparked a new chain of events. It was one thing to declare baseball to be "all American," but it was another to actually name a creator and a place of origin. A Doubleday Memorial Fund was started, as well as efforts to turn an old pasture in Cooperstown into a permanent baseball field for the village. Apparently, the property was pointed out in the letter that Abner Graves sent to the Mills Commission as the location where he saw Doubleday teach and play baseball. Doubleday Field was officially opened on September 6, 1920.

One of the leading citizens in the development of Cooperstown was Stephen Clark. He had inherited a great deal of money and possessed an entrepreneurial spirit. One of Clark's employees in one of his business ventures in New York City was Alexander Cleland. Clark, originally from Cooperstown, met Cleland in 1934 for a business discussion in Cooperstown. While there, they saw a number of men grading the site of Doubleday Field, which was expanding and improving thanks to the WPA project of the 1930s.

After one of the workers exclaimed to Cleland that the town was looking forward to the centennial of baseball, Cleland was struck with an idea. He thought of constructing a building that would store a collection of all past, present, and future historical data of the game. Upon Cleland's suggestion to his boss, Clark agreed to the idea. Townspeople in Cooperstown as well as the leaders of professional baseball also agreed. Cleland was then appointed secretary of the museum.

Then, as baseball's centennial commemoration gathered steam and publicity, a new development occurred. In December 1935, Bruce Cartwright Jr., who was living in Honolulu, wrote Alexander Cleland concerning his grandfather's role in developing the national pastime. Bruce claimed that his grandfather was the organizer of the Knickerbocker Base Ball Club and thus the "'Father of Organized Base Ball' as he was known locally during his life." In addition, he stated, "My grandfather told many local people that he organized it, drew up the rules they played under and also laid out the first 'base-ball diamond' which was officially approved by the Club and the measurements used by all other clubs for years. " Bruce also stated that he had a copy of his grandfather's gold rush diary from 1849, and he offered to furnish the museum with a number of items related to his grandfather.[9]

Cleland responded to Cartwright and thanked him for anything that he could pass along about his grandfather's connection with baseball. Cleland also mentioned that they had received a request from the St. Louis Baseball Club for information on Cartwright, which they wanted to use for a radio broadcast. However, Cleland did not mention to Bruce that a letter had been sent in response to the St. Louis ball club declaring that Abner Doubleday had the honor of having invented the game.[10]

Evidently, Bruce Cartwright Jr. came to feel that he needed some help to make a case for his grandfather. On May 25, 1938, he wrote to John Hamilton, the Honolulu city manager, and asked Hamilton to write to Alexander Cleland in support of Cartwright. Bruce listed the facts Hamilton was meant to cite, and some of the wording in this letter would end up on his grandfather's induction plaque:

> He laid out the first "base-ball" diamond, with permanent non-movable bases 90 feet apart, on which they played; He organized the first base-ball team limiting the number to nine players, so that they could cover the base-ball diamond that he had invented; That Alexander Joy Cartwright, Jr. started from New York City, (his home) to California on March 1, 1849 and arrived in California in July, 1849. That along his route he introduced

the new game "Base-ball" all the way to California. This is referred to in his letter of April 6, 1865 to Charles De-Borst [sic], an original "Knickerbocker."[11]

John Hamilton didn't waste time: two days later, on May 27, 1938, he wrote to Alexander Cleland as Bruce requested, and in his letter he essentially said that the Mills Commission had gotten it wrong when, twenty-one years ago, they had declared Abner Doubleday the inventor of baseball:

> It is a matter of history that Alexander J. Cartwright organized the Knickerbocker Base Ball Club and also a matter of history that he laid out the diamond . . . We desire to ask your further consideration and if necessary, further study in order that the records may be kept straight for the future.[12]

Cleland must have needed a little help in answering Mr. Hamilton. A few weeks later, on June 14, he received a letter from the National League president Ford Frick directing him about how to respond:

> The point I think you want to make in answering all queries such as you mention is simply this:
> The Centennial of baseball is a centennial of a game rather than of individuals. It is nation-wide in its scope and every village and town in the country can participate. It naturally centers around Cooperstown because, so far as the records show, the first baseball diamond in history was laid out in Cooperstown.
> However, there is no tendency on the part of organized

215

baseball at least to give all the credit to Abner Doubleday and to overlook Cartwright, Chadwick and the other
men who played so important a part in the development
of our national game. Mr. Cartwright certainly will be
included among the immortals whose names will be
perpetuated in the museum.[13]

About a week later, Alexander Cleland wrote a three-page
response to Mr. Hamilton in Honolulu, and this letter reflects
some of the wording Frick suggested. Yet, Cleland also added
a few choice words revealing his own stressful moments in
the matter:

> Your letter has forced our hands to some extent but we
> feel that you have a right to advanced information and
> are willing to say, in strict confidence, that we expect
> to hold a special Cartwright Day as one of the principal
> features of the celebration, commemorating the orga-
> nization of the Knickerbockers, and Mr. Cartwright's
> part in the development of the game. On this day it is
> planned to unveil a bronze plaque in memory of Mr.
> Cartwright in the Hall of Fame, and produce a pag-
> eant delineating his journey across the continent, orga-
> nizing clubs as he went . . . We will welcome any data
> which gives information regarding Mr. Cartwright's
> trip across the country; how many accompanied him;
> where he made stops, etc.[14]

After Hamilton received this letter from Cleland, he sent it
along to Bruce Cartwright. Bruce responded to Hamilton on July

12, 1938, and thanked him for sending Cleland's letter. Bruce also offered a few more details about Cartwright's gold rush journey: he said it took his grandfather 156 days to travel from Newark, New Jersey, to San Francisco. In addition, his grandfather walked the whole distance, and whenever they rested and had enough people to form two baseball nines, they played "baseball," according to his letters to old "Knickerbockers."

Lastly, Bruce stated, "I can work out his 'log' day by day from March 1, 1849, when he left Newark, N.J., to August 10, 1849, when he arrived in San Francisco if it is desired, but it will take a little time."

The newspaper of Cooperstown, New York, *The Glimmerglass*, published by the Freeman's Journal Company, announced the arrival of the log on August 13, 1938. The article's title declared, "Authentic Log of Cartwright's Trip Received," and the article itself states, "This week the National Base Ball Hall of Fame received from John A. Hamilton, manager of the Honolulu Chamber of Commerce, a complete log of the long journey made by Mr. Cartwright and his associates, which was compiled by Bruce Cartwright, Jr., his grandson, from his letters and diary." The title of the article is misleading. It gives the reader the impression that what was received was the actual log of Cartwright's journey west. Instead, later in the article, it is revealed that "a copy of the log has been placed in the Museum, and a duplicate turned over to Lester G. Bursey, chairman of the Program committee for the Centennial, who in turn is planning to give a copy to Prof. Randolph Somerville, director of the Washington Square Players at Duke's Oak. Prof. Somerville has promised to prepare a pageant for the Centennial."

John Hamilton wrote a letter to Alexander Cleland on July 19, 1938, which accompanied the log that Bruce Cartwright Jr. provided. The log was typewritten by Bruce and entitled "The 'Log' of Alexander Joy Cartwright, Jr., from New York City to Honolulu, compiled by Bruce Cartwright, Jr., his grandson, from his letters and diary." In regard to the entry for April 16 Bruce comments, "His journal says 'it was comical to see Mountain men and Indians playing the new game,'" while the April 23 entry states, "During the past week we have passed the time in fixing wagon-covers, stowing property, etc., varied by hunting and fishing, and playing base-ball. I have the ball with me that we used back home."

What is puzzling, however, is that just prior to the April 27 entry, Bruce interjects with a statement to the reader, "These extracts to give local color! From now on will just give the log." This statement makes one wonder if Bruce inserted a bit of oral history (or information from letters lost) about baseball up until that point. The rest of his typed log gives no mention of baseball. Alexander Cleland acknowledged receipt of the log in a letter to John Hamilton dated August 10, 1938, in which he says that several copies of the log were made for Professor Somerville, a professor of dramatics at New York University, with a request that he use it as a basis for the proposed pageant of Cartwright Day.

The following month Bruce Cartwright wrote Alexander Cleland and mentioned that a park in Honolulu had been renamed and dedicated that month to his grandfather. Makiki Park became Cartwright Park in Honolulu. Bruce reminisced,

This park, while very small, seems to be a fitting memorial as it formerly was the only baseball park in Honolulu, and I remember viewing several games there with "The Father of Organized Base Ball." On one occasion, I remember seeing him draw a circle in the dust with his umbrella and then draw a cross through the circle. He then explained to a crowd who had gathered how he divided the "Baseball Square," as I remember it. There are quite a few men in Honolulu who remember seeing him at this old baseball field on numerous occasions.[15]

In March 1936, a few months after Bruce Cartwright Jr. first wrote to Alexander Cleland about his grandfather, Bruce forwarded a book to Cleland authored by someone who, Bruce claimed, knew his grandfather. The book was *Base Ball, 1845–1871*, by Seymour R. Church. The author was a resident of San Francisco. The section of the book describing the early history of baseball cited Cartwright as the person who proposed the first regular organization in the spring of 1845.[16] Other than that, Church does not mention that he personally knew Alexander Cartwright or provide any other details surrounding Cartwright's direct involvement in the creation of baseball.

Among the items that were donated from the Cartwright family for display during the festivities and celebrations of the grand opening of the Hall of Fame were a daguerreotype of six people (believed to be Cartwright and other Knickerbockers), two banquet receipts, Seymour Church's book, and a chart that showed Cartwright's ancestry.[17]

One may wonder why Cartwright was singled out as the only Knickerbocker to include in the festivities. Were there not other significant founding members of the Knickerbockers to celebrate as well—such as Duncan Curry, William Wheaton, William Tucker, and Daniel Adams? There are two main reasons why Cartwright was commemorated and given a "Cartwright Day" to celebrate his baseball accomplishments. Both reasons are reflected in a letter sent to Alexander Cleland by Walter Littell, secretary of the local county historical society and editor of the local newspaper, the *Otsego Farmer*. In a letter dated March 11, 1939, Littell commends Cleland:

> You are absolutely right about the importance of sewing up the Leagues and College Groups and I think you did a great job when you did it. Menke's poison will pass.
>
> The final nail was driven when the Cartwright negotiations were made some time ago and on this account it is very important that you and the New York and Cooperstown authorities make sure that Cartwright Day is a real success.[18]

Littell's remark about "Menke's poison" referred to an article written by Frank G. Menke and published in a new magazine named *Ken*.[19] The article, supposedly based on a great deal of research, stated that the claims made about Doubleday were false. According to Menke, not only was Doubleday a student at a military academy at the time in 1839, but baseball really derived from cricket. He also criticized the Mills Commission for their inaccuracies and guesswork. Yet, the most surprising of his claims was that it was Alexander Cartwright who first introduced the game in *1839*!

The biggest problem with Menke's claim about Cartwright was that he offered no evidence, then as well as in later years. A book he published in 1944, *The New Encyclopedia of Sports*, for example, shows a diagram of a baseball diamond with a caption claiming that it was "made by Alexander Cartwright."[20] This book also lists no sources. As such, Littell rebutted Menke's many claims in the *Otsego Farmer*. However, Littell did not diminish Cartwright's place in baseball history.

One reason, then, to create a "Cartwright Day" and to play up Cartwright's particular accomplishments was to appease critics of Doubleday (such as Menke), but it was also done to appease the descendents of Alexander Cartwright and the City of Honolulu. Celebrating Alexander Cartwright on a special day was a diversion the organizers of the museum felt was needed to draw attention away from the doubt being shed on Doubleday's connection with baseball.

Ironically, Cartwright was inducted into the Baseball Hall of Fame on the same day as Henry Chadwick, whose argument with Spalding had initiated the controversy that led to the Mills Commission. The men were voted on in a "pioneers" category of the Veterans' Committee ballot by the Centennial Commission. Currently, pioneers are considered for induction every other year, along with managers, umpires, and executives.

Bruce Cartwright Jr. would not live to see his grandfather honored at the Baseball Hall of Fame in August 1939. Bruce died in March of that year and is buried in the Cartwright family plot in Oahu Cemetery in Honolulu.

Cartwright Day took place on August 26, 1939, and was a great success in both New York and Hawaii. In addition to the festivities going on in Cooperstown, another celebration occurred at Ebbets Field in Brooklyn, New York. The *New York Times* reported that during a doubleheader, Alexander Cartwright was celebrated: "In honor of the memory of Alexander Cartwright, native Hawaiian girls hung leis about the necks of players of both teams after a pineapple juice drinking ceremony at the plate between the games. The pioneer was born in Honolulu, hence the Hawaiian touch."[21]

As this report shows, even the *New York Times* can get it wrong, and the actual details of Alexander Cartwright's life were already blurred by legend and myth. Perhaps the *Times* reporter was guessing at why there was a "Hawaiian touch" to the game's festivities, or perhaps no one there really understood the life of the person they were celebrating.

In 1939, television had just been introduced to the general public at the New York World's Fair. Though virtually no Americans had a television, Major League Baseball made its television debut on Cartwright Day. The National Broadcasting Company's station w2xbs broadcast the game from the Empire State Building, and the signal was picked up by television sets as far away as fifty miles.[22]

In Hawaii, another pineapple-juice toast was celebrated at Honolulu City Hall, where a duplicate of the plaque in the Baseball Hall of Fame was placed in honor on the wall.[23] Bruce Cartwright had the duplicate plaque made as a gift to the City of Honolulu in memory of his grandfather. Bruce had written a letter to Hamilton in October 1938 stating, "I would like to know if we could buy a duplicate of this bronze plaque to place in 'Cartwright Park' in Honolulu during the Baseball celebration in 1939, and what such a plaque would cost."[24]

Hamilton wrote a letter that same month to Cleland with Bruce's request, and after Bruce's death a few months later, the duplicate plaque that he purchased was unveiled on June 11, 1939, at Honolulu Stadium after the first game of a Hawaii league doubleheader between the Braves and the Wanderers. Bruce had intended to have the plaque installed at Cartwright Park, but it was later hung and dedicated at the Honolulu City Hall on Cartwright Day, August 26, 1939.[25] The plaque now resides in a private collection.

CONCLUSION

*Alexander Cartwright, Father of Modern Baseball**

In baseball, the asterisk is the symbol of a disputed achievement. For example, some still think Roger Maris's single-season home run record doesn't count because he achieved it over more games than Babe Ruth played; and some will always think Barry Bonds's home run records don't count because of the suspicion that he took steroids. And yet the records remain. Alexander Cartwright has been bestowed with the most respected designation in baseball's history, and yet there is some dispute over his record. While the popular account is that Cartwright is the "father of modern baseball," like the crowning of the "home run king," this is another title that deserves an asterisk.

Henry Chadwick, known as "The Father of Baseball" in the nineteenth century, was inducted into the Baseball Hall of Fame in 1938, the same year as Alexander Cartwright. Chadwick's plaque reads "Baseball's Preeminent Pioneer," while Cartwright's plaque reads "Father of Modern Baseball." On the one hand, the differences between "pioneer" and "father" seem semantic; there are no standards that determine what they mean or how they were achieved. They are characterizations, not official titles. Both men were selected for their 1938 induction by the Centennial Commission, which was a small committee that selected inductees that year for their outstanding service to baseball apart from playing the game.

However, on the other hand, the different titles imply different accomplishments: pioneers discover; fathers create. And politics as much as merit seem to have determined who was named what. Would Chadwick have remained baseball's "father" if Albert Spalding and professional baseball itself hadn't become caught up in nationalistic fervor? Would Cartwright have been inducted when and how he was without the persistence of his grandson Bruce in his correspondence with Cleland? And why did the Centennial Commission choose to honor Cartwright in this way and at this time and not other important Knickerbockers as well, such as Duncan Curry, the first president of the Knickerbockers; or Daniel Adams, who headed the committee to revise rules and by-laws in 1848 as well as being the club's president that year; or William Wheaton, a founder of the earlier Gotham Club who served on the Knickerbockers' first by-laws committee? What, in fact, happened to the National League president Ford Frick's reasonable perspective that "the Centennial of baseball is a centennial of a game rather than of individuals"?

Regardless of the actual reasons for Cartwright's induction, documentation for Cartwright must have been nearly as scarce then as it is now—but this clearly wasn't an obstacle. Baseball may be a game of statistics, but sentiment has always played a huge role in how its history has been told. Documentation for Abner Doubleday was scarce, too—resting on a single letter—yet he was originally dubbed baseball's founder, and the Baseball Hall of Fame and Museum was erected in the little town of Cooperstown, Doubleday's hometown.

Still, why *isn't* there more documentation? Looking beyond politics and mythology, we are left to wonder why there isn't more evidence on Cartwright's behalf, since he was clearly a significant person in baseball's development. Most recently, my opinion on this was swayed by an intriguing, inconspicuous little article that appeared in the *Hawaiian Gazette* in 1868. It begins, "We have several times been indebted to A. J. Cartwright, Esq., for facts and dates connected with the personal history of our residents . . . his records run back many years, they often prove most convenient and valuable for reference."[1] Efforts to locate these records, named by the article as belonging to the Pioneer Society, were unsuccessful.

Originally, as I learned about the full scope of Cartwright's many family, business, political, and social involvements, I had thought that perhaps he simply never had the time to write about his experiences or be interviewed by any newspaper. However, considering that he was a frequent letter writer to family and friends in the United States, and that according to at least one newspaper account he wrote and recorded the personal history of *others* in Honolulu, it would have been consistent with his character that he would have made the time to write about *his own* history.

I feel he must have. But *if* he did, it was likely destroyed or lost before the 1930s. If anything of this nature had existed during the time of Bruce's letter-writing campaign with the Baseball Hall of Fame, he would have been certain to produce it. In the ensuing years after Alexander Cartwright's induction in 1938, many original letters and possessions were sold off. Many items reside now in private collections unrelated to the Cartwright family, and they sometimes reenter circulation through auction Web sites. Individual Cartwright items have sold for hundreds to thousands of dollars.

I have gained access to or have knowledge of some of the private collections directly related to Alexander Cartwright, primarily via connections through the Society for American Baseball Research. The Cartwright descendents have very few original items left in their possession, from what I was able to gather during research for this book. I have seen, and I reference in this book, a number of original Cartwright items contained in other private collections, but out of respect to the current owners of these items, I am not at liberty to divulge them by name. Some collection owners refused to grant me access, but I was able to learn about the items they possess through auction site descriptions. Sometimes that was enough to determine the nature of the original.

In addition to the material in private collections, there is informational material related to Cartwright in the New York Public Library, the National Baseball Hall of Fame Research Library, the Library of Congress, the Cleveland Public Library, the Hawaii State Archives, the Mission Houses Museum and Library, the Bishop Museum, the Punahou School, and Hawaiian Island Stamp and Coin, among others. In fact, it never ceases to amaze me how much information is actually out there pertaining to Cartwright.

So why isn't Cartwright's baseball legacy more clearly documented? There is no solid answer, but I believe that some of those answers were burned shortly after his death. There is plenty of circumstantial evidence that Cartwright's baseball legacy is substantial, even if we leave out the more dubious claims made on his behalf. Based on what I have found and describe in this book, I feel Alexander Cartwright deserves to be honored as one of baseball's "pioneers." Yet to call him the *sole* "Father of Modern Baseball" is more than a stretch. It conflicts with the evidence: while there is certainly a group of men who deserve, for different reasons but in almost equal measure, to be considered baseball's pioneers or founders, like the game itself—which may celebrate the individual but is won only by a team—it took a team effort to develop baseball into a "modern" game.

Most likely, Cartwright will continue to be revered and honored more than his fellow teammates, even if the documented evidence for his accomplishments remains weak. Any myth or legend, once embedded in the culture, is difficult to amend. There are a great many people today who still insist that Abner Doubleday invented baseball—after all, baseball's Hall of Fame is in Cooperstown! An established and celebrated location surely signifies legitimacy, doesn't it?

Not always—especially when the story justifying it sounds and feels satisfying. The biographer Shirley A. Leckie talks about this in her book *Elizabeth Bacon Custer and the Making of a Myth*. Elizabeth was the widow of General George Armstrong Custer, who died at the Battle of Little Bighorn in 1876 during the Indian

Wars. Elizabeth became somewhat famous in her own right after her husband's death; she was in demand as a speaker and traveled extensively, promoting her husband's heroism and his memory throughout the rest of her life.

Mrs. Custer referred to her late husband as a "sincere friend of the reservation Indian." According to Leckie, what Elizabeth meant by this was that her husband had accepted the Indian who knew his place—the one assigned to him by white men.[2] Leckie labels Elizabeth Custer a "professional widow" because she made a good living at glorifying her late husband. However, Leckie states, this good living was based on the "perpetuation of an idealized version of the past." Elizabeth Custer lived so well, in fact, that at the end of her life, she made her home on Park Avenue in New York City—in the Murray Hill district. Elizabeth died in 1933.

The story of how Alexander Cartwright founded baseball and spread it across the country is, most likely, based on a similar "idealized version of the past." What the current evidence (or lack thereof) proves about Cartwright's particular baseball accomplishments has been overshadowed by a desire to mythologize a more compelling tale. I'm hopeful we may yet learn more about Cartwright, for we are left with some very curious areas for further research. I believe that somewhere out there—tucked away in an attic, or buried in a basement or the back of a closet—are significant pieces of the puzzle yet to be discovered or understood for what they are. Such historical discoveries are made all the time, and they may yet settle the debate and allow us to erase the asterisk from Cartwright's name.

Regardless of what may or may not be discovered about

baseball's "father," the legacy of Alexander Cartwright the man is complex and significant. Depending on the circumstances, he could be warm and wise or stubborn and opinionated. He was civic-minded, energetic, and involved, and he moved in politically influential circles; yet he seemed as adept at making powerful enemies as powerful friends. He was not just one of baseball's founders, but a gold rush pioneer and one who was associated with Hawaii's annexation movement. He needs to be remembered in all of these ways. Cartwright played a notable role during one of the nation's most dynamic and profound eras and has thereby earned himself a place in American history.

NOTES

Introduction
1. Berman, *Madison Square*.
2. *Boston Daily Globe*, April 9, 1891.
3. Leckie, "Biography Matters," 13, 14.
4. Leckie, "Biography Matters," 18.

1. Cartwright and Nineteenth-Century New York
1. Peterson, *Man Who Invented Baseball*, 100.
2. Peterson, *Man Who Invented Baseball*, 100.
3. Peterson, *Man Who Invented Baseball*, 103.
4. Steele, *Ebbets*, 61.
5. Peterson, *Man Who Invented Baseball*, 104.
6. Family genealogy papers, Cartwright family letters and manuscripts, private collection.
7. Peterson, *Man Who Invented Baseball*, 56.
8. Peterson, *Man Who Invented Baseball*, 54.
9. Beresniak, *Symbols of Freemasonry*.
10. Burrows and Wallace, *Gotham*, 455.
11. SABR Office, "1791 Baseball in Pittsfield, Mass.," *SABR-Zine*, May 13, 2004, http://www.sabr.org/sabr.cfm?a=cms,c,739,34,0.

12. Seymour, *Baseball*, 28.

2. The Knickerbocker Base Ball Club of New York

1. Freyer and Rucker, *Peverelly's National Game*. Speculation among baseball historians is that Henry Chadwick was Peverelly's source for the information on baseball; however, there is no documented source to confirm this.

2. Hans, comp., *100 Hoboken Firsts*, 114.

3. Winfield, "Hoboken, a Pleasure Resort for Old New York."

4. Winfield, "Hoboken, a Pleasure Resort for Old New York."

5. New Jersey Title Guarantee and Trust Company, "Castle Point and the Elysian Fields"; Seymour, *Baseball*, 15.

6. Knickerbocker dinner receipt, photocopy of original, Cartwright family letters and manuscripts, private collection.

7. Seymour, *Baseball*, 17.

8. Seymour, *Baseball*, 17.

9. Seymour, *Baseball*, 19.

10. Zoss and Bowman, *Diamonds in the Rough*, 232.

11. Qtd. in Spink, *The National Game*, 56.

12. Knickerbocker Score Book, Spalding Baseball Collection, Humanities Manuscripts and Archives, New York Public Library, New York NY.

3. The Rush for Gold

1. Clark, ed., *Off at Sunrise*, xiii.

2. Clark, ed., *Off at Sunrise*, xiii.

3. Clark, ed., *Off at Sunrise*, xiii–xiv.

4. *St. Louis Daily Union*, March 19, 1849.

5. *Newark Daily Advertiser*, April 5, 1849.

6. The quote is from the diary of Joseph Waring Berrien, who traveled with Colonel Jarrot and Captain Lafferty. Berrien begins his journal entries from aboard the *Alice* on March 31, 1849, in St. Louis; his impressions of the men from New York are from his April 3 entry, the day before the ship's arrival in Independence (Ted Hinckley and Caryl Hinckley, "Overland from St. Louis to the California Gold Field in 1849: The Diary of Joseph Waring Berrien," *Indiana Magazine of History* [1960]).

7. Rieck, ed., "Cyrus Currier," 1.

8. *Newark Daily Advertiser*, April 13, 1849.

9. Cartwright, Gold rush journal.

10. Rieck, ed., "Cyrus Currier," 5.

11. Rasmussen, *California Wagon Train Lists*, 10.

12. Bruce Cartwright Jr., "Alexander Joy Cartwright Jr.," Cartwright family letters and manuscripts, private collection.

13. Cartwright, Gold rush journal.

14. Rieck, ed., "Cyrus Currier," 3.

15. Erickson, *Daily Life in a Covered Wagon*, 11.

16. Erickson, *Daily Life in a Covered Wagon*, 24.

17. Cartwright, Gold rush journal.

18. Cartwright, Gold rush journal.

19. Cartwright, Gold rush journal.

20. Rieck, ed., "Cyrus Currier," 20.

21. Rieck, ed., "Cyrus Currier," 22.

22. Rieck, ed., "Cyrus Currier," 25.

23. Society of California Pioneers, San Francisco CA.

24. Clark, ed., *Off at Sunrise*, 138.

25. Clark, ed., *Off at Sunrise*, 150.

26. Clark, ed., *Off at Sunrise*, 170.

27. Erikson, "Alexander Joy Cartwright."

28. Records of Passenger Arrivals and Departures, 1843–1900, Collector General of Customs Records, Hawaii State Archives, Honolulu HI.

29. *Pacific Commercial Advertiser*, July 13, 1892.

30. Browne, ed., *J. Ross Browne*.

31. *Hawaiian Gazette*, July 1892.

32. Soule, Gihon, and Nisbet, *Annals of San Francisco*, 243.

33. Soule, Gihon, and Nisbet, *Annals of San Francisco*, 260.

34. Lockwood, *Suddenly San Francisco*, 34.

35. Steele, *Ebbets*, 68.

36. Steele, *Ebbets*, 102.

4. The Allure of Paradise

1. Records of Passenger Arrivals and Departures, 1843–1900, Collector General of Customs Records, Hawaii State Archives, Honolulu HI.

2. Erikson, "Alexander Joy Cartwright."

3. Records of Passenger Arrivals and Departures, 1843–1900, Collector General of Customs Records, Hawaii State Archives, Honolulu HI.

4. *Hawaiian Gazette*, July 19, 1892.

5. Cartwright Diary, Bishop Museum Archives, Honolulu HI, Manuscript Document 55.

6. Records of Passenger Arrivals and Departures, 1843–1900, Collector General of Customs Records, Hawaii State Archives, Honolulu HI.

7. Grant, Hymer, and Bishop Museum Archives, *Hawaii Looking Back*, 29.

8. Whitsell, *100 Years of Freemasonry in California*, 350.

9. Gardiner, "Prince Lot Kapuaiwa Kamehameha," 2.

10. Whitsell, *100 Years of Freemasonry*, 355.

11. Erikson, "Alexander Joy Cartwright."

12. Whitsell, *100 Years of Freemasonry*, 355.

13. *The Polynesian*, December 27, 1851.

14. Parke, *Personal Reminiscences*, 17–18.

15. *Hawaiian Gazette*, February 10, 1875. As an aside, it's interesting to note that the article in the *Hawaiian Gazette* was actually a correction to an earlier article commemorating the twenty-fifth anniversary of the fire department. The paper had mistakenly announced that Cartwright's appointment was in 1850, when in fact it was 1851. The correction now declared that dating from the appointment of Alexander Cartwright as chief engineer, the Honolulu Fire Department would celebrate their twenty-five years as of February 3, 1876.

16. The privy council was a committee of advisors selected by the sovereign who met to provide confidential advice to the monarch.

17. Smith, "History of the Honolulu Fire Department."

18. Smith, "History of the Honolulu Fire Department."

19. *The Polynesian*, Saturday, April 24, 1852.

20. Smith, "History of the Honolulu Fire Department."

21. Erikson, "Alexander Joy Cartwright."

22. Ship passenger log, Cartwright family letters and manuscripts, private collection.

23. "Death Announcement," *The Polynesian*, November 22, 1851.

24. "A Card," *The Polynesian*, November 22, 1851.

25. Thrum, *Thrum's Almanac and Annual*, 99.

26. Notations on a photograph of the house, private collection.

27. Notations and diagram of house location among family genealogy papers, Cartwright family letters and manuscripts, private collection.

28. Whitsell, *100 Years of Freemasonry*, 357.

29. Whitsell, *100 Years of Freemasonry*, 357.

30. Whitsell, *100 Years of Freemasonry*, 358.

31. Gardiner, "Prince Lot Kapuaiwa Kamehameha."

5. An American in Kamehameha's Kingdom

1. American Club announcement, *Pacific Commercial Advertiser*, July 2, 1856.

2. Alexander Cartwright to Prince Lot Kamehameha, February 26, 1857, Cartwright Manuscript Collection, Hawaii State Archives, Honolulu HI.

3. Gardiner, "Prince Lot Kapuaiwa Kamehameha," 2.

4. Gardiner, "Prince Lot Kapuaiwa Kamehameha," 2.

5. Gardiner, "Prince Lot Kapuaiwa Kamehameha," 2.

6. Gardiner, "Prince Lot Kapuaiwa Kamehameha," 2.

7. Daws, *Honolulu*, 210.

8. Karpiel, "Mystic Ties of Brotherhood," 51.

9. *The Polynesian*, December 13, 1851.

10. Records of Passenger Arrivals and Departures, 1843–1900, Collector General of Customs Records, Hawaii State Archives, Honolulu HI.

11. Letters in the Cartwright family letters and manuscripts, private collection.

12. On the fire engine, see Thrum, *Thrum's Almanac and Annual*, 66.

13. Alexander Cartwright to Arthur Ebbetts, May 24, 1856, Cartwright family letters and manuscripts, private collection.

14. Information on the marriages and divorces comes from the family genealogy papers in the Cartwright family letters and manuscripts, private collection. Information on the donation/provenance of Cartwright's journal is from Mary Check Taylor, from the Will of Mary Check Taylor, dated January 31, 1974, Bishop Museum Archives, Honolulu HI. (This will is kept in donor files and is not available to the public.)

15. King, ed., *Diaries of David Lawrence Gregg*, 272, 307, 353, 370, 371.

16. King, ed., *Diaries of David Lawrence Gregg*, 417–19.

17. King, ed., *Diaries of David Lawrence Gregg*, 420.

18. King, ed., *Diaries of David Lawrence Gregg*, 425.

19. King, ed., *Diaries of David Lawrence Gregg*, 453.

20. Joerger, "A Political Biography of David Lawrence Gregg," 200–202.

21. Whitsell, *100 Years of Freemasonry in California*, 367.

22. "Lemuel Lyon Biography" [family history compiled for library readers], Independence Public Library, Independence OR.

23. Karpiel, "Mystic Ties of Brotherhood," 54.

24. Karpiel, "Mystic Ties of Brotherhood," 55.

25. Karpiel, "Mystic Ties of Brotherhood," 58.

26. Karpiel, "Mystic Ties of Brotherhood," 59.

27. Karpiel, "Mystic Ties of Brotherhood," 59.

28. Karpiel, "Mystic Ties of Brotherhood," 60.

29. King, ed., *Diaries of David Lawrence Gregg*, 478–79.

30. King, ed., *Diaries of David Lawrence Gregg*, 477.

31. "Honolulu Merchants' Looking Glass," 11.

32. "Honolulu Merchants' Looking Glass," 17.

33. A short history of the Queen's Medical Center can be found on the hospital's Web site, http://www.queens.org/about/history.html.

34. Erikson, "Alexander Joy Cartwright."

6. America's National Pastime in Hawaii

1. Biography of Abner Doubleday from the Web site of Arlington National Cemetery, http://www.arlingtoncemetery.net/doubledy.htm.

2. Vlasich, *A Legend for the Legendary*.

3. "Audience at Iolani Palace," *Pacific Commercial Advertiser* Supplement, September 29, 1877.

4. Ardolino, "Missionaries, Cartwright, and Spalding."

5. Alexander and Dodge, *Punahou*, 118.

6. *Hawaiian Gazette*, August 28, 1867.

7. *Punahou School Directory*.

8. *Hawaiian Gazette*, August 28, 1867.

9. Brown, *Reminiscences of a Pioneer Kauai Family*, 45.

10. *Pacific Commercial Advertiser*, July 30, 1906.

11. *Hawaiian Gazette*, August 18, 1875.

12. Cartwright may have used the word *lares* in one of two ways: *Lare* is from the Old Frisian language, similar to English meaning "learning." This word is now known as the word *lore*. Or, he could have meant *lares*, which is the plural of *lar*, which means "household deities."

13. The phrase "Sound the Goose" meant those who favored a slaveholding Kansas. The word *goose* was code for the slavery question.

14. Alexander Cartwright to Charles DeBost, April 6, 1865, original in a private collection of Cartwright letters and manuscripts.

7. Cartwright and the Monarchy

1. Fred Hutchinson to Alexander Cartwright, 1872, Cartwright family manuscripts and letters, private collection.

2. Gardiner, "Prince Lot Kapuaiwa Kamehameha."

3. "Time Capsule Buried in 1870s Is Found in Honolulu Building," *New York Times*, December 12, 2005.

4. "Memorandum of Agreement," January 31, 1867. Manuscript Group 70, box 77.5, Judd papers, Bishop Museum Archives, Honolulu HI.

5. Cartwright Manuscript Collection, Hawaii State Archives, Honolulu HI.

6. Stone, "Chamber of Commerce of Hawaii Celebrates."

7. Cartwright family letters and manuscripts, private collection.

8. On the morning of August 17, 1858, Charles Reed Bishop and William A. Aldrich opened the Bank of Bishop & Company in a corner of Cartwright's office. Samuel Mills Damon eventually became a partner; on May 31, 1895, Mr. Damon became the sole owner of Bishop & Co. Mr. Damon died in 1924. His land holdings and other assets were placed in trust to be managed by the trustees of the estate of Samuel Mills Damon.

On November 9, 2004, Joan Damon Haig, the last living grandchild of Samuel Mills Damon, died, marking the termination and eventual dissolution of the estate of Samuel Mills Damon. Among the estate's holdings were a coin collection that likely originated from the beginnings of the bank in a corner of Cartwright's office (http://www.doylenewyork.com/damoncoins/damncoins.htm).

9. See http://www.doylenewyork.com/damoncoins/damncoins.htm.

10. Cartwright Manuscript Collection, Hawaii State Archives, Honolulu HI.

11. General information about Bernice Bishop can be found at http://www.pauahi.org.

12. Alexander Cartwright to A. Reimers. Esqr., September 25, 1878, transcription copy, Cartwright family letters and manuscripts, private collection.

13. Alexander Cartwright to his sister Kate, August 18, 1874, Cartwright family letters and manuscripts, private collection.

14. Alexander Cartwright to Esther Cartwright, July 16, 1862, Cartwright family letters and manuscripts, private collection.

15. Alexander Cartwright to Esther Cartwright, May 31, 1858, Cartwright family letters and manuscripts, private collection.

16. Alexander Cartwright to his brother Benjamin Cartwright, December 21, 1865, Cartwright family letters and manuscripts, private collection.

17. Alexander Cartwright to his son DeWitt Cartwright, January 20, 1868, Cartwright family letters and manuscripts, private collection.

18. Alexander Cartwright to his daughter Mary Cartwright Maitland, August 29, 1868, Cartwright family letters and manuscripts, private collection.

19. Alexander Cartwright to his son-in-law Adolf G. Maitland, May 27, 1869, Cartwright family letters and manuscripts, private collection.

20. "In Memory of Our Daughter Mary" (1869), Robert Van Dyke papers, Bishop Museum Archives, Honolulu HI; *Hawaiian Gazette*, June 9, 1869.

21. *Hawaiian Gazette*, March 21, 1870.

22. Alexander Cartwright to Washington Durbrow, March 11, 1872, transcription copy, Cartwright family letters and manuscripts, private collection.

23. Bruce Cartwright Jr., *Paradise of the Pacific*, July 1, 1913. The Birthday Club booklet is found in Cartwright Manuscript Collection, Hawaii State Archives, Honolulu HI.

24. Gardiner, "Prince Lot Kapuaiwa Kamehameha."

25. Gardiner, "Prince Lot Kapuaiwa Kamehameha."

26. Gardiner, "Prince Lot Kapuaiwa Kamehameha."

27. Twigg-Smith, *Hawaiian Sovereignty*, 39.

28. Twigg-Smith, *Hawaiian Sovereignty*, 39.

29. Twigg-Smith, *Hawaiian Sovereignty*, 42.

30. Twigg-Smith, *Hawaiian Sovereignty*, 42.

31. Ardolino, "Missionaries, Cartwright, and Spalding."

32. Ardolino, "Missionaries, Cartwright, and Spalding."

33. Ardolino, "Missionaries, Cartwright, and Spalding."

34. Ardolino, "Missionaries, Cartwright, and Spalding."

35. "Centennial Celebration of American Independence," July 4, 1876, Cartwright Manuscript Collection, Hawaii State Archives, Honolulu HI.

36. "Centennial Celebration of American Independence," July 4, 1876, Cartwright Manuscript Collection, Hawaii State Archives, Honolulu HI.

37. Loomis, *Best of Friends*, 6.

38. Loomis, *Best of Friends*, 6.

39. Loomis, *Best of Friends*, 6.

40. Loomis, *Best of Friends*, 6.

41. Loomis, *Best of Friends*.

42. Burbank, "Story of the Honolulu Library and Reading Room Association."

43. Thrum, *Thrum's Almanac and Annual*, 38.

44. Hawaiian Lodge No. 21 F. & A. M., *Centennial Anniversary 1852–1952*, 82.

8. Annexation and the Hawaiian League

1. Tootle, "The Arch," 1.

2. Tootle, "The Arch," 5.

3. *Morning Journal* (Columbus OH), April 14, 1866.

4. "Audience at Iolani Palace," *Pacific Commercial Advertiser* Supplement, September 29, 1877.

5. Burbank, "Story of the Honolulu Library and Reading Room Association."

6. Twigg-Smith, *Hawaiian Sovereignty*, 44.

7. *Pacific Commercial Advertiser*, August 21, 1880.

8. Allen, *Kalakaua*, 96–97.

9. Moreno, Celso Cesar, "The Position of Men and Affairs in Hawaii," Open letter to His Majesty King Kalakaua, August 7, 1886, Hamilton Library, University of Hawaii, Manoa.

10. Some details of the history of the Iolani Palace are from its Web site, http://www.iolanipalace.org/history/.

11. Allen, *Kalakaua*.

12. Allen, *Kalakaua*.

13. Blount, Blount Report: Affairs in Hawaii.

14. For a brief history of the Hawaii Sugar Planters' Association, see the Hawaii Agriculture Research Center Web site, http://www.hawaiiag.org/harc/HARCHSII.htm.

15. E. H. Allen papers, Manuscript Division, Library of Congress.

16. *Hawaiian Gazette*, August 30, 1882.

17. *Hawaiian Gazette,* August 30, 1882.

18. *Pacific Commercial Advertiser,* February 4 and February 11, 1882.

19. Photocopy of certificate designating Alex J. Cartwright as a lifetime member of the Honolulu Athletic Association, Cartwright Manuscript Collection, Hawaii State Archives, Honolulu HI.

20. *Pacific Commercial Advertiser,* February 18, 1882.

21. Decree of Divorce between Theresa Cartwright and A. J. Cartwright, April 7, 1883. From the records of the First Circuit Court, Hawaii State Archives, Honolulu HI.

22. See http://www.iolanipalace.org/history.

23. See http://www.iolanipalace.org/history.

24. Both the Dayton toast and this one are quoted in Herbert G. Gardiner, PGS, "The Glory and Travail of a Bygone Era," http://www.calodges.org/ncrl/glory.html.

25. Gardiner, "Glory and Travail."

26. Appointment as attorney for Kalakaua, Kapiolani, Liliuokalani, Dominis, Likelike, and Cleghorn, Cartwright Manuscript Collection, Hawaii State Archives, Honolulu HI.

27. Alexander Cartwright to Emma Kaleleonanlani, Dowager Queen, September 20, 1874, in a private collection of Cartwright letters and manuscripts.

28. Last Will and Testament of Queen Emma Kamehameha, 1884, Queen Emma Foundation, Honolulu HI.

29. The gold watch from Queen Emma to Alexander Cartwright is held in a private collection.

30. Historical file, 1875–1895, Hawaii State Archives, Honolulu HI.

31. Historical file, 1875–1895, Hawaii State Archives, Honolulu HI.

32. Bob Dye, "Royal Visit to the Bay," *Spirit of Aloha Inflight Magazine,* May/June 2003, Aloha Airlines, http://www.spiritofaloha.com/features/0503/royal.html.

33. Dye, "Royal Visit to the Bay."

34. Letter to Alex J. Cartwright from Bank of California thanking him and citizens of Honolulu for contributions, Cartwright Manuscript Collection, Hawaii State Archives, Honolulu HI.

35. King David Kalakaua, Opening session of 1887 Hawaiian Legislature,

Treaty of Reciprocity between the United States of America and the Hawaiian Kingdom. Located on the Web site of the Independent and Sovereign Nation-State of Hawaii, http://www.hawaii-nation.org/treaty1875.html.

36. Coffman, *Nation Within*, 80.

37. Lorrin Thurston Collection, Hawaii State Archives, Honolulu HI. In this collection is a roster from 1887 of member names of the Hawaiian League; Alexander Cartwright and his two sons, Bruce and Alexander, are on that list.

38. Honolulu Rifles Subscriptions, 1857, Cartwright Manuscript Collection, Hawaii State Archives, Honolulu HI.

39. Hawaiian League oath, Lorrin Thurston Collection, Hawaii State Archives, Honolulu HI.

40. Allen, *Betrayal of Liliuokalanai*, 218–19.

41. Tom Coffman, e-mail message to author, December 25, 2005.

9. Spalding Comes to Hawaii

1. Many of the details of Spalding's visit are taken from the description published in the *Hawaiian Gazette*, November 26, 1888.

2. *Hawaiian Gazette*, November 26, 1888.

3. Spalding Scrapbook on microfilm, SABR Lending Library, Cleveland OH.

4. Spalding Scrapbook on microfilm, SABR Lending Library, Cleveland OH.

5. Spalding Scrapbook on microfilm, SABR Lending Library, Cleveland OH.

6. Spalding Scrapbook on microfilm, SABR Lending Library, Cleveland OH.

7. *Hawaiian Gazette*, November 26, 1888; Spalding Scrapbook on microfilm, SABR Lending Library, Cleveland OH.

8. Spalding Scrapbook on microfilm, SABR Lending Library, Cleveland OH.

9. *Hawaiian Gazette*, November 26, 1888.

10. Diary excerpt of anonymous ballplayer with Spalding World Tour, 1888, National Baseball Hall of Fame, Cooperstown NY.

11. *Hawaiian Gazette*, November 26, 1888.

12. *Hawaiian Gazette*, November 26, 1888.

13. Spalding, *America's National Game*, 53.

14. Charter of Incorporation of the Hawaiian Base Ball Association, 1890, Lorrin Thurston Collection, Hawaii State Archives, Honolulu HI.

15. Van Dyke, "Alexander Joy Cartwright," 24; image of stock certificate, Mission Houses Museum and Library, Honolulu HI.

10. The Death of Cartwright, a King, and a Kingdom

1. Allen, *Kalakaua*, 209.

2. *Hawaiian Gazette*, March 13, 1888.

3. Allen, *Kalakaua*, 215.

4. Allen, *Kalakaua*, 215.

5. Allen, *Kalakaua*, 215.

6. Allen, *Kalakaua*, 217.

7. Allen, *Kalakaua*, 218.

8. Zambucka, *Kalakaua: Hawaii's Last King*.

9. *San Francisco Examiner*, December 21, 1890.

10. Allen, *Kalakaua*, 228.

11. Zambucka, *Kalakaua: Hawaii's Last King*, 99.

12. Zambucka, *Kalakaua: Hawaii's Last King*, 100.

13. Zambucka, *Kalakaua: Hawaii's Last King*, 103.

14. *Hawaiian Gazette*, February 24, 1891.

15. Alexander Joy Cartwright, Certificate of Death, Hawaii Health Department Vital Record Archives, Honolulu HI.

16. Letter from Mrs. Judd to her son, July 18, 1892, private collection.

17. *San Francisco Examiner*, March 9, 1893.

18. Coffman, *Nation Within*, 308.

19. The discussion of Sanford Dole and his role in Hawaii's provisional government is largely taken from essays by Kenneth R. Conklin, PhD, http://www.angelfire.com/hi2/hawaiiansovereignty/dole.html.

11. "Dear Old Knickerbockers"

1. "How Baseball Began—A Member of the Gotham Club of Fifty Years Ago Tells about It," *San Francisco Daily Examiner*, November 27, 1887.

2. Freyer and Rucker, *Peverelly's National Game*, 10–11. This book reprints from Peverelly's *American Pastimes* (1866).

3. Brown, "How Baseball Began," 51–54.

4. Alexander Cartwright to Charles DeBost, April 6, 1865, original in a private collection of Cartwright letters and manuscripts.

5. John Thorn, "A Really Good Find: The Magnolia Ball Club of 1843," *Woodstock Times*, November 14, 2007 http://www.ulsterpublishing.com/index.cfm?fuseaction=article&articleID=439584.

6. DiClerico and Pavelec, *The Jersey Game*, 14.

7. Bruce Cartwright Jr. to James E. Sullivan regarding receipt of Albert Spalding's book *America's National Game*, December 14, 1911, Spalding Scrapbook on microfilm, SABR Lending Library, Cleveland OH.

8. Spalding, *America's National Game*, 51–53.

9. Spalding Scrapbook on microfilm, SABR Lending Library, Cleveland OH.

10. Albert G. Spalding to George W. Smith, date unknown, private collection.

11. All Knickerbocker team officers and players are from Freyer and Rucker, *Peverelly's National Game*, 12, 13.

12. Spalding Baseball Collection, Humanities Manuscripts and Archives, MssCol 2835, New York Public Library, New York.

13. *New York Herald*, October 21, 1845.

14. DiClerico and Pavelec, *The Jersey Game*, 19.

15. Thompson, "New York Baseball 1823."

12. "Baseball on Murray Hill"

1. *Knickerbocker Base Ball Club By-laws and Rules*, 1848, private collection.

2. Chadwick and Petersen, *Beadle's Dime Base-ball Player*.

3. See Robert W. Henderson's article for the June 1939 issue of *Current History* (excerpted from a longer article published in the April 1939 *Bulletin of the New York Public Library*, where he was a librarian); Henderson asks if baseball was celebrating a "fake centennial," considering that it had already been proved that Abner Doubleday was at West Point throughout all of 1839, and that he did not like outdoor sports.

4. First Day Cover Envelope, Robert Van Dyke papers, Bishop Museum Archives, Honolulu HI.

5. Furukawa, "Originator of Organized Baseball," 24.

6. Furukawa, "Originator of Organized Baseball," 24.

7. Rankin's original article appeared in various newspapers during the summer of 1886. In some, it bore the title "Our National Game," and elsewhere it was called "Early History of Baseball." A reprint of the latter is located in Box 8, "New York Clipper articles by Rankin, 1904–1912," among the baseball scrapbooks originally included in the Charles W. Mears Collection on Baseball at the Cleveland Public Library, Cleveland OH; it can also be found in the "Scrapbook of William Rankin's Weekly Base Ball Letter, 1904–1912," part 9 of the Baseball Scrapbooks microfilm collection, University of Notre Dame Memorial Library, South Bend IN.

    8. Spink, *The National Game*, 54–56.

    9. Rankin, "Base Ball's Birth."

    10. Rankin, "Base Ball's Birth."

    11. Rankin, "Game's Pedigree."

    12. Rankin, "Game's Pedigree."

    13. Rankin, "Game's Pedigree."

    14. "Dr. D. L. ADAMS."

    15. E-mail from John Thorn to the author, July 21, 2008.

13. "On Mountain and Prairie"

    1. Peterson, "Baseball's Johnny Appleseed," 61.

    2. Peterson, "Baseball's Johnny Appleseed," 61.

    3. Peterson, "Baseball's Johnny Appleseed," 61.

    4. Peterson, "Baseball's Johnny Appleseed," 76.

    5. Quote by Mary Check Taylor from the Will of Mary Check Taylor, dated January 31, 1974, Bishop Museum Archives, Honolulu HI. (This will is kept in donor files, and is not available to the public.)

    6. Reed Hayes, handwriting analysis of journal, report to author (August 2005).

    7. These observations about gold rush trail diaries are from July 2004 interviews with historians and docents at the National Frontier Trails Museum, Independence, Missouri (including Kathleen Tuohey).

    8. Conversation between Reed Hayes and author, April 2006.

    9. Cartwright, Gold rush journal.

    10. E-mails from D. T. Barriskill, Guildhall Library, London, to author, October 10 and 15, 2007.

    11. Cartwright family letters and manuscripts, private collection.

12. Cartwright family letters and manuscripts, private collection.

13. Cartwright family letters and manuscripts, private collection.

14. Cartwright family letters and manuscripts, private collection.

15. Cartwright family letters and manuscripts, private collection.

16. Letter from Anne E. Cartwright to the author, August 29, 2005.

17. Mike Jay, "Archives of Hawaii Get Letter Giving Names of Knicker-bocker Ball Team," *Honolulu Star Bulletin*, October 1926.

18. Jack McDonald, "'Twas Big Thing that Event 101 Years Ago Today," *San Francisco Call-Bulletin*, June 19, 1947, 22.

19. McDonald, "'Twas Big Thing that Event 101 Years Ago Today."

20. McDonald, "'Twas Big Thing that Event 101 Years Ago Today."

21. Kathleen Tuohey, phone interview with author, October 7, 2006.

22. Macfarlane, "The Knickerbockers," 8.

14. "On the Sunny Plains of Hawaii nei"

1. In 1933 Herb Hunter would again visit Cartwright's grave, this time with Babe Ruth, who was in town for an exhibition game (*Honolulu Star-Bulletin*, October 20, 1933, 12, photo with caption "Ruth Pays Tribute to Baseball Originator").

2. "Tribute Paid to Founder of Organized Baseball in Impressive Ceremony Here," *Honolulu Star-Bulletin*, January 23, 1923.

3. "Tribute Paid to Founder of Organized Baseball in Impressive Ceremony Here," *Honolulu Star-Bulletin*, January 23, 1923.

4. Smith, *Heroes of Baseball*, 16.

5. "Tells of Old Time Baseball," *Honolulu Advertiser*, February 24, 1926, 11.

6. "Tells of Old Time Baseball," *Honolulu Advertiser*, February 24, 1926, 11.

7. *Pacific Commercial Advertiser*, August 3, 1867, 3.

8. Tally Book of the Punahou Baseball Club (October 1869–February 1875), Henry Poor, Tally Keeper, Punahou School Archives, Honolulu HI.

9. "Mount Tantalus Got Its Name from Punahou Boys," *Pacific Commercial Advertiser*, October 7, 1901, 3.

10. "Game of Ball," *The Polynesian*, April 7, 1860, 3.

11. "Sports in Honolulu," *The Polynesian*, December 26, 1840, 114.

12. Castle, "Introduction of Baseball," 70.

13. Castle, "Introduction of Baseball," 70.

14. Castle, *Reminiscences of William Richards Castle*, 51–52.

15. "Introduction of Baseball to Hawaii Told in Book," *Honolulu Star-Bulletin*, May 14, 1941, 15.

16. "Introduction of Baseball to Hawaii Told in Book," *Honolulu Star-Bulletin*, May 14, 1941, 15.

17. "National Pastime Has Rich Heritage in the Territory," *Honolulu Star-Bulletin*, July 15, 1948, 19.

18. Goto, "The Early Baseball in Hawaii," in *The Japanese Baseball-dom of Hawaii*.

19. Thrum, *Compendium of All Articles of Historical and Cultural Interest from* Thrum's Almanac and Annual, 29.

20. Bruce Cartwright Jr. to Arthur C. Alexander, December 9, 1938, private collection.

21. Spalding, *America's National Game*, 51–53.

15. Baseball and the "Family Lare"

1. Schiff, *Father of Baseball*, 49.

2. Schiff, *Father of Baseball*, 59.

3. Schiff, *Father of Baseball*, 158. See Chadwick and Petersen, *Beadle's Dime Base-ball Player*.

4. Seymour, *Baseball*, 9.

5. Vlasich, *A Legend for the Legendary*, 10.

6. Vlasich, *A Legend for the Legendary*, 17.

7. Vlasich, *A Legend for the Legendary*, 18.

8. Vlasich, *A Legend for the Legendary*, 18.

9. Bruce Cartwright Jr. to Alexander Cleland, December 4, 1935, Cleland Files, National Baseball Hall of Fame, Cooperstown NY.

10. Alexander Cleland to Bruce Cartwright Jr., December 18, 1935, Cleland Files, National Baseball Hall of Fame, Cooperstown NY.

11. Bruce Cartwright Jr. to John Hamilton, May 25, 1938, Cleland Files, National Baseball Hall of Fame, Cooperstown NY.

12. John Hamilton to Alexander Cleland, May 27, 1938, Cleland Files, National Baseball Hall of Fame, Cooperstown NY.

13. Ford Frick to Alexander Cleland, June 14, 1938, Cleland Files, National Baseball Hall of Fame, Cooperstown NY.

14. Alexander Cleland to John Hamilton, June 23, 1938, Cleland Files, National Baseball Hall of Fame, Cooperstown NY.

15. Bruce Cartwright Jr. to Alexander Cleland, September 13, 1938, Cleland Files, National Baseball Hall of Fame, Cooperstown NY.

16. Bruce Cartwright Jr. to Alexander Cleland, March 20, 1936, Cleland Files, National Baseball Hall of Fame, Cooperstown NY.

17. All these items are in the Cleland Files, National Baseball Hall of Fame, Cooperstown NY.

18. Walter Littell to Alexander Cleland, March 11, 1939, Cleland Files, National Baseball Hall of Fame, Cooperstown NY.

19. Vlasich, *A Legend for the Legendary*, 140.

20. Menke, *New Encyclopedia of Sports*, 89.

21. "Dodgers and Reds Split Double Bill," *New York Times*, August 27, 1939, Sports section, 4.

22. "Games Are Televised," *New York Times*, August 27, 1939, Sports section, 4.

23. Campbell, "Cartwright Day," *Paradise of the Pacific*, August 1939, 17.

24. Bruce Cartwright Jr. to John Hamilton, October 18, 1938, Cleland Files, National Baseball Hall of Fame, Cooperstown NY.

25. Campbell, "Cartwright Day," *Paradise of the Pacific*, August 1939, 17.

Conclusion

1. *Hawaiian Gazette*, September 16, 1868.

2. Leckie, *Elizabeth Bacon Custer*, 301.

BIBLIOGRAPHY

Manuscript Collections

Allen, E. H. Papers. Manuscript Division, Library of Congress.

Cartwright Family Letters and Manuscripts. Private Collection.

Cartwright Manuscript Collection. Hawaii State Archives, Honolulu HI.

Cleland Files. National Baseball Hall of Fame, Cooperstown NY.

Collector General of Customs Records. Hawaii State Archives, Honolulu HI.

Judd Papers. Bishop Museum Archives, Honolulu HI.

Spalding Baseball Collection. Humanities Manuscripts and Archives, New York Public Library, New York NY.

Spalding Scrapbook on microfilm. SABR Lending Library, Cleveland OH.

Lorrin Thurston Collection. Hawaii State Archives, Honolulu HI.

Van Dyke, Robert. Papers. Bishop Museum Archives, Honolulu HI.

Other Sources

Alexander, Mary Charlotte, and Charlotte Peabody Dodge. *Punahou, 1841–1941.* Berkeley: University of California Press, 1941.

Allen, Helena G. *The Betrayal of Liliuokalanai.* Honolulu HI: Mutual Publishing, 1982.

———. *Kalakaua: Renaissance King.* Honolulu HI: Mutual Publishing, 1994.

Ardolino, Frank. "Missionaries, Cartwright, and Spalding: The Development of Baseball in Nineteenth-Century Hawaii." *NINE: A Journal of Baseball History and Culture* 10, no. 2 (Spring 2002): 27–45.

Beresniak, Daniel. *Symbols of Freemasonry*. Assouline NY: Assouline Publishing, 2000.

Berman, Miriam. *Madison Square: The Park and Its Celebrated Landmarks*. Layton UT: Gibbs Smith, 2001.

Berrien, Joseph Waring. Diary. Indiana Historical Society Library, Indianapolis IN.

Block, David. *Baseball before We Knew It: A Search for the Roots of the Game*. Lincoln: University of Nebraska Press, 2005.

Blount, James H. Blount Report: Affairs in Hawaii. *The Executive Documents of the House of Representatives for the Third Session of the Fifty-third Congress, 1895–1985, in Thirty-five Volumes*. University of Hawaii at Manoa, Special Collections.

Brown, Malcolm. *Reminiscences of a Pioneer Kauai Family with References and Anecdotes of Early Honolulu, 1804–1919*. Honolulu HI: T. McVeach, 1918.

Brown, Randall. "How Baseball Began." *The National Pastime: The Society for American Baseball Research* 24 (May 2004): 51–54.

Browne, Lina Fergusson, ed., *J. Ross Browne, His Letters, Journals, and Writings*. Albuquerque: University of New Mexico Press, 1969.

Burbank, Mary A. "Story of the Honolulu Library and Reading Room Association." *Hawaiian Historical Society Annual Report No. 36*. Honolulu: Hawaiian Historical Society, 1927.

Burrows, Edwin G., and Mike Wallace. *Gotham: A History of New York City to 1898*. New York: Oxford University Press, 2000.

Cartwright, Alexander Joy, Jr. Gold rush journal [Journal of Alexander Joy Cartwright Jr.]. Manuscript, Document 55, Bishop Museum Archives, Honolulu HI.

Castle, William R. "The Introduction of Baseball." *The Friend* (March 1924): 70.

———. *Reminiscences of William Richards Castle*. Honolulu HI: Advertisers Publishing Company, 1960.

Chadwick, Henry, and Philip Petersen. *Beadle's Dime Base-ball Player: A compendium of the game comprising elementary instructions of this*

American game of ball: together with the revised rules and regulations for 1860, rules for the formation of clubs, names of the officers and delegates to the general convention, &c. New York: Irwin P. Beadle, 1860.

Clark, Thomas D., ed. *Off at Sunrise: The Overland Journal of Charles Glass Gray.* San Marino CA: Huntington Library, 1976.

Coffman, Tom. *Nation Within: The Story of America's Annexation of the Nation of Hawaii.* Kaneohe HI: EPICenter, 2003.

Daws, Gavan. *Honolulu: The First Century.* Honolulu HI: Mutual Publishing, 2006.

DiClerico, James M., and Barry J. Pavelec. *The Jersey Game.* New Brunswick NJ: Rutgers University Press, 1991.

Dougherty, Michael. *To Steal a Kingdom: Probing Hawaiian History.* Honolulu HI: Island Style Press, 1992.

"Dr. D. L. ADAMS; Memoirs of the Father of Base Ball; He Resides in New Haven and Retains an Interest in the Game." *Sporting News,* February 29, 1896. Rpt. in *Early Innings: A Documentary History of Baseball, 1825–1908,* ed. and comp. Dean A. Sullivan, 13–18. Lincoln: University of Nebraska Press, 1995.

Erickson, Paul. *Daily Life in a Covered Wagon.* New York: Puffin Books, 1994.

Erikson, Jerry E. "Alexander Joy Cartwright." *Royal Arch Mason* (1962): n.p.

Freyer, John, and Mark Rucker. *Peverelly's National Game.* Chicago IL: Arcadia Publishing, 2005.

Furukawa, S. F. "Originator of Organized Baseball." *Paradise of the Pacific,* May 1947, 24.

Gardiner, Herbert G. "Prince Lot Kapuaiwa Kamehameha: The First Full-Blooded Hawaiian Freemason." Article on Web site for the Grand Lodge of Free and Accepted Masons of the State of Hawaii, 2002, http://hawaiifreemason.org/resources/prince_lot.html.

Goto, Reverend Chimpei P. *The Japanese Baseballdom of Hawaii.* Honolulu HI: 1940.

Grant, Glen, Bennett Hymer, and the Bishop Museum Archives. *Hawaii Looking Back: An Illustrated History of the Islands.* Honolulu HI: Mutual Publishing, 2000.

Hans, Jim, comp. *100 Hoboken Firsts*. Hoboken NJ: Hoboken Historical Museum, 2005.

Hawaiian Lodge No. 21 F. & A. M. *Centennial Anniversary 1852–1952*. Honolulu HI: Hawaiian Lodge No. 21, 1952.

Hinckley, Ted, and Caryl Hinckley. "Overland from St. Louis to the California Gold Field in 1849: The Diary of Joseph Waring Berrien." *Indiana Magazine of History* 56 (1960): 273–352.

"The Honolulu Merchants' Looking Glass." Mission Houses Museum and Library, Honolulu HI. N.d.

Joerger, Pauline King. "A Political Biography of David Lawrence Gregg." PhD thesis, University of Hawaii, 1976.

Kahn, James M. *The Umpire Story*. New York: G. P. Putnam's Sons, 1953.

Karpiel, Frank J. "Mystic Ties of Brotherhood." PhD dissertation, University of Hawaii, 1998.

King, Pauline, ed. *The Diaries of David Lawrence Gregg: An American Diplomat in Hawaii, 1853–1858*. Honolulu: Hawaiian Historical Society, 1982.

Leckie, Shirley A. "Biography Matters." In *Writing Biography*, ed. Lloyd E. Ambrosius. Lincoln: University of Nebraska Press, 2004. 1–26.

————. *Elizabeth Bacon Custer and the Making of a Myth*. Norman: University of Oklahoma Press, 1993.

Lockwood, Charles. *Suddenly San Francisco: The Early Years of an Instant City*. San Francisco: The San Francisco Examiner, Division of the Hearst Corporation, 1978.

Loomis, Albertine. *The Best of Friends: The Story of Hawaii's Libraries and Their Friends, 1879–1979*. Honolulu HI: Press Pacifica, 1979.

Mcfarlane, Angus. "The Knickerbockers: San Francisco's First Baseball Team?" *Base Ball: A Journal of the Early Game* 1, no. 1 (Spring 2007): 7–21.

Menke, Frank G. *The New Encyclopedia of Sports*. New York: A. S. Barnes & Company, 1944.

The New Jersey Title Guarantee and Trust Company. "Castle Point and the Elysian Fields." January 1912. Hoboken Public Library, Hoboken NJ.

Palmer, Henry Clay. *Athletic Sports in America, England, and Australia.* Philadelphia: Hubbard Brothers, 1889.

Parke, William Cooper. *Personal Reminiscences of William Cooper Parke, Marshall of the Hawaiian Islands from 1850–1884.* Cambridge MA: Cambridge University Press, 1891.

Peterson, Harold. "Baseball's Johnny Appleseed." *Sports Illustrated,* April 14, 1969, 57–76.

———. *The Man Who Invented Baseball.* New York: Charles Scribner's Sons, 1973.

Punahou School Directory: A Catalogue of Trustees, Officers of Administration and Instruction, Students, First Classes and Graduating Classes, 1841–1934. Honolulu HI: Punahou School, 1935.

Rankin, William. "Base Ball's Birth." *Sporting News,* April 8, 1905, 2.

———. "Game's Pedigree." *Sporting News,* April 2, 1908, 2.

Rasmussen, Louis J. *California Wagon Train Lists.* Colma CA: San Francisco Historic Records, 1994.

Rieck, Richard L., ed. "Cyrus Currier: Journal to California by the Northern Overland Route from Newark, State of New Jersey." 1999. Wyoming State Archives, Cheyenne WY.

Schiff, Andrew. *The Father of Baseball: A Biography of Henry Chadwick.* Jefferson NC: McFarland, 2008.

Seymour, Harold. *Baseball: The Early Years.* New York: Oxford University Press, 1960.

Smith, H. A. "History of the Honolulu Fire Department," rev. ed. Honolulu HI: Honolulu Fire Department, November 19, 1950.

Smith, Robert. *Heroes of Baseball.* Cleveland OH: World Publishing Company, 1952.

Soule, Frank, John J. Gihon, and James Nisbet. *The Annals of San Francisco.* Berkeley CA: Berkeley Hills Books, 1999.

Spalding, Albert G. *America's National Game.* New York: American Sports Publishing Company, 1911. Rpt. Lincoln: University of Nebraska Press, 1992.

Spink, Alfred. *The National Game,* 2nd ed. Carbondale: Southern Illinois University Press, 1910, 2000.

Steele, Edward. *Ebbets: The History and Genealogy of a New York Family.* St. Louis MO: E. E. Steele, 2005.

Stone, Scott C. S. "The Chamber of Commerce of Hawaii Celebrates Its 150th Birthday." *Island Business* (March 2000).

Tally Book of the Punahou Baseball Club (October 1869–February 1875). Henry Poor, Tally Keeper. Punahou School Archives, Honolulu HI.

Thompson, George, Jr., "New York Baseball 1823." *The National Pastime: The Society for American Baseball Research* 24 (January 2001): 6–8.

Thrum, Thomas G. *A Compendium of All Articles of Historical and Cultural Interest from* Thrum's Almanac and Annual, *1873–1933, by Thomas G. Thrum.* Compiled and edited by Richard Bordner. SRSC Press, 2006. CD-ROM.

———. *Thrum's Almanac and Annual.* Honolulu HI: Hawaiian Historical Society, 1880.

Tootle, James R. "The Arch." *Columbus Historical Society* 14 (Winter 2004): 1–5.

Twigg-Smith, Thurston. *Hawaiian Sovereignty: Do the Facts Matter?* Honolulu HI: Goodale Publishing, 1998.

Van Dyke, Robert E. "Alexander Joy Cartwright." *Coins* (October 1964): 24.

Vlasich, James A. *A Legend for the Legendary: The Origin of the Baseball Hall of Fame.* Bowling Green OH: Bowling Green State University Popular Press, 1990.

Whitsell, Leon O. *100 Years of Freemasonry in California.* San Francisco CA: 1916.

Winfield, Charles H. "Hoboken, a Pleasure Resort for Old New York." N.d. New Jersey Historical Society, Newark NJ.

Zambucka, Kristin. *Kalakaua: Hawaii's Last King.* Honolulu HI: Mana Publishing, 2002.

Zoss, Joel, and John Bowman. *Diamonds in the Rough: The Untold History of Baseball.* New York: McGraw-Hill/Contemporary Books, 1996.

INDEX

Carter, Hannah, 53
Carter, Henry A. P., 134
Cartwright, Alexander, III, 181; adult
life of, 83, 88, 92, 93; baseball
played by, 77, 195–96, 202, 204;
birth and childhood of, 60–61; education of, 77; journals written by,
184; transcription of Alexander Joy
Cartwright Jr.'s diaries by, 182
Cartwright, Alexander Joy (father of
A. J. Cartwright Jr.), 6–7, 89
Cartwright, Alexander Joy, Jr.: arrival
in Hawaii of, 44–45; banking industry and, 7–8, 84–85, 113–14; baseball
rules developed by, 161–64; birth
and childhood of, 6–7; business
ventures by, 48–49, 58–59, 79–80,
81, 117–18; and the California Gold
Rush, 24–36, 187–90; children of,
7–8, 24, 40, 51–53, 60–61, 77, 88,
90–92, 112–13; death of, 137–38; enemies of, 68–71; grandchildren and
great-grandchildren of, 61, 83–84,
112–13, 154–55, 181–82; Hawaiian
homes of, 52; honored in Hawaii,
222–23; legacy of, 143–44, 174–78,
193–95, 227–31; marriage of, 7–8,
51–52, 86–87; monarchy of Hawaii
and, 81–83; newspaper columns
of, 85–86; parents of, 6–7, 87–89,
92; professional organizations and,
84; siblings of, 6–7, 39, 40–41, 45,
59. See also letters and diaries of
Alexander Joy Cartwright Jr.
Cartwright, Alfred, 24, 39, 70; American Relief Fund Association and,
84; death of, 136–37; in Hawaii, 45,
48–49, 59; letters from Alexander

Joy Cartwright Jr. to, 98; in San
Francisco, 40–41
Cartwright, Benjamin, 89–90
Cartwright, Bruce: adult life of, 88,
92, 93, 109, 112; baseball played
by, 77, 195–96, 202, 204; birth
and childhood of, 60, 61; educa-
tion of, 77; letters of Alexander Joy
Cartwright Jr. and, 180–81, 188–89;
transcriptions of Alexander Joy
Cartwright Jr.'s letters by, 185–87
Cartwright, Bruce, III, 61
Cartwright, Bruce, Jr., 61, 154–55,
164–66, 178, 213–21, 222–23, 228
Cartwright, Coleman, 61
Cartwright, Daisy Napulahaokalani,
60, 113
Cartwright, DeWitt Robinson, 7–8, 51,
77, 88, 90–91, 196
Cartwright, Eliza Ann Gerrits Van
Wie, 7–8, 24, 51–52, 60–61, 86–88,
112–13
Cartwright, Esther Burlock, 6–7,
87–89
Cartwright, Eva Kuwailanimamao,
60, 113
Cartwright, Kathleen DeWitt, 61
Cartwright, Kathleen Lee, 8, 51–52
Cartwright, Mary Groesbeck, 7–8, 51,
77, 88, 90–91, 181
Cartwright, Mary Muriel, 61
Cartwright, Ruth Joy, 61
Cartwright, William, 187
Cartwright Park, 218–19
Castle, Carrie, 97
Castle, James, 76
Castle, Samuel N., 198
Castle, William R., 76, 109, 198–203

Newark Daily Advertiser, 24, 39
Newark Overland Company, 23–29, 38, 190
The New Encyclopedia of Sports (Menke), 221
New York Base Ball Club, 151, 152
New York Central Railroad, 5
New York City: banking industry, 6–7; firefighters, 8; immigrants to, xxiii–xxiv; Madison Square Park, xxi–xxiii; Masons, 8–9; nineteenth-century development of, 3–6; Wall Street, 5–6, 8
New York Clipper, 196
New York Cricket Club, 151
New York Evening Post, 3, 4
New York Giants, 127
New York Herald, 152, 153, 159–60
New York Magnolia Ball Club, 152
New York Times, xii, 3, 222
New York World, 173
Niebuhr, Fraley C., 158

Oahu College, 75
Oakley, Walter, 158
Ohio State Journal, 101
Onderdonk, Henry M., 158
Oregon Trail, 36, 190
origins of baseball, ix–xiii, xxvii–xxviii, xxxiii–xxxiv, 10–11, 73–74, 219; Albert Goodwill Spalding on, 153–57; Bruce Cartwright on, 213–21; Charles Peverelly on, 148–50; Duncan Curry on, 171–73, 211–12; early clubs and, 151–53; Knickerbocker club and, 12–13, 144–50, 153–54, 213–15; Mills Commission on, 210–15, 220; William Rankin on,

168, 171–74; William Wheaton on, 144–47. *See also* baseball
Otsego Farmer, 221

Pacific (ship), 43, 44, 45
Pacific Commercial Advertiser, 84, 98, 197, 204
Paradise of the Pacific (Furukawa), 164
Parke, William C., 49–50, 83, 109
Parker, Samuel, 127
Paty, John, 117
Personal Reminiscences (Parke), 49
Petersen, Charles, 136
Peterson, Harold, xxvii, xxviii, xxx, 179–82, 187
Peverelly, Charles, xxx, 12, 148–50, 157, 162, 172
Pickard Nine, 134
Pierce, Franklin, 58
Pierce, Henry, 96, 97, 102
Planter Labor and Supply Company, 108
Plunkett, Eugene, 158, 162
Poe, Edgar Allen, 5, 8
politics, Hawaiian, 68–69, 82, 110–11; elections and, 94–95; militias and, 120–23; Reform government and, 132–33; Treaty of Reciprocity and, 119–20; and U.S. annexation, 56–58, 102–5, 106, 123, 139–40. *See also* Hawaii
The Polynesian, 52, 53, 197, 198
Pratt, Franklin, 113
Punahou Reporter, 77
Punahou School Baseball Club, 76, 97, 195–201, 203–4

Rankin, William, xi–xii, 168, 171–74, 211–12, 246n7